EARLY JUDAISM
and the
NEW TESTAMENT

EARLY JUDAISM
and the
NEW TESTAMENT

Troubling Misunderstandings

Warren Carter and Ariel Feldman

Baker Academic
a division of Baker Publishing Group
Grand Rapids, Michigan

© 2025 by Warren Carter and Ariel Feldman

Published by Baker Academic
a division of Baker Publishing Group
Grand Rapids, Michigan
BakerAcademic.com

Printed in the United States of America

All rights reserved. No part of this publication may be reproduced, stored in a retrieval system, or transmitted in any form or by any means—for example, electronic, photocopy, recording—without the prior written permission of the publisher. The only exception is brief quotations in printed reviews.

Library of Congress Cataloging-in-Publication Data
Names: Carter, Warren, 1955– author. | Feldman, Ariel, 1974– author.
Title: Early Judaism and the New Testament : troubling misunderstandings / Warren Carter and Ariel Feldman.
Description: Grand Rapids, Michigan : Baker Academic, a division of Baker Publishing Group, [2025] | Includes bibliographical references and index.
Identifiers: LCCN 2025003646 | ISBN 9781540968111 (paperback) | ISBN 9781540969552 (casebound) | ISBN 9781493451630 (ebook) | ISBN 9781493451647 (pdf)
Subjects: LCSH: Judaism—Relations—Christianity. | Christianity and other religions—Judaism. | Bible. New Testament—Criticism, interpretation, etc.
Classification: LCC BM535 .C374 2025 | DDC 261.2/6—dc23/eng/20250312
LC record available at https://lccn.loc.gov/2025003646

Unless otherwise indicated, Scripture quotations are from the New Revised Standard Version Updated Edition. Copyright © 2021 National Council of Churches of Christ in the United States of America. Used by permission. All rights reserved worldwide.

Scripture quotations labeled ESV are from The Holy Bible, English Standard Version® (ESV®), copyright © 2001 by Crossway, a publishing ministry of Good News Publishers. Used by permission. All rights reserved. ESV Text Edition: 2016

Scripture quotations labeled NJPS are from the New Jewish Publication Society Version © 1985 by The Jewish Publication Society. All rights reserved.

Scripture quotations labeled NRSV are from the New Revised Standard Version Bible, copyright © 1989 National Council of the Churches of Christ in the United States of America. Used by permission. All rights reserved worldwide.

Baker Publishing Group publications use paper produced from sustainable forestry practices and postconsumer waste whenever possible.

25   26   27   28   29   30   31   7   6   5   4   3   2   1

Contents

Abbreviations of Ancient Texts   vii
A Note to Readers   ix

1. What Is This Book About?   1
2. Reusing Biblical Traditions   19
3. The Temple in Early Jewish Texts   35
4. Groups   51
5. Torah/Law   67
6. Messiah/Christ   83
7. Demons and Angels   97
8. Crucifixion   113
9. Resurrection   127
10. Eschatology   141
11. Revealing God: Traditions About Wisdom   155
12. Prayer   171
13. People: Women and Non-Jews/Gentiles   185

Postscript   201
Appendix: The Dead Sea Scrolls and Hungry Caterpillars   203
Bibliography   205
Scripture and Ancient Sources Index   209

Abbreviations of Ancient Texts

Apocrypha

Add. Esth.	Additions to Esther
Bar.	Baruch
1–2 Esd.	1–2 Esdras
Jdt.	Judith
Let. Jer.	Letter of Jeremiah
1–4 Macc.	1–4 Maccabees
Pr. Azar.	Prayer of Azariah
Pr. Man.	Prayer of Manasseh
Ps. 151	Psalm 151
Sir.	Sirach/Ecclesiasticus
Sus.	Susanna
Tob.	Tobit
Wis.	Wisdom of Solomon

Pseudepigrapha

ALD	Aramaic Levi Document
2 Bar.	2 Baruch
1 En.	1 Enoch
Jub.	Jubilees
LAE	Life of Adam and Eve
Let. Aris.	Letter of Aristeas
Pss. Sol.	Psalms of Solomon
T. Benj.	Testament of Benjamin
T. Dan	Testament of Dan
T. Iss.	Testament of Issachar
T. Jos.	Testament of Joseph
T. Sol.	Testament of Solomon

Josephus

Ag. Ap.	*Against Apion*
Ant.	*Jewish Antiquities*
J.W.	*Jewish War*
Life	*The Life*

Philo

Abraham	*On the Life of Abraham*
Contempl. Life	*On the Contemplative Life*
Decalogue	*On the Decalogue*
Embassy	*On the Embassy to Gaius*
Hypoth.	*Hypothetica*
Moses	*On the Life of Moses*
QE	*Questions and Answers on Exodus*
Spec. Laws	*On the Special Laws*
Virtues	*On the Virtues*

Dead Sea Scrolls

For the Dead Sea Scrolls references, see chapter 1 and the appendix.

A Note to Readers

This book is written for college and seminary students, for church and synagogue groups, for anyone interested in understanding the texts of Early Judaism and the New Testament. We are very aware that Jewish life did not end in the second century and that issues of troubling interactions between Jews and Christians have extended across two millennia, yet we have restricted our focus to this period and to these literatures.

Each chapter recognizes troubling misunderstandings that people often have about the interactions between Early Judaism and the New Testament. Some misunderstandings arise from not knowing information, some from religious traditions, some from more nefarious motives. We trouble these misunderstandings by supplying accurate information and attending to the continuities and discontinuities that exist between the two traditions.

With each chapter, we suggest you begin by reading the chapter. In the chapter, we include some of the key texts that we are discussing. But you might want to read more of those texts. In the end of the book, we list the sources we used to cite these texts.

Each chapter ends with several questions to assist any readers, classes, or groups to process the chapter's material. Depending on the group, you might take up a further issue and consider the implication of the material for contemporary Jewish-Christian interactions.

We want to thank Wendy Davidson and Emma Norton for their contributions to this book.

CHAPTER 1

What Is This Book About?

We begin with three images: an illustration, a carving, and a statue. First, a manuscript illustration (see fig. 1.1).

There are two women. The woman on the left sets the scene's point of view. She is upright, crowned, well-dressed, dominant, and confident, looking down and directly at the figure on the right. Her pose is one of superiority. She is located next to a church building and spire. That identifies her as Ecclesia (Church).

The woman on the right has a bowed and uncrowned head. She is turned away from Ecclesia. She does not look at her. Her face is turned down, dejected and defeated. Her eyes are covered; she is blindfolded. In her right hand, a tablet or document looks to be falling out of her grip. Perhaps it is too heavy. Perhaps it is not important. She is lesser, subordinated, dismissed. Her name is Synagoga (Synagogue).

The image comes from a thirteenth-century manuscript. The two figures present a common Christian perspective on the relationship of the Christian church and Jewish synagogue. The church is presented as superior to, dominant over, and dismissive of the synagogue. The latter is dismissed, inferior, defeated, blind to the church's glorious gospel that has replaced the law of Moses.

Figure 1.1. From f. 93 of *Historia scholastica* (the "Ashridge Petrus Comestor"), at the beginning of Deuteronomy. Written in Latin (1283–1300).

1

The tablet slipping from Synagoga's hand represents the law given to Moses on Mount Sinai. It is dropping away to be replaced by the gospel.

The image is located in an illustrated manuscript of the Scriptures. It appears at the beginning of the book of Deuteronomy, which presents an account of God giving the law to Moses. The image interprets Deuteronomy's account of the law. It presents it as defeated and, like the synagogue itself, inferior to the Christian gospel and church.

The scene illustrates a nasty and hostile relationship between the church and the synagogue. It visualizes Christian supersessionist claims that the church is triumphant, victorious, and dominant while the synagogue is surpassed, irrelevant, defeated, obsolete. It denotes and participates in the wider cultural-societal despising of Jews fed by Christian bigotry. In the medieval era, Jews were persecuted in various ways: banned from occupations, victimized by violence and murders, expelled from cities and countries, scapegoated for tragedies such as the Black Death.

Second, two statues (see figs. 1.2 and 1.3).

These two carved stone statues also come from the thirteenth century. They were positioned on either side of one of the entrances to Strasbourg Cathedral. The statues are large, about six and a half feet tall.

Again we have two women, Ecclesia on one side and Synagoga on the other. Ecclesia carries the distinctive Christian symbol of the cross. She is crowned and the more dominant of the two. Her head is positioned so she looks confidently ahead and with a resolute expression toward the other figure. One hand carries another Christian symbol of salvation, the chalice. This represents the blood of Christ spilled from the cross and made available in the church's Mass.

Synagoga appears downcast and dominated. She looks down and away. She is blinded with her eyes covered, representing her inability to see and understand the Christian gospel. She carries a spear, perhaps representing the

Figure 1.2. Statue representing the church.

Claude Truong-Ngoc / CC BY-SA 3.0 / Wikimedia Commons

Figure 1.3. Statue representing the synagogue.

Vassil / Public Domain / Wikimedia Commons

(mistaken) view that Jews or the synagogue killed Jesus. It particularly evokes the spear thrust into Jesus's side at his crucifixion (John 19:34). The spear seems broken, suggesting that Jews could not keep Jesus dead in the face of God's resurrecting power. In her left hand—oftentimes the side that represents a curse—the tablet of the law has a low position. Is it slipping away? Is it too heavy and burdensome to hold aloft? Either way, the Christian dismissal of the law is clear.

The two statues are located at the entrance to the cathedral, the place of Christian worship. Framed by the full weight of the building, they communicate to Christian worshipers entering the cathedral the messages of Christian superiority and Jewish inferiority. The church is much greater than the synagogue. The gospel of Jesus's salvation is greater than the law of Moses. The statues participate in and depict the larger societal-cultural disdain for and violence against Jews.

Figure 1.4. Synagoga and Ecclesia.
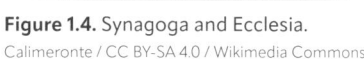
Calimeronte / CC BY-SA 4.0 / Wikimedia Commons

Again, the Christian agenda of triumphalism and supersessionism is on display.

Third, a sculpture (see fig. 1.4).

From an illustration and carved stone figures to a sculpture.

From a manuscript and a cathedral to a university.

From the thirteenth century to the twenty-first century.

In 2015 this statue was unveiled at Saint Joseph's University in Philadelphia. What makes it different?

This sculpture, located outside the chapel of Saint Joseph's University in Philadelphia, was created by sculptor Joshua Koffman in 2015. That year, 2015, was the fiftieth anniversary of a significant document, *Nostra aetate* (In our time), released by the Second Vatican Council. The document recognized and appreciated numerous world religions. Specifically for our purposes, the document proposed a respectful and open relationship marked by mutual understanding between Christians and Jews. The document acknowledged the church's location in continuity with

> Israel's patriarchs and prophets. The document also drew back from its traditional accusation that all Jews were responsible for Jesus's death: "What happened in His passion cannot be charged against all the Jews, without distinction, then alive, nor against the Jews of today." In addition, it declared that the church "decries hatred, persecutions, displays of anti-Semitism, directed against Jews at any time and by anyone."[1] While the document did not go far enough for some, it nevertheless marked a significant change in the church's attitude to and interactions with Judaism.

Again we have two women. The two figures are the same height. One does not look down on the other. They sit side by side. They are turned toward each other. The figure on the left, Synagoga, carries an open or unrolled scroll representing Jewish sacred writings. The figure on the right, Ecclesia, carries an open book, the Bible including the New Testament.

Both documents are equally valued. Neither is slipping away. In fact, the open texts suggest dialogue, not domination, dismissal, and defeat. The open texts affirm the wisdom of each tradition and the openness of each figure to the other.

This statue suggests a very different relationship between church and synagogue, Christianity and Judaism. It images mutuality, openness, reciprocity, respect. And it represents repentance on the part of the church, a letting go of claims of arrogant superiority and judgment. It depicts a changed narrative about the interaction of two traditions.

Reading This Book

We're pleased you're reading this book. We think it addresses an important topic.

For a long time, Christians have had some troubling misunderstandings about Jews and Judaism. In this book we trouble those misunderstandings by attending to some of the continuities and discontinuities that exist between the two traditions.

These images remind us that conflict between church and synagogue, Christianity and Judaism, has a long and vicious history. In this book, we cannot discuss this nasty history that spans two millennia in any detail. That would be too big a task for one book.

---

1. See https://www.vatican.va/archive/hist_councils/ii_vatican_council/documents/vat-ii_decl_19651028_nostra-aetate_en.html.

Rather, we focus on just one piece of this larger history. Numerous studies have discussed possible relationships between the "Old" and "New" Testaments. But few studies have examined the interaction between the texts and traditions of Early Judaism and the New Testament writings. "Early Judaism" refers to the time period immediately preceding and overlapping with New Testament texts. We're dialing in on these texts and a time span from around 250 BCE to about 150 CE.

> The Judaism that we study in this book is an ancient religion. As every other religious tradition, it has changed and morphed throughout the millennia. To help track these changes, scholars divide its long history into periods. In this book we are zooming in on the time between 250 BCE and 150 CE. This stretch of time is a part of the Second Temple period. Nowadays, scholars call the variety of Jewish religious life in this period "Second Temple Judaism" or "Early Judaism." These respectful names do away with the imprecision of a term such as "postbiblical Judaism" or the supersessionism expressed by "intertestamental period" or the dismissiveness of "Late Judaism." For similar reasons, we use the term "Hebrew Bible" rather than "Old Testament" throughout this book.

In the subsequent chapters, we highlight significant continuities between the texts of Early Judaism and the New Testament writings. We also outline various ways in which New Testament texts interpret these traditions in relation to Jesus. Throughout, without denying differences and instances of vicious hatefulness, we highlight more amicable relationships, shared contexts and traditions, and continuities in understandings rather than the traditional antithetical and hostile interactions. That is, our work rejects centuries of bigotry and prejudice, vitriol and claims of Christian triumphalism, in favor of a model emphasizing shared traditions, mutuality, and respect.

Why Is This Book Necessary?

This book is necessary because while the relationship between Judaism and Christianity has shown some improvement since the thirteenth century, there is still a considerable way to go. We have only to recall the appalling genocide of European Jews in the mid-twentieth century, the Holocaust. In the timeline of human history, the genocide of the 1930s and '40s is shockingly recent.

Or we can note that anti-Jewish actions (assault, harassment, vandalism, etc.) are on the rise in the United States. The Anti-Defamation League (ADL) reported 2,026 such incidents in 2020; 2,717 in 2021 (a 34 percent increase); and 3,697 in 2022 (a 36 percent increase). The 2022 number is the highest since the ADL started recording incidents in 1979. It is dangerous to be a Jewish person in the United States.[2] The Foundation to Combat Antisemitism has launched a $25 million social media and television campaign (#StandUpToJewishHate) to counter anti-Jewish hate. The causes of this increase are multiple and have certainly been fueled in recent years by right-wing politicians and white supremacist groups, who often evoke some form of Christian identity to justify their hateful claims.

But anti-Jewish prejudice is not the preserve of extremist groups. It cannot be denied that there remains a long-standing cultural prejudice fed by anti-Jewish readings of the New Testament in Catholic and Protestant churches. It would be rare for a churchgoer not to have heard the reading of nasty New Testament passages such as the following.

After the Roman governor Pontius Pilate condemns Jesus to death, a Jerusalem crowd surprisingly takes responsibility and cries,

> His blood be on us and on our children! (Matt. 27:25)

Or in John's Gospel, Jesus addresses the Jewish leaders with some nasty name-calling:

> You are from your father the devil, and you choose to do your father's desires. He was a murderer from the beginning and does not stand in the truth because there is no truth in him. When he lies, he speaks according to his own nature, for he is a liar and the father of lies. (John 8:44)

Or in the book of Acts, the apostle Peter blames the Jewish council in Jerusalem for crucifying Jesus:

> The God of our ancestors raised up Jesus, whom you had killed by hanging him on a tree. (Acts 5:30)

And it would be rare for a churchgoer not to have heard some of these nasty claims that mischaracterize Judaism and assert Christian superiority:

- Jews didn't know about love until Jesus taught about it.
- In the temple, Jews went through the motions with ritual and sacrifice for a distant or absent God, whereas Christians know and practice spiritual worship in intimate relationship with God as "Abba" (Daddy).

---

2. See "Audit of Antisemitic Incidents 2022," ADL, March 23, 2023, https://www.adl.org/resources/report/audit-antisemitic-incidents-2022.

- In futility, Jews relied on works and the law to earn God's favor, whereas Christians confidently rely on God's grace through faith.
- All Jews were expecting a Messiah but rejected and killed Jesus because he did not meet their expectations.
- Jews didn't believe in resurrection, so they didn't believe Jesus had been raised.
- Since God is either absent, uncaring, or distant, Jewish prayers are not answered, but since Jesus taught Christians to pray, God only answers prayers in Jesus's name.
- Some Christians even think that Judaism is a religion that is not currently practiced!

These common claims are simply not true, as we demonstrate in the following chapters.

When Jesus teaches about love, he borrows verses from Deuteronomy and Leviticus (see chap. 2). Jewish traditions are full of accounts of encounters with God (see chap. 3), and "Abba" does not mean "Daddy." Jews did not rely on works and the law to earn God's favor; they already had divine blessing by being born into the covenant (see chap. 5). Not all Jews were expecting a messiah, and there was not one standard expectation (see chap. 6). Jews did not crucify Jesus; his death was ordered by the Roman governor Pontius Pilate (see chap. 8). Among various views of the afterlife, some Jews did expect resurrection (see chap. 9). Jews had an extensive experience of prayer and did not regard God as absent or distant (see chap. 12).

These errant claims are uninformed and attest prejudices and assertions of superiority among (some) Christians. The claims have been around for centuries. Sadly, they remain just one Google search away. We are not interested in targeting specific groups or naming and shaming specific individuals here. Rather, we highlight thinking that sustains bigotry and can escalate to disrespectful and hateful actions. Our discussions in the subsequent chapters will address these matters.

The Texts

In each chapter we identify some of the important texts in both Early Judaism and the New Testament related to the chapter's topic. Some of this material will be unfamiliar; some will be familiar. We cannot discuss every relevant text because of space limitations.

We have selected texts that we think are especially relevant and representative. Those texts primarily belong to four collections: the Apocrypha, the Pseudepigrapha, the Dead Sea Scrolls, and the New Testament. We also consider other Jewish writings from around the time of the New Testament. For example, Philo of Alexandria and Josephus, who writes from Rome where he was an "adviser" in the emperor's court, produced significant writings. In the bibliography you will find a list of the English translations that we used for these texts.

Here is some orientation to the four main collections of texts.

The Apocrypha

The Apocrypha is a collection of Jewish texts written between around 250 BCE and 100 CE. The texts were not included in the Jewish Bible or the Protestant Bible but were included in the Greek translation of the Jewish Bible known as the Septuagint (often indicated by its abbreviation in Roman numerals, LXX). The word "apocrypha" is a transliteration of a Greek word that means "hidden things." The term probably denotes the noncanonical status of these writings.

The Roman Catholic Church included most of this collection of writings in its "Old Testament" at the Council of Trent in 1546 and referred to them as deuterocanonical texts. In recent decades, versions of the Bible used particularly by Protestants have included the texts of the Apocrypha without giving them canonical or authoritative status. Their inclusion reflects a renewed interest in Judaism in the aftermath of the Holocaust and was stimulated by the discovery and publication of the Dead Sea Scrolls in the second half of the twentieth century.

The collection comprises sixteen documents, some written originally in Hebrew or Aramaic and subsequently translated into Greek, and some written originally in Greek. The collection comprises different genres.

1. "Historical" Books

First and Second Maccabees focus on the violent assertion of Hellenistic culture by Antiochus IV Epiphanes in the 160s BCE and his attack on Judaism. Jewish resistance overcomes Antiochus's attack. First Maccabees legitimates the emergent Hasmonean dynasty. Second Maccabees emphasizes God's protection of the people when they are loyal to the covenant.

2. Wisdom Writings

These writings expand on the wisdom writings in the Hebrew Bible such as Proverbs, Ecclesiastes, Job, and wisdom psalms. *Wisdom of Sirach* (or *Ben Sira*) sets out a teacher's instruction for elite male students. The author instructs them to resist assimilating Hellenistic culture and thus compromising their observance of Torah and their covenant loyalty.

The *Wisdom of Solomon*, written not by Solomon but in his name, probably in Alexandria, Egypt, exhorts the righteous to faithfulness in circumstances of opposition. It assures them of God's care for God's people, even postmortem, and of God's condemnation of enemies and Hellenistic religion.

3. Treatises

The *Letter of Jeremiah*, neither a letter nor by Jeremiah, warns readers away from gentile idolatry and dominant Hellenistic culture. *Fourth Maccabees* is a first-century CE philosophical treatise arguing that reason is the means of mastery of passions. The writer addresses other Hellenistic Jews, urging faithfulness to the Jewish law, which redefines reason and which fulfills the Hellenistic ideal. His primary exhibit consists of Jewish martyrs from the crisis of the 160s BCE.

4. Rewritten Bible / Expansions and Reformulations of Scripture

This is the largest group.

First Esdras offers a retelling of 2 Chronicles 35–36, Ezra 1–10, and Nehemiah 7:73–8:13. It emphasizes Zerubbabel's significance and the line of David.

The *Greek version of Esther* in the Apocrypha differs significantly from the Hebrew Bible's version. It contains six additions that result in 150 more verses than the Hebrew Bible text. The additions emphasize God as the savior of the Jews in a context of gentile hostility. The edict against Jews becomes more anti-Jewish than in the Hebrew text. Mordecai gains more prominence, and Esther becomes a romantic heroine.

The *Greek version of Daniel* includes three additions. The *Prayer of Azariah and the Song of the Three Jews* presents their prayers in the furnace. Daniel saves *Susanna* from a terrible injustice. In *Bel and the Dragon*, Daniel exposes the ineffectiveness of gentile idolatry, and King Cyrus recognizes Daniel's God as the true God.

Psalm 151 celebrates God's actions through David and his victory over the gentile Goliath.

The *Prayer of Manasseh* supplies the repentance and confession of the wicked Manasseh, after which God restores his kingship. The prayer is mentioned in 2 Chronicles 33:12–13, but that passage does not supply the prayer. Someone fills this gap with the Prayer of Manasseh.

Baruch comprises three parts, echoing Daniel 9, Job 28, Deuteronomy 30, and Deutero-Isaiah (Isa. 40–55). The document consoles Jews in exile and promises deliverance from gentile domination, perhaps that of Antiochus IV Epiphanes.

5. Folktales/Romances

Tobit tells the story of Jews living faithfully in the difficult circumstances of exile and foreign domination. The story exhorts faithfulness to the Torah. In line with Deuteronomic theology, obedience brings blessing, while disobedience brings disaster. Suffering tests faithfulness.

Judith tells the story of Nebuchadnezzar as gentile king and Holofernes as invading general. They threaten the town of Bethulia. Judith, the heroine, bravely delivers the town by seducing and beheading Holofernes. God defends the oppressed. Observing the law is central.

Third Maccabees has nothing to do with the Maccabees. Its focus is the effort of the Egyptian king Ptolemy IV to suppress Judaism and remove Jews from Egypt. The writing provides assurance that God cares for Jews outside the land in the diaspora.

6. Eschatology

Second Esdras includes a Jewish apocalypse (2 Esd. 3–14 = 4 Ezra) from the late first century, after the Romans destroyed Jerusalem and the temple. It concerns God's providence and justice. After their deaths, God rewards the faithful and punishes those who don't obey Torah. A future messiah will condemn Rome and bring an age of peace. Chapters 1–2 and 15–16 are Christian additions.

These writings that make up the Apocrypha employ these diverse genres. Yet running through many of them is an exhortation to live faithfully to the law in the midst of pressures and tribulations from gentile (Hellenistic and Roman) cultures.

Pseudepigrapha

While the Apocrypha has had fixed contents for millennia, the collection known as the Pseudepigrapha has not. The German scholar and manuscript collector Johann Albert Fabricius first brought a collection of diverse texts together in 1713. These texts were not in the Bible, nor were they part of the Apocrypha. However, some of the writings have been part of the canons of some Christian communities across the ages. We should note that the dating of some of the texts is not clear.

The Pseudepigrapha includes texts that bear the names of authoritative or ideal figures from Jewish traditions, such as patriarchs (Abraham), kings (Solomon), prophets (Moses, Elijah, Isaiah), and other leading figures (e.g., Adam and Eve, Enoch, Baruch, Ezra). These figures did not write the texts bearing their names. Rather, their names were "borrowed" to supply authority and legitimacy to the writing's content.

The Pseudepigrapha also includes texts associated with biblical figures or stories. Some rewrite sections of biblical texts (Jubilees). Others elaborate a scriptural reference and create a new story. For example, Joseph and Aseneth creates a story around the brief mention of Genesis 41:45 that Joseph married Aseneth, the daughter of an Egyptian priest.

The term "pseudepigrapha" is controversial. To some, it sounds like forgery and fraud marked by false and misleading attributions of authorship. It is important for us to remember that different conventions of authorship operated in the ancient world. Writing a work but attributing its authorship to a famous figure was not considered fraudulent or spurious. Rather, it was a sign of homage, a recognition and borrowing of a leading figure's prestige and authority for the work's content. Often it was a way for an author or student to align with the famous figure's teaching or actions. While the term has been challenged, it has remained in use for centuries.

One popular edition of the Pseudepigrapha includes some sixty-three writings. It consists of two volumes and some nineteen hundred pages.[3] And the number of texts included in the Pseudepigrapha keeps growing.[4] These writings date from around 250 BCE to around 300 CE.

The Pseudepigrapha attests the extensive number, range, and vibrancy of writings that Jews produced. And there is no doubt other texts have been either destroyed or not found. A number of pseudepigraphic texts emerged from the Dead Sea Scrolls (see the Dead Sea Scrolls section below). The clear conclusion is that Early Judaism was diverse, living, creative. Old stereotypes among some Christians that it was dead and constrained by the law are simply not true.

Further, throughout the time period in which these texts were produced, Jews were not isolated from the dominant cultures and armies of leading powers. Persians, Greeks, Syrians, Egyptians, and Romans threatened Jewish identity, practices, and commitments. The Pseudepigrapha attests different ways in which Jewish folks negotiated these challenges in seeking to remain faithful to the covenant and its way of life.

The texts also provide insight into some of the theological thinking and practices of Early Judaism. One major emphasis concerns the origin of evil and sin and the problem of theodicy. For example, interpreting Genesis 3, some texts blame Eve for human sinfulness (LAE 18:1). Some blame Adam (4 Ezra 3:20). Others blame individual choices (2 Bar. 54:15–19). Others, interpreting Genesis 6, blame evil angels (1 En. 6–16). Some recognize the oppressive economic, social, and political practices of "kings, governors, high

---

3. James H. Charlesworth, ed., *The Old Testament Pseudepigrapha*, 2 vols. (New York: Doubleday, 1983–85).

4. Alexander Panayotov, James Davila, and Richard Bauckham, eds., *Old Testament Pseudepigrapha: More Noncanonical Scriptures*, vol. 1 (Grand Rapids: Eerdmans, 2013).

officials, and landlords" (1 En. 62:1), notably of invading Romans (Pss. Sol. 17:11–20).

Another major emphasis concerns divine workings. Conventional affirmations of God as monotheistic, creator, maker of covenants, giver of the law, active in history, and the righteous judge of all utilize Hebrew Bible traditions. Nevertheless, the ways of God are not always evident in difficult circumstances, so apocalyptic texts anticipate divine action in a final judgment and establishment of divine rule. In these texts, God communicates with humans, whether by oracles (Sibylline Oracles), angels (Jubilees), Lady Wisdom (1 Enoch), or visions and announcements of seers (1 Enoch; 4 Ezra). God is also accessible through the numerous prayers expressed in the texts.

A further emphasis concerns appropriate living, especially in contexts of hostility to Judaism. One genre in particular, that of the testament (e.g., Testaments of the Twelve Patriarchs), provides moral teaching. It usually employs the scenario of a patriarch or distinguished figure on his deathbed who instructs his children on how to live faithfully.

> While the Pseudepigrapha is significant for the study of Early Judaism, their value was not always affirmed, even in the ancient world. For example, the New Testament writing of Jude attacks false teachers. It quotes from the pseudepigraphic text of 1 Enoch (Jude 14–15; 1 En. 1:9), and some think it draws from another pseudepigraphic text, the Assumption of Moses, in verses 9–10. Interestingly, 2 Peter includes most of Jude in its second chapter. Yet significantly, it omits the passages that evoke 1 Enoch and the Assumption of Moses. These omissions suggest that the author of 2 Peter did not consider them worthy of or authoritative for inclusion.

Dead Sea Scrolls

The Dead Sea Scrolls are a trove of Jewish texts that were discovered in the caves near the western shore of the Dead Sea in the 1940s and '50s. These caves are located near the remains of an ancient settlement called Khirbet Qumran in Arabic, which provides the other name often used to describe the scrolls: Qumran scrolls. There are more than one thousand texts in this collection; some are well-preserved and some are badly damaged.

As scholars sorted and gradually identified the scrolls, they also named them. Often, these names are abbreviated (see the appendix for more details). For example, 11QT^a stands for a scroll found in Cave 11 of Qumran (Q). It is called the Temple Scroll (T). And the superscript *a* indicates that this is one of several copies of this composition found in Cave 11. Most scrolls also have a number assigned to them. For instance, Genesis Apocryphon from Cave 1 can be signified both as 1QapGen and as 1Q20.

The scrolls are dated between the third century BCE and the first century CE. Several theories explain how all these texts found their way into the caves. The most popular one assumes that Khirbet Qumran was a home for a Jewish group known as the Essenes. This group used the scrolls and placed them in the caves to protect them when the First Jewish War broke out against Rome in 66 CE.

Figure 1.5. Caves of Qumran.

The Dead Sea Scrolls fall into three groups.

Group 1 comprises some two hundred scrolls containing books that are now a part of the Hebrew Bible. These are our earliest copies of the Jewish Scriptures in their original languages, Hebrew and Aramaic.

Group 2 comprises many texts—all in Hebrew—written by and for a particular Jewish community, possibly the Essenes. Here we identify some of the more prominent and different types of these writings.

Some texts guide the life of this community:

The *Community Rule* (S) addresses various aspects of the communal life and the worldview of a group that called itself *Yahad*, a Hebrew word meaning "together." Several manuscripts of S have been found in the caves. They often differ significantly from one another. The best-preserved manuscript is 1QS.

The *Damascus Document* (CD) elaborates the group's origins, its controversies with its opponents, and its way of life. For example, it includes

Figure 1.6. A Dead Sea Scroll.

regulations for those who wish to join the group and details Sabbath observances. Scholars were aware of two manuscripts of this work before multiple copies of CD were discovered at Qumran.

Some texts are treatises:

Some Precepts of the Law (4QMMT) is a polemical treatise written as a letter to an unknown addressee, perhaps the high priest of the Jerusalem temple. In it, the group outlines multiple issues on which they held a different opinion and explains why they formed their own community.

Some texts are biblical commentaries:

The Dead Sea Scrolls brought to light the earliest known biblical commentaries. These commentaries interpret biblical prophecies as being fulfilled in the life of the community. For example, a commentary on Habakkuk from Qumran reads Habakkuk's description of a foreign invader as referring to the Romans. These actualizing interpretations are often introduced with the word *pesher*, a Hebrew word for "meaning." Scholars then used this word to name these texts: *Pesher Habakkuk* (1QpHab), *4QPesher Isaiah^a* (4Q161), and more.

Some texts contain prayer and religious poetry:

Hodayot / Thanksgiving Hymns (H) is a collection of hymns offering a unique glimpse of the sectarian view of humanity and the world in general.

Many of the hymns begin with the phrase "I thank you, O Lord/God." The most often cited copy of this work is the scroll 1QH^a found in Qumran Cave 1. Several fragmentary manuscripts of H were discovered also in Cave 4.

Some texts provide wisdom teaching:
    4QInstruction is a wisdom text that reflects some of the views held by the sectarian community. There are multiple copies of this writing.

Some texts are eschatological, concerned with the completion of the divine purposes:
    11QMelchizedek (11Q13) is a fragmentary text featuring a heavenly figure named Melchizedek. Through an interpretation of several biblical texts, he is presented as God's agent of forgiveness of sins at the end of days.

    Group 3 of the Dead Sea Scrolls comprises a wide variety of texts. Some of them were known before the Qumran discoveries, while others were not. Among the familiar writings are copies of 1 Enoch and Jubilees (in the Pseudepigrapha) and Sirach and Tobit (in the Apocrypha). Of the many previously unknown texts, two kinds are particularly noteworthy.
    Numerous writings rewrite or expand biblical writings in Hebrew and Aramaic. Many of them are concerned with the books of the Torah (Pentateuch). *Genesis Apocryphon* (1QapGen), for example, is a rewriting—often with significant embellishments—of the Genesis stories about Enoch, Noah, Abraham, and Sarah. It is written in Aramaic.
    Another example is the *Temple Scroll*. It rewrites significant portions of Exodus–Deuteronomy. It envisions a temple in Jerusalem that, as a structure, differed greatly from the contemporary temple. It elaborates various matters pertaining to sacrificial worship.
    Other writings contain prayers. The Dead Sea Scrolls yield the earliest known Jewish prayer books. These include a cycle of prayer for one week (*Words of the Luminaries* [4Q504–506]), a cycle of prayers for a month (*4QDaily Prayers* [4Q503]), and *Prayers for the Festivals* (1Q34 + 1Q34bis; 4Q507–509).
    The Dead Sea Scrolls thus comprise three groups: manuscripts of books in the Hebrew Bible; texts written by and for the community itself; and various other texts, including rewritings of scriptural texts and prayers.

New Testament

We have identified three big collections of texts from Early Judaism: the Apocrypha, the Pseudepigrapha, and the Dead Sea Scrolls.
    The fourth corpus or collection of texts that we discuss in this book is the New Testament or Second Testament. This collection comprises twenty-seven

writings that, along with the Hebrew Bible texts, Christians regard as canonical or authoritative for understanding and practices. The word "canon" means "rule" or "definitive measure."[5]

Jesus was crucified around 30 CE. All the New Testament texts were written between around 50 CE and the 120s CE. All of them are concerned with faithful living for the followers of Jesus.

Although they were not placed first in the New Testament, the letters of Paul were the first works in the New Testament to be written. Scholars generally think Paul wrote seven letters between the late 40s and 50s CE. Five of these are addressed to Jesus-groups in cities: 1 Thessalonians, 1–2 Corinthians, Philippians, and Romans. One was sent to the Galatian believers, though there is debate about exactly where these folks lived. And one was sent to an individual, Philemon, along with the group of Jesus-followers meeting in his house.

The writers of the rest of the New Testament did not date their works, so we don't know for sure when they were written. Some scholars claim they were written in the 50s–70s CE. Others claim a later date, the 70s–100 CE. Among these writings are six letters probably written by followers of Paul in Paul's name after his death: Colossians, Ephesians, 1–2 Timothy, Titus, and 2 Thessalonians. The Gospels were likely written during this period too: first Mark, probably in the early 70s, then Matthew, Luke, and John in the 80s–100 CE. These Gospels tell stories about Jesus and narrate both his actions and his teachings. Most of the remaining writings (James, 1 Peter, 1–3 John, Hebrews, Jude, Revelation) probably come from the 70s–100 CE. Acts and 2 Peter might be the latest, written in the early 100s CE.

In the first couple of centuries CE, there was no "New Testament," no collection of definitive texts, no official New Testament selection committee. Rather, followers of Jesus produced lots of other writings in these centuries, including church manuals (the Didache), letters (Ignatius of Antioch), gospels (of Thomas, of Mary, etc.), and longer treatises. All these writings were used in churches for teaching, preaching, pastoral work, and worship.

Churches evaluated these writings and compiled collections of texts on the basis of their use in church life: the most useful, the somewhat useful, and the not helpful. Some texts gained wide support in many churches early on. Other texts, like Revelation, had a divided response and struggled for wide acceptance. The process was pragmatic and informal.

In the year 367 CE, Bishop Athanasius wrote an important letter at Easter. In it he recognizes that twenty-seven texts seem to have widespread recognition in churches. Whether Athanasius was describing the situation accurately or

---

5. For elaboration, see Warren Carter, *Seven Events That Shaped the New Testament World* (Grand Rapids: Baker Academic, 2013), 107–54.

prescribing what he wanted is debatable. Either way, his proposal was debated at length and gained support.

In 397 CE the Council of Carthage ratified the twenty-seven writings of the New Testament canon, proclaiming them authoritative for the church's doctrine and practice.

Predictably, not everyone agreed!

Matters for Reflection

1. Look back at the first section of this chapter. What are your reactions to the images, texts, statistics, and claims cited there?
2. We identify four big collections of Jewish texts. Remind one another what the four collections are. Can you name some of the writings that belong to each collection? Many recent publications of the Bible include the Apocrypha. If you are not familiar with these writings, sample some of them. Try the Prayer of Manasseh, the first two chapters of 1 Maccabees, 2 Maccabees 7, Judith, Susanna, or parts of Tobit.
3. The discovery of the Dead Sea Scrolls in the twentieth century was a huge archaeological discovery that has had a big impact on our understanding of first-century Judaism. There are multiple documentaries about their discovery that may be available through your library and numerous YouTube videos on the topic.
4. How was the list of the twenty-seven books of the New Testament established? When were these books written? How do these dates relate to the dating of other early Jewish texts we discuss in this chapter?

CHAPTER 2

Reusing Biblical Traditions

In this chapter we focus on a troubling misunderstanding that claims that the Hebrew Bible points only to Jesus—in other words, that parts of the Hebrew Bible made no sense until Jesus came along. Students who have heard this teaching in churches are often surprised to learn that Hebrew Bible texts addressed their own situations for centuries before Jesus and that Jesus-followers were the ones who started the practice of reading the Scriptures through "Jesus glasses."

For example, two of the New Testament Gospels present Jesus citing Psalm 22:1 on the cross when he dies: "My God, my God, why have you forsaken me?" (Mark 15:34; Matt. 27:46). Some Christian interpreters have claimed that the psalm predicted or envisioned Jesus's death centuries before it happened and that people did not understand the psalm until they discovered it referred to Jesus.

In this chapter we trouble that misunderstanding or misreading of the Hebrew Bible. First, the writings of the Hebrew Bible addressed their own contexts long before the events of Jesus's life. Second, and very important for this book, the Hebrew Bible is a common source of material and understandings for both Early Judaism and the New Testament. Both textual traditions draw on the Hebrew Bible in a variety of ways. Their practice of reusing Hebrew Bible texts and characters provides an important continuity between Early Judaism and the New Testament writings.

Yet this act of reusing or rereading Hebrew Bible material is also an act of interpreting it for diverse and often contemporary circumstances. So we look at six instances of this practice of reinterpretation in the writings of both Early Judaism and the New Testament.

Reading Through Qumran Glasses and Jesus Glasses

The community of the Dead Sea Scrolls believed that texts found in the Hebrew Bible spoke about their community and had been fulfilled in their times and experiences. Scholars call such an interpretation *pesher* (singular; plural: *pesharim*). As mentioned in chapter 1, this is the Hebrew word for "meaning." The community's writings often use pesher to introduce an actualizing interpretation of oracles that they regarded as prophetic about themselves.

> Pesher Habakkuk (1QpHab) is a commentary on the book of Habakkuk. Found at Qumran, it reflects the worldview of the sectarian community that preserved the Dead Sea Scrolls.

One remarkable example of this technique involves the book of Habakkuk. The biblical book of Habakkuk was written at the turn of the seventh and sixth centuries BCE. Its first chapter speaks of the imminent invasion of the ruthless Chaldeans (Hab. 1:5–11). These are the Babylonians responsible for the sacking of Jerusalem in 587 BCE.

Pesher Habakkuk (1QpHab) was written some five hundred to six hundred years later. It interprets "Chaldeans" as referring not to the Babylonians but to the dominant power of its own time, the Romans. By doing so, the pesher operates on the assumption that the ancient writer of Habakkuk did not understand the full meaning of the oracles he delivered—in other words, what he wrote had greater meaning than he knew.

So the pesher assumes that the writer of Habakkuk did not fully understand what he wrote and that the leader at Qumran gained full understanding centuries later. The author claims that

> God told Habakkuk to write down that which would happen to the final generation, but He did not make known to him when time would come to an end. (1QpHab 7:1–2)

The full meanings were revealed to the founding figure of the Qumran group. Pesher Habakkuk and other scrolls refer to this figure as the Teacher of Righteousness:

> This concerns the Teacher of Righteousness, to whom God made known all the mysteries of the words of His servants the Prophets. (1QpHab 7:3–5)

Elsewhere, Pesher Habakkuk mentions "the priest" in whose heart "God set [understanding] that he might interpret all the words of His servants the Prophets" (1QpHab 2:8–9). And there was indeed a need for some explaining. For instance, we learn from this scroll that this group expected a divine intervention that had not yet occurred. Pesher Habakkuk interprets Habakkuk's words as encouraging patience. Habakkuk says,

> For there is still a vision for the appointed time; . . . If it seems to tarry, wait for it; it will surely come; it will not delay. (Hab. 2:3)

Interpreting this passage, Pesher Habakkuk calls for patient waiting "when the final age is prolonged." It reassures the faithful that "all the ages of God reach their appointed end as he determines for them" and asks them not to "slacken in the service of truth" (1QpHab 7:10–13).

The inhabitants of Qumran read the Hebrew Bible book of Habakkuk through their "Qumran glasses." They saw what nobody else had ever seen in Habakkuk—namely, the history and experience of their own community.

A similar approach to Hebrew Bible passages is evident in New Testament writings. But instead of reading through Qumran glasses, the New Testament writers read through their "Jesus glasses." They interpreted Hebrew Bible passages in a way that provides insight into Jesus's identity and shapes the identity of Jesus-followers.

One example involves several Hebrew Bible writings that employ a spirituality, or paradigm of understanding God's workings, called "lament." This paradigm involves three parties: a person who is faithful to God, hostile opponents who cause them suffering, and God. The faithful person feels God has abandoned them and laments or whines about their circumstances to God, who seems absent and uncaring. Then suddenly, somehow, God intervenes to rescue and restore the situation. The faithful person then praises God.

Think Job, Jeremiah, lament psalms like Psalms 22 and 69.

The Gospels of Mark and Matthew reuse this paradigm of the faithful or righteous sufferer to shape the story of Jesus's death (Mark 14–15; Matt. 26–27). These narratives present Jesus as faithful to God's purposes. His opponents include the Rome-allied Jerusalem leaders and the Roman governor Pontius Pilate. They abuse Jesus and crucify him.

Jesus cries from the cross by borrowing the words of Psalm 22:1: "My God, my God, why have you forsaken me?" (Mark 15:34; Matt. 27:46). Psalm 22 is a lament psalm. The Gospel narrative also borrows other features of this lament paradigm from Psalm 22: mocking (Ps. 22:6–8; Mark 15:16–32), being surrounded by enemies (Ps. 22:6–8, 12–13; Mark 15:1–38), head shaking (Ps. 22:7; Mark 15:29), casting lots for clothing (Ps. 22:18; Mark 15:24), and being vindicated by divine intervention (Ps. 22:21b; Mark 16:1–8 [resurrection]).

The point is that Psalm 22 did not refer to Jesus until Jesus-followers read it in relation to Jesus's death. For centuries, the psalm was read in the context of Jewish worship. Countless faithful people saw themselves and their nation in the psalm's scene. They experienced harassment from hostile enemies.

They felt God had abandoned them. But then, they testified to experiencing God's deliverance. And for centuries no one attributed this psalm to Jesus.

That is, until Jesus-followers read it through Jesus glasses. They borrowed the spirituality of lament. They reused the psalm's paradigm to make sense of Jesus's horrible crucifixion. He was faithful to God. Hostile people like Pilate opposed him and killed him. He experienced God's apparent indifference and absence. Subsequently, he knew God's faithful deliverance in resurrection.

New/Renewed Covenant (Jer. 31:31–34)

A prophecy in Jeremiah 31:31–34 envisions a time when God will make "a new covenant with the house of Israel and the house of Judah" (31:31). The reason for a new covenant is simple: Israel failed to keep the covenant that God made with them at Sinai. Will the new covenant be different from the previous one?

Jeremiah says that God will put God's "law" or "torah" ("teaching") "within them" and "write it on their hearts" (31:33). As a result, they will obey God, and God "will forgive their iniquity" (31:34).

Jeremiah's words offered consolation to the people and the land desolated by the Babylonian invasion in 587 BCE. Centuries later, the Dead Sea Scrolls community believed that God established this new covenant with them and with them alone. In their view, when Israel went astray, God delivered Israel to the sword but spared a remnant.

> The Damascus Document (CD) tells about the origins of a sectarian community, its opponents, and its way of life. Several copies of this text were found among the Dead Sea Scrolls.

According to the Damascus Document (CD), which was written some four hundred years after Nebuchadnezzar's sacking of Jerusalem, a group of penitent faithful emerged from the remnant (CD 1:1–11). God established with them God's "Covenant with Israel forever" (CD 3:13). Moreover, God revealed to them where the rest of Israel failed by not observing "His holy Sabbaths and His glorious feasts, the testimonies of His righteousness and the ways of His truth, and the desires of His will" (CD 3:14–16).

The Damascus Document describes this covenant as the "new covenant." And it associates this new covenant with careful observance of the Torah, especially in matters related to purity, Sabbath, and festivals. It also highlights the importance of separating from the wicked and their wealth and refraining from oppressing the less fortunate (CD 6:14–21).

The Qumran texts reveal that not all who initially accepted the terms of the new covenant remained faithful to it. They are called "traitors" (1QpHab

2:4; CD 19:34) who have no part in the community (CD 19:33–20:1, 12–13). This new covenant is also called "a pledge" (CD 20:12). This term recalls the "pledge" to observe certain laws of the Torah by those who came back from the Babylonian exile in Nehemiah 10.

As in Nehemiah 10, these writings do not claim to replace the Torah of Moses with another set of regulations. Rather, they call for a more perfect observance of it. Hence, some suggest that a translation of "renewed covenant" would be more accurate.

New Testament writers employ "covenant" especially as a means of interpreting Jesus's death. Describing the Passover meal that Jesus shares with his disciples, Mark's Gospel narrates that Jesus takes the cup and says to them,

> This is my blood of the covenant . . . poured out for many. (Mark 14:24)

The blood that seals the covenant at Sinai (Exod. 24:8) is reinterpreted here in relation to Jesus's death. As with previous covenants, Jesus's death benefits many. This is not a brand-new covenant but another form of God's covenant with God's people. Just as in Genesis the covenant with Abraham promises blessing for all people or nations (Gen. 12:3; 17:2–7), so in Mark's Gospel, "many," Jews and gentiles, benefit from Jesus's death.

Matthew's Gospel elaborates the benefit of Jesus's poured-out blood. His blood effects forgiveness of sin (Matt. 26:28). This is not a new reality. The claim evokes and repeats Jeremiah's proclamation of a (re)new(ed) covenant that is marked by forgiveness of sin (Jer. 31:34).

Paul also evokes the link with Jeremiah by using the language of "new covenant" to refer to Jesus's death. He reminds the Jesus-followers of what Jesus said:

> This cup is the new covenant in my blood. (1 Cor. 11:25; cf. Luke 22:20)

How new is "new"? There is no indication in Paul that this new covenant in Jesus's blood replaces covenants with Israel or renders them obsolete. Paul affirms continuity in recognizing that the covenants belong to Israel (Rom. 9:4). The covenant made with Abraham promises divine blessing for all people, Jew and gentile (Gen. 12:3). Accordingly, Paul is adamant that God is the God of both Jews and gentiles (Rom. 3:29). The language of "renewed" covenant seems most appropriate.

Likewise in 2 Corinthians 3, Paul continues to follow Jeremiah 31:31–34 in presenting the (re)new(ed) covenant as a development of the previous covenant, even an improvement of it. That's because the covenant is renewed in being written on hearts, not stone tablets. It deals in life, not death (2 Cor. 3:14–16).

The book of Hebrews develops this process of previous and renewed covenants with a sharp contrast between old and new. This contrast creates a different, less charitable interaction with regard to previous expressions of covenant. It indicates a break, a starting over with something new that discards the past. It frames the "old" covenant as now obsolete and disappearing (Heb. 8:13).

New Testament writers thereby evoke covenant in different ways. Most emphasize continuity in a renewed covenant and align Jesus's death and its benefits with the covenants associated with Abraham, Sinai, and Jeremiah. Others, such as the author of Hebrews, seem to highlight discontinuity to assert both Christian superiority and exclusivism in claiming a Christocentric interpretation. This presentation is inconsistent with the inclusive covenant with Abraham, in which divine blessing extends to all.

Reusing Isaiah 40

Isaiah 40 opens with an oft-cited message of consolation:

> Comfort, O comfort my people, says your God.

Written in the sixth century BCE with the Judean exiles in Babylon in view, the oracles of Isaiah 40 envision an imminent return of the exiles to their homeland of Judea:

> A voice cries out: "In the wilderness prepare the way of the LORD; make straight in the desert a highway for our God." (40:3)

Since ancient Hebrew did not have punctuation marks, this passage can also be read differently:

> A voice cries out *in the wilderness*: "Prepare the way of the LORD; make straight in the desert a highway for our God."

When Isaiah was translated into Greek in the second century BCE, the translators favored the latter rendering. This is the reading found also in the Gospels. On the other hand, the key writing from Qumran, Community Rule, favors the first reading.

Like Pesher Habakkuk, the Community Rule takes up Isaiah's vision and reads it through Qumran glasses. This approach results in a distinctive and important interpretation (1QS 8:12–16). It understands Isaiah 40:3 as calling community members to separate from the "people of injustice." The community members are to "go into the wilderness to prepare there the way of Him [God]." This "wilderness" is apparently the area near the Dead Sea. Another copy of the Community Rule interprets this "way" as a metaphor: "the way of the Truth" (4Q259 [4QS^c] 3:4).

Next comes a citation, a prooftext from Isaiah 40:3: "As it is written, 'Prepare in the wilderness prepare the way of · · · ·, make straight in the desert a path for our God'" (1QS 8:14).

> Quoting from Isaiah 40:3, the ancient Jewish scribe who copied 1QS replaced the Hebrew name of God—the so-called Tetragrammaton—with four dots, one dot for each letter. Apparently, this was the scribe's way of indicating to the readers that this name should not be pronounced. Several early Jewish texts attest to the emergence of such a prohibition in this period.

What is this going to "the wilderness" to prepare the "highway" or the "path" all about? According to the Community Rule, it's about the "expounding of the Torah" that takes place in the community's location near the Dead Sea. The community believed that, in that place, God would continue to reveal God's will to this faithful community "from age to age." The community would receive these revelations by the "expounding of" or "searching in" the words of "the prophets" who wrote "by His holy Spirit" (1QS 8:12–16).

This same passage from Isaiah 40:3 is important for the Gospels of Mark (1:2–3), Matthew (3:3), and Luke (3:4–6). Each Gospel continues the same practice of interpreting this Scripture in relation to its particular circumstances, thereby creating new meaning for Isaiah's verse. These Gospels apply the passage to John the Baptist and his role in preparing for Jesus's ministry.

> The Community Rule, or S, as scholars have designated it, regulates the life of a sectarian community and explains its worldview. It was found among the Dead Sea Scrolls. Its best-preserved copy is 1QS.

Of course, Isaiah's declaration had nothing whatsoever to do with John the Baptist. As we noted above, originally it addressed sixth-century exiles from Judea who had been taken as captives to Babylon. It announced that God was preparing for them to return to their homeland. This took place in 539 BCE and the following years. Wearing Jesus glasses centuries later, the Gospels reinterpret the verse in relation to John's ministry. The voice of one crying in the wilderness is neither God nor a member of the heavenly council, as in Isaiah, but is now John the Baptist in the Gospel.

The circumstances are not exile in sixth-century Babylon but the wilderness of first-century, Rome-controlled Judea in anticipation of Jesus's activity. And in relation to John's role of being a witness, the "way of the Lord" refers not to God's activity but to Jesus's activity.

"Prepare the way" and "make his paths straight" refer to John's preaching of repentance and practice of baptism before Jesus Messiah/Christ comes.

While the citation is short and identical in Matthew and Mark, Luke's citation in 3:4–6 is longer. It cites not only Isaiah 40:3 but also Isaiah 40:4 and rewrites part of verse 5. Isaiah 40:4, cited in Luke 3:5, envisions considerable geographical transformation:

> Every valley shall be lifted up, and every mountain and hill be made low; the uneven ground shall become level, and the rough places a plain.

Perhaps this geographical transformation signifies the reengineering of a road in preparation for the arrival of an important person to a city or town. Perhaps it imagines transformed lives—smoothed out and made straight—that result from a response of repentance to John's proclamation.

Luke 3:6 adds a further piece, a declaration that "all flesh shall see the salvation of God." Just as Isaiah expects that "all flesh shall see it [God's saving action] together" (Isa. 40:5) as God frees the exiles from Babylon to return home, so too does Luke's Gospel expect *everyone*, Jews and gentiles, to experience God's transforming, saving work effected by Jesus. The Gospel sounds this theme in the previous chapters. Mary envisions a transformed and just world (Luke 1:47–55). Angels announce peace on earth (2:14). The elderly Simeon sees Jesus as "a light for gentiles and glory for Israel" (2:32). This universal expectation differs from the Gospels of both Mark and Matthew, as well as the "in-house" focus of the Qumran reading of the Isaiah passage.

Different communities read the same text—Isaiah 40:3–5—in different circumstances with different perspectives and with quite different meanings.

Reconstructing Abraham

Several writings in the Hebrew Bible rewrite existing writings. The books of Chronicles, for example, rewrite or rework the books of Samuel and Kings by omitting, expanding, and paraphrasing. These rewritings are not mere duplications of the earlier texts. Rather, they recast and mold them in numerous ways to create new meanings.

Many early Jewish texts rewrite or rework stories found in the Hebrew Bible. The Dead Sea Scrolls, for example, include many previously unknown texts with rewritten narratives and laws from the Torah and the Prophets. One example is the badly damaged scroll named Genesis Apocryphon (1QapGen). As its name suggests, it rewrites portions of the book of Genesis.

Genesis Apocryphon is written in Aramaic. Its treatment of Genesis suggests it represents views of wider Jewish communities of the time. Four of its surviving twenty-three columns (cols. 19–22) are devoted to events involving Abraham narrated in Genesis 12–15. While rewriting these stories, the scroll sometimes greatly expands them.

The scroll presents Abraham as an ideal figure. He is renowned for his wisdom, which draws Egyptian nobles searching for scribal knowledge, wisdom, and truth (1QapGen 19:23–25). Abraham has dream visions (21:8–14; 22:27–34), including a prophetic one (19:14–17). Abraham is a man of prayer. He prays "through sorrow and streaming tears" when Sarah is taken away (20:12–16), and he heals Pharaoh and his house with prayer and the laying on of hands (20:21–23, 28–29).

In biblical Genesis, Abraham does not always behave well. In Egypt, Pharaoh abducts Sarah, whom Abraham presented as his sister, not his wife (Gen. 12:10–20). But in Genesis Apocryphon, Abraham gets a makeover. His decision to present Sarah as his sister is said to result from his prophetic dream (1QapGen 19:14–21). Abraham is freed of responsibility. It was God's idea!

Further, it is word of Abraham's wisdom that brings the Egyptian courtiers to his home, leading to Sarah's exposure after five years of hiding (19:23–24). Sarah's beauty, when reported to Pharaoh, appears to set the disturbing events in motion (20:2–8). God miraculously protects Sarah's chastity (20:17). Pharaoh formally divorces her (20:9, 23) and swears that he has not defiled her (20:30). This makes it clear that Abraham can lawfully have her as his wife (cf. Deut. 24:4).

Other constructions of Abraham in both early Jewish and New Testament writings portray Abraham in a way that serves a particular agenda. For example, Ben Sira presents Abraham as the model faithful Jew in covenant with God (cf. Gen. 17:2–7) and obedient to the law. He

> kept the law of the Most High and entered into the covenant with him. He certified the covenant in his flesh [circumcision]. (Sir. 44:19)

This presentation is so keen to emphasize Abraham as a model that it has Abraham keeping Israel's law *before* God had granted it to Moses. Abraham is constructed as the father of Israel, God's chosen people: "You chose the descendants of Abraham above all the nations" (Pss. Sol. 9:9).

Yet Abraham is also constructed as an international figure. The divine promise to Abraham that he would be the father of many nations and that in him all the peoples of the earth would be blessed is often repeated (Gen. 12:3; 17:4–6).

> Abraham was the great father of a multitude of nations. . . . The nations would be blessed through his offspring. (Sir. 44:19, 21; cf. Jub. 12:22–24)

Josephus portrays Abraham as a man of international learning (*Ant.* 1.161–68). In Egypt Abraham instructs the Egyptians and Greeks in arithmetic and astronomy (*Ant.* 1.168). He is the progenitor not of an exclusive people but of "a multitude of nations" (*Ant.* 1.235).

Philo's Abraham also operates internationally. He rejects the idolatry and astronomy of the Chaldeans while he continues his search for God (*Abraham* 68–88). He discovers God through reason but not through the Mosaic law. This God is "the maker and ruler" of all. Abraham's quest is a model for all. His children are not limited to ethnic descent but are marked by openness to the discernment of divine purposes in creation and appropriate living.

> Josephus was a Jewish general during the First Jewish War with Rome in 66–74 CE. Early in the war, he defected to the Roman side. After the war, he wrote several important works about the war and the history of the Jewish people.

> Philo was a Jew who lived in first-century CE Alexandria. In his many writings in Greek, Philo explains the Torah using tools and ideas borrowed from Hellenistic philosophy.

New Testament writings continue this tradition of constructing Abraham in different ways.

Paul's Abraham is a Jew (Rom. 4:1). Yet God reckoned him righteous *before*, not *after*, he was circumcised (4:10; cf. Gen. 15:6). This order of events establishes Abraham as an example of the faithfulness that God desires (Rom. 4:12). It proves for Paul that God justifies gentiles as well as Jews by faithfulness (4:11–12). Abraham is the father of many nations (gentiles) because of his trust in God's promises (4:13–22).

Matthew's Gospel constructs Abraham as both Jewish and international. The Gospel opens by identifying Jesus as a descendant of Abraham (Matt. 1:1). The following genealogy (1:1–17, with a few exceptions) traces Jesus's genealogy from Abraham through Israel's history.

Yet the Gospel troubles reliance on ethnicity. When Jewish leaders oppose John the Baptist's baptism, John challenges them to "bear fruit worthy of repentance" (Matt. 3:8). They reply by appealing to Abraham as their ancestor (3:9). John the Baptist dismisses an appeal to ancestry; God can "raise up children to Abraham" from stones (3:9). True children of Abraham bear the "fruit" of faithfully doing God's will. Gentiles and Jews are both children of Abraham and God.

John's Gospel takes a different approach. It viciously redefines and curtails Abraham's fatherhood (John 8:39–47). In an exchange with Jesus, Jewish leaders identify themselves as children of Abraham (8:39). Jesus denies them this identity because, he says, they do not act as Abraham does. Instead of receiving Jesus as Abraham would, they are trying to kill Jesus, who is an agent and revealer of God (8:40). If they were children of Abraham, they would love Jesus and understand his teaching (8:41–43). John's Jesus presses the attack. Their behavior, in fact, suggests they are not children of Abraham but children of the devil. The devil lies and murders. The Jewish leaders are, in the Gospel's construction, liars and murderers like their father, the devil (8:44–47).

This attack on the Jewish leaders—not all Jews—is appalling. It is not the norm in the New Testament or normative for Christian understanding. It might have emerged from bitter conflicts between Jesus-followers and synagogue members. It certainly functions to distinguish the latter from the former and to ally Abraham exclusively with Jesus and his followers.

Love God, Love Neighbor

Some Christians sing a Christmas carol with words written by the nineteenth-century English poet Christina Rossetti (d. 1894). It includes these lines:

> Love came down at Christmas. . . . Love was born at Christmas.

The carol expresses a common Christian claim that Jesus taught something new. He brought love into a loveless world. After all, he did teach,

> You shall love the Lord your God with all your heart and with all your soul and with all your mind. . . . You shall love your neighbor as yourself. (Matt. 22:34–40)

This claim that love is something unique to Christians is not accurate. It embodies an inaccurate and unsustainable claim of Christian superiority.

First, Jesus's teaching of love for God and neighbor draws together two Hebrew Bible verses. Deuteronomy 6:5 states Moses's first command to love God wholeheartedly. And Leviticus 19:18 teaches love for neighbor.

This neighbor love is not primarily about being "nice" (though that can help). It is more about a societal vision in which practices of love and justice ensure that everyone has what they need for a good life.

Love for the neighbor in Leviticus 19 includes supplying the poor and foreigner with food (19:10), paying wages to the laborer (19:13), and caring for kinsfolk and "any of your people" (19:1–18). Neighbor love creates a network of human interactions that includes respect for parents (19:3); dealings without stealing, lying, falsity, or swearing (19:11–12); not taking advantage of the vulnerable (19:13–14); not showing partiality (19:15); not slandering (19:16); and not taking vengeance (19:17–18).

Second, this double command to love God and neighbor is not Jesus's creation. It is teaching found regularly in Early Judaism. For example, various testaments, in which a patriarch or significant figure is dying, include this teaching:

> Keep the law of God, my children. . . . Love the Lord and your neighbor; be compassionate toward poverty and sickness. (T. Iss. 5:1–2)

> Throughout all your life love the Lord, and one another. (T. Dan 5:3)[1]

Other texts express the same commitments to God and people with slightly different language. Philo identifies both love of people and love of God as necessary for an honorable and virtuous life (*Decalogue* 110). Philo also presents Abraham as exhibiting his duty to God in piety and holiness and his duty to people in humanity and justice (*Spec. Laws* 2.63). In his farewell instructions, Abraham is said to teach his children to "guard the way of the Lord . . . and love your neighbor" (Jub. 20:2). Other testaments link duty to God and neighbors.

> Fear the Lord and love your neighbor. (T. Benj. 3:3–4)

> In every act keep the fear of God before your eyes and honor your brothers/siblings. (T. Jos. 11:1)

Jesus's double command to love God and neighbor, then, is not a Christian creation. Jesus did not invent love. Jewish traditions know, teach, and practice love for God and neighbor. This love constitutes societal practices and networks that ensure the inclusion and well-being of all.

Jesus emphasizes an all-inclusive understanding of "neighbor":

> You have heard that it was said, "You shall love your neighbor and hate your enemy." But I say to you: Love your enemies and pray for those who persecute you. (Matt. 5:43–44)

---

1. These two passages come from a document (Testaments of the Twelve Patriarchs) that has in several places brief additions or insertions that refer to Jesus. The passages cited in this chapter are not impacted by these later editings.

Nowhere does the Bible explicitly teach hatred toward enemies, though it does sanction genocide against "the Hittites and the Amorites, the Canaanites and the Perizzites, the Hivites and the Jebusites" (Deut. 20:17). In Matthew 5 Jesus emphasizes that the notion of neighbor extends to all members of the human family, including enemies and those who actively seek to cause harm to others. This all-inclusive love imitates God's indiscriminate love and mercy for all people; for God

> makes his sun rise on the evil and on the good, and sends rain on the righteous and on the unrighteous. (Matt. 5:45 NRSV)

Matthew 5:43 claims that there is a command to hate enemies. While this is not a biblical command, some parts of the non-biblical tradition do instruct hate for enemies. At Qumran, the Sons of Light are to hate the Sons of Darkness (1QS 1:10–11). Josephus says the Essenes "practice piety towards the Deity and . . . justice towards people," but they will "forever hate the unjust" (*J.W.* 2.129).

More broadly, Jesus's act of summarizing the law's teaching in terms of love for God and neighbor belongs to a larger discourse about how to live a good life in a just society. There are other summaries of the divine will in the Bible. Micah 6:8 is a well-known example, where the Lord requires the people "to do justice and to love kindness and to walk humbly with . . . God." The summary in Amos 5:4 is brief: "Seek me and live" (cf. v. 6). Isaiah 56:1 summarizes, "Maintain justice, and do what is right." Jesus sums up the tradition with the double love command to love God and love neighbor.

Divorce

The Dead Sea Scrolls community believed that the end of all wickedness was near. Meanwhile, the demonic forces were left "unrestrained in Israel" under their leader, Belial. According to the Damascus Document, one of the "nets" or "traps" in which Belial "catches Israel" is "fornication." The Document provides a specific example of "fornication": "taking two wives in their lifetimes" (CD 4:13–5:6).

This succinct phrase allows for several interpretations. Is the text prohibiting having more than one wife at any given time (polygamy), remarrying while the first divorced wife is alive, or both? Good arguments can be offered in support of each scenario. What stands out, however, is the text's use of Scripture to back up its position, whatever it might be.

A careful reader will notice that the Hebrew Bible does not preclude polygamy or divorcing and remarrying. Abraham had multiple wives (Gen. 16:3; 25:1). And the Torah explicitly allows for a man to divorce his wife (Deut. 24:1).

To support its views on marriage, the Damascus Document provides two biblical prooftexts. In their original contexts, neither has anything to do with either marriage or divorce. One verse comes from the Genesis flood story, in which "those who entered the ark went in two by two" (CD 5:1). Here the animals seem to model monogamy! The other text is borrowed from Genesis 1:27: "The principle of creation is, male and female He created them" (CD 4:21).

The use of the creation story in this context of forbidding divorce invites a comparison with the Gospels' views on divorce.

In Mark 10:2–12, "some" Pharisees test Jesus by asking him whether it is "lawful for a man to divorce his wife." The question is somewhat strange since divorce was widely recognized in both Jewish tradition and Greco-Roman culture. Mark's Jesus recognizes Moses's allowance of divorce (10:3–4). But Jesus goes on to say that this was a concession for hardness of heart. He cites a prooftext from Genesis 1:27: "But from the beginning of creation 'God made them male and female'" (Mark 10:6). God's will is that the two become one flesh and are not to be separated (10:5–9). Jesus adds that divorcing one's spouse and marrying another is an act of adultery.

Matthew's account redirects the scene somewhat. In Matthew 19:3 the Pharisees' question is slightly different: "Is it lawful for a man to divorce his wife for any cause?" The addition of "for any cause" heightens attention to male power. In patriarchal marriage, is a husband's power over his wife absolute, or are there limits?

Framed by this question, Jesus's response, which emphasizes the divine will for married people to be one flesh and not to be separated, limits male power (Matt. 19:5–6; Gen. 1:27). In addition, like Mark's, Matthew's Jesus disallows remarriage after divorce "except for unchastity" (Matt. 19:9). This exception allows divorce and remarriage in just one set of circumstances. Just what these circumstances might be has been much debated. Does the exception refer to forbidden marriages (Lev. 18) or adultery?

Like the Damascus Document, the New Testament appeals to a limited selection of Hebrew Bible texts to address the issue of divorce. It does not include texts that highlight other considerations of human relations, such as the presence of violence in the marriage, the absence of love, or the ending of a marriage motivated by mercy.

Matters for Reflection

1. We have identified six examples of how texts from both Early Judaism and the New Testament draw on Hebrew Bible writings. Identify some similarities in the ways that early Jewish and New Testament texts do this. What differences do you notice?
2. Read through the lament Psalm 22. Identify the roles and characteristics of the three characters: the victimized psalmist, the enemies, and God. Then read Matthew 27 and identify ways in which the story of Jesus's death incorporates the spirituality of a lament psalm.
3. Consider how Jesus's command to love God and neighbor aligns with the other early Jewish expressions of the importance of love for God and other human beings.
4. In this chapter we used the metaphor of glasses to describe attempts to apply Scripture to new contexts. What are contemporary examples of such applications?

CHAPTER 3

The Temple in Early Jewish Texts

Some Christians have regarded Jewish practices of worship in the Jerusalem temple in a negative light, as marked by empty ritual, continuous animal sacrifices, and priests going through the motions. This chapter addresses these troubling misunderstandings, troubling them by examining early Jewish attitudes and practices, as well as New Testament presentations.

New Testament references recognize that good things happen in the temple. In Luke's Gospel, for example, an angel interrupts the offering of incense and of prayers to tell Zechariah that Elizabeth will give birth to John the Baptist. Subsequently, Simeon and Anna welcome the newborn Messiah-Jesus in the temple (Luke 1–2).

Yet there is also bad news. Jesus announces judgment on the temple. He condemns it. And he locates its destruction as a sign that the end is near (Matt. 21:1–11; 24:1–3).

Why the contrasting perspectives?

In this chapter we identify from early Jewish and New Testament texts the temple's multiple functions: religious, political, economic, cultural, slaughterhouse. We note how it is honored, attacked, condemned. We observe how the notion of temple is reinterpreted as community, not a building. And we establish the existence and imaginings of other temples, including geographical, heavenly, and eschatological end-time temples.

Clearly, various peoples in various circumstances found it very important to think about temples.

Early Jewish Attitudes to the Temple

Today, the word "temple" often brings to mind a place of worship where believers come for prayer and fellowship. But what about the ancient Jewish temple in Jerusalem?

Sources tell us that Jews prayed (Sir. 50:19) and conversed in the temple (Luke 2:46; 21:37). However, first and foremost, they came there to offer sacrifices to the God of Israel. The Torah prescribes a wide variety of temple-based rituals, many of which involve sacrifices. Sacrifices of domestic animals, grain, oil, and wine were offered every day, even on Sabbath. During major festivals such as Passover, Pentecost, the Day of Atonement, Sukkoth, and Hanukkah, when pilgrims from all around the ancient world came to Jerusalem, "many tens of thousands of animals" were sacrificed (Let. Aris. 88).

> The Letter of Aristeas, written in Greek, is a pseudepigraphic letter. It tells the story of the translation of the Hebrew Bible into Greek. This translation is known as the Septuagint, often signified by LXX.

Imagine how those animals were supplied and stored, bought and sold, killed and sacrificed. The temple was a massive economy and slaughterhouse.

The temple's personnel came from the male members of one of the twelve tribes, the tribe of Levi. One family within this tribe, the family of Aaron, Moses's brother, supplied the priests who took care of the sacrificial procedures. Perhaps hundreds of priests were in action each week. Other Levites assisted in running the temple. Priests and Levites were materially supported through an intricate system of gifts or taxes from the people. The Torah/Law—Exodus, Leviticus, Numbers, and Deuteronomy—outlines procedures.

The high priest or chief priest presided over the temple. He was also a political leader. After the return from the Babylonian exile in the 530s BCE, the high priests served as the chief administrators of the land. In that period, the high priesthood was a lifelong office that passed from father to son. For centuries, high priests came from the family of Zadok, David's high priest.

After the Maccabean revolt (160s BCE), the priestly family who led the uprising, the Hasmoneans, also known as the Maccabees, began to supply chief priests. Later, Hasmonean high priests declared themselves kings of Judea.

After the Romans established their rule in the first century CE, the Roman governor appointed and removed high priests. These appointments positioned the chief priests awkwardly between being accountable to their Roman political masters, on the one hand, and to Israel's and the temple's traditions and commitments, on the other. Josephus calls the chief priests the rulers of the people (*Ant.* 20.251). As one way of keeping chief priests dependent on Rome, Roman governors stored the chief priest's garments in the Antonia fortress that was next to and overlooked the temple area. The chief priest had to ask the Romans for the garments in order to get dressed to do chief priestly duties.

Priests offered sacrifices twice a day in the temple *for* but not *to* the Roman emperor. One source, Philo, says the emperor Augustus funded these sacrifices (*Embassy* 317). The refusal by some lower-ranked priests to offer these sacrifices was one of the reasons for the outbreak of the war for independence from Rome in 66 CE. Some leaders and chief priests counseled unsuccessfully against war. They warned, rightly, that the temple would be a casualty (Josephus, *J.W.* 2.400).

> Josephus was a Jewish general during the First Jewish War with Rome in 66–74 CE. Early in the war, he defected to the Roman side. After the war, he wrote several important works about the war and the history of the Jewish people.

> Philo was a Jew who lived in first-century CE Alexandria. In his many writings, Philo explains the Torah using tools and ideas borrowed from Hellenistic philosophy.

Temple Economy

Temple worship required an extensive economy (1 Macc. 1:23; 2 Macc. 3:6). It involved supplies of animals for daily sacrifice (bulls, rams, lambs, doves) and grain, wine, incense, and oil for offerings. Salt, water, building materials, linens, and other supplies were needed for the temple's functioning and decoration. An annual temple tax on males in Judea and the diaspora supplied cash flow and provoked some resentment. Money changers provided acceptable coins to purchase sacrifices.

Accordingly, the temple was part slaughterhouse from the numerous daily sacrifices. It was also part bank. People stored money and valuables there (2 Macc. 3:10–12; Josephus, *J.W.* 2.293–308). They assumed that this holy place would not be violated or plundered. Warehouses stored these valuables as well as temple supplies. Several Roman governors, however, did plunder these riches (e.g., Josephus, *J.W.* 6.282).

Temple Buildings

In the biblical story, the temple is a latecomer. According to 2 Samuel 7:1–16, it was King David who wished to replace the portable wilderness sanctuary, the tabernacle, with a permanent house of God.

The tabernacle was a simple structure with two compartments: the Holy and the Holy of Holies. In the Holy, there was a candlestick with seven branches, a table with twelve loaves of bread, and a small incense altar. The Holy of Holies housed the ark of the covenant. Adjacent to the tabernacle were an altar for sacrifices and a water basin.

Figure 3.1. A miniature replica of the Jerusalem temple renovated by King Herod (now in the Israel Museum, Jerusalem).

The first and the second temples followed this basic pattern. The first temple, constructed by Solomon, was destroyed by the Babylonians in 587 BCE. In this destruction, the ark of the covenant was lost. When the Judeans returned from the Babylonian exile in the 530s BCE, they built the second temple.

Late in the first century BCE, the Rome-appointed Judean king, Herod "the Great," undertook a massive renovation of the second temple. He doubled its area (Josephus, *J.W.* 1.401) and introduced several new features. Among them were specially designated areas or "courts" for Jewish women and for non-Jews. The latter was part of Herod's agenda to open up Judea to the rest of the Roman Empire.

The renovated temple was an impressive structure. Its facade was covered with plates of gold. Josephus remarks that "its magnificence [was] never surpassed" (*J.W.* 1.401). He also reports that the Holy of Holies was an empty space without the ark of the covenant (*J.W.* 5.219). Likewise, the Letter of Aristeas describes the work of the priests in the temple as "absolutely unsurpassable" (Let. Aris. 92). And Ben Sira, a Jerusalemite, compares the high priest in his priestly garbs to a brilliant star shining from amid the clouds (Sir. 50:5–11). So significant was the temple for many Jews that several early Jewish texts claim that it is the center of the earth (Jub. 8:12, 19; 1 En. 26:1).

It was utterly devastating, therefore, when in 70 CE, after some Jews revolted against Rome in a quest for independence, Roman troops burned down the temple. It was not rebuilt.

Attacks on the Temple

The temple had vast reach into people's lives. Predictably, interactions with it were diverse. For many it was a special and inspiring place in which God was encountered and honored, sins were atoned for, and national identity and community were celebrated and secured.

But it was not always so for everybody. A long tradition of prophets, such as Amos (Amos 4:4–5; 5:21–24), Micah (Mic. 6:6–8), Isaiah (Isa. 1:11–17), and Jeremiah (Jer. 7:1–15), attacked inconsistencies between acts of worship and the societal practices marked by injustice and the exploitation of the poor by ruling elites. In the years immediately before Rome destroyed the temple in 70 CE, a peasant prophet, Jesus ben Hananiah, protested the temple by announcing a curse on it: "A voice against Jerusalem and the sanctuary." Despite a severe whipping he continued his protest until he was killed (Josephus, *J.W.* 6.300–309).

The temple was both honored and criticized. This ambivalence is evident in texts from Early Judaism and the New Testament.

For example, in the Book of Dreams, a text that became a part of 1 Enoch, the temple is depicted as impure (1 En. 89:73). Concerns with the temple's purity occur also in several texts from the community at Qumran. The writers of Some Precepts of the Law (4QMMT) say that they decided to separate from the rest of the people because the temple priests were mishandling Torah regulations, rendering the temple impure.

Pesher Habakkuk condemns a certain "priest," also called the "Wicked Priest," for committing "abominable deeds," for defiling "the Temple of God," and, in particular, for oppressing the poor by robbing "the poor of their possessions" (1QpHab 12:2–3, 6–10). Elsewhere, it says that this priest started well. Yet when he "became ruler over Israel," he "betrayed the precepts for the sake of riches," which he "amassed" by force (8:8–13). A similar critique is leveled in the pesher against "the last priests of Jerusalem" who "amass money by plundering the peoples" (9:5–6).

> First Enoch is not really one book but a collection of several early Jewish texts written in Aramaic. Different as they are, they all highlight the biblical figure of Enoch from Genesis 5:21–24.

> Some Precepts of the Law (4QMMT) is a text from Qumran. It is written as a letter listing matters related to the observance of the Torah. The writers claim that they separated from the rest of the people because the people were not observing the Torah properly.

> Pesher Habakkuk (1QpHab) is a commentary on the book of Habakkuk. Found at Qumran, it reflects the worldview of the sectarian community that preserved the Dead Sea Scrolls.

The Damascus Document denounces fellow Jews in general for defiling the temple by failing to observe the Torah's ordinances on sexual matters, such as marrying one's niece (CD 5:6–8).

In Malachi 1, God criticizes people for defiling the "food" on the altar by offering blind animals (vv. 7–9). This critique is followed by a call: "Oh, that someone among you would shut the temple doors, so that you would not kindle fire on my altar in vain!" (v. 10). Damascus Document 6:11–13 takes up this text and argues that none of those who enter the new "covenant shall enter the Temple to light His altar in vain." Rather, they should be the "closers of the door." The text calls its hearers to stay away from "the Temple treasure" and not to "rob the poor of His people, to make of widows their prey and of the fatherless their victim." Yet while the Damascus Document seems to be calling members of the new covenant to avoid the temple, it also seems to assume that the group participates in the temple (e.g., CD 11:16–21).

> The Damascus Document (CD) tells about the origins of a sectarian community, its opponents, and its way of life. Several copies of this text were found among the Dead Sea Scrolls.

Thus the writings of the community of the Dead Sea Scrolls (along with other early Jewish texts) were highly critical of the temple and its priesthood. This community thought that the priests' improper handling of the Torah procedures, on the one hand, and their unethical behavior, on the other, rendered the temple impure.

In 66 CE Judeans took up arms against Rome. Romans brutally subdued this revolt in 74 CE. In 132–135 CE Judeans rebelled once again. This uprising was led by Simeon bar Koseva, who is better known as Simeon Bar Kokhba, "son of a star." This pun on his name points to Numbers 24:17, a passage that was often understood as a messianic prophecy. This revolt, too, was crushed by the Romans.

During the Bar Kokhba uprising, the rebels minted their own coins. One such coin features an image of the temple's facade. It is surrounded by the word "Shimon," a reference to Bar Kokhba.

Figure 3.2. A Bar Kokhba coin, with the temple on the left and, on the right, items associated with the Festival of Tabernacles. The Hebrew text reads, "To the freedom of Jerusalem."
Classical Numismatic Group, Inc. http://www.cngcoins.com / CC BY-SA 3.0 / Wikimedia Commons

The Qumran Community as a Temple

Perhaps it was these critical attitudes that gave rise to the understanding that the Qumran community itself was (like) a temple. While this idea appears in texts from the community at Qumran, there is no systematic discussion of this concept. Rather, all we have are a few scattered references.

The Damascus Document offers one glimpse. According to this text, the Qumran community considered itself the faithful remnant of Israel. This community presented itself as faithfully seeking God while other Jews went astray. As a result, God established a new or renewed covenant with them. God revealed to them the "hidden things." These "things" were the correct interpretations of God's commandments, which the rest of Israel had failed to observe (CD 3:12–16). God "forgave them their sin and pardoned their wickedness" (CD 3:18). By doing so, God "built them a sure house in Israel whose like has never existed from former times till now" (CD 3:19–20). Those who "hold fast" to this "house" "are destined to live forever."

Underlying this statement is a pesher interpretation of Nathan's prophecy to David in 2 Samuel 7:3–16. There Nathan declares that God will build a house for David. This "house" has a double meaning. It refers to both a dynasty of David's descendants and the future temple that Solomon will build. The Damascus Document claims that the community at Qumran is this sure house. They are the temple.

Nathan's oracle to David is interpreted in a similar way in another text from Qumran, 4QFlorilegium (4Q174). This fragmentary scroll offers an actualizing interpretation of 2 Samuel 7:10–11 (4Q174 1–2 i 21 1–13). Once again, while the text plays with the double meaning of the word "house" in 2 Samuel 7 ("dynasty" and "temple"), it is interested only in the second meaning of the word: "temple."

> 4QFlorilegium (4Q174) is a fragmentary text from Qumran that interprets several biblical texts. It explains how these passages are or will be fulfilled in the life of the sectarian community.

It interprets 2 Samuel 7 with reference to two temples.

First, it claims that the house that God promised to David is a future eschatological temple. This future temple or sanctuary will not be desolated by foreigners, unlike the first temple destroyed by Babylonians in 587 BCE. We return to this notion of eschatological temples below.

Second, it says that God "has commanded that a sanctuary of men be built for Himself, that there they may send up, like the smoke of incense, the works of Torah" (4Q174 1–2 i 21 6–7). Scholars disagree on the precise meaning of the phrase "a sanctuary of men." Some prefer to read it as a "sanctuary *by* men"—in other words, as a reference to the first temple. However, an interpretation assuming that the temple *of* men stands for the Qumran community itself fits far better. This temple-community offers its "works of Torah" as incense.

Like the Damascus Document and 4QFlorilegium, the Community Rule, too, refers to the Qumran community itself as a temple (1QS 8:1–10; 9:3–5). It describes this community with biblical terms that denote the temple: "a House of Holiness for Israel, an Assembly of Supreme Holiness for Aaron" (8:5–6), and "a Most Holy Dwelling for Aaron" (8:8–9).

> The Community Rule, or S, as scholars have designated it, regulates the life of a sectarian community and explains its worldview. It was found among the Dead Sea Scrolls. Its best-preserved copy is 1QS.

This temple's task is to "atone for guilty rebellion and for sins of unfaithfulness" and "to atone for the land" (1QS 9:4; 8:6, 10). The text describes this atoning in terms reminiscent of the temple sacrifices. The community does it by the "offering of the lips," which is like "an acceptable fragrance of righteousness," and by their "perfect conduct," which is like "a delectable free-will offering" (9:4–5).

Perhaps this emphasis on conduct not only protests the Jerusalem temple officials but also stands in continuity with Isaiah's protest that God hates sacrifices without ethics. In the prophet Isaiah's words, people are to "do good; seek justice; rescue the oppressed; defend the orphan; plead for the widow" (Isa. 1:17).

Other Temples of Early Judaism

The temple that stood in Jerusalem until 70 CE was not the only Jewish temple mentioned in early Jewish writings. These writings refer to temples in other locations too. Some texts envision a new temple. Some imagine a heavenly temple. And some imagine an eschatological or "last days" temple.

First, there have been three temple buildings outside of Jerusalem.

- Under Persian rule (539–332 BCE), a group of Jewish mercenaries was stationed in the Egyptian village of Elephantine. These mercenaries built a temple to the God of Israel in which they offered sacrifices.
- A demoted high priest, Onias, fled from a persecution instigated by Antiochus IV Epiphanes (160s BCE) to Leontopolis, Egypt. He built there a temple in which he officiated.
- Not far from Jerusalem, the Samaritan community, claiming to be the Israelites who did not go into exile in Babylon, established their temple on Mount Gerizim (John 4:20).

Second, there is an alternative plan for the Jerusalem temple in the Temple Scroll.

The Temple Scroll (11QTemple^a) is the longest scroll found at Qumran. The fact that there are multiple copies of this text suggests its importance. The scroll offers a vision of a new, magnificent Jerusalem temple. Like the temple depicted in Ezekiel 40–42, it was idealistic and never built.

The temple described in the Temple Scroll both resembles and differs from its contemporary, the second temple. It is enormous, probably the size of the city of Jerusalem in the second century BCE, when this text was written. It also has several new features. One is a large outer court surrounded by a wall. This court is designated for Israelite women, children, and proselytes. Moreover, the scroll provides a festive calendar that governs this temple. It includes several festivals that are not mentioned in the Torah/Law: Wood Festival, Festival of the New Wine, and Festival of the New Oil.

Third, several early Jewish texts make a claim that, in addition to an earthly sanctuary, there is a heavenly or celestial temple in which God resides. This idea has biblical roots (Isa. 6:1). Detailed descriptions of the heavenly sanctuary are attributed to biblical figures, such as Enoch (1 En. 14:8–23). Moreover, some writings suggest that the earthly sanctuaries—the tabernacle and the Jerusalem temples—were copies of this heavenly temple (Wis. 9:8). While the earthly temple is served by priests, in the heavenly sanctuary angels are the ministers (Jub. 31:14).

Fourth, early Jewish texts feature visions of an eschatological temple. This temple will be established at the end of the days. One such source, 4QFlorilegium, interprets Nathan's prophecy to David about a future "house" in 2 Samuel 7:13 as an eschatological temple: "This is the house which [he will establish] for h[im] in the latter days" (4Q174 1–2 i 21 1–13).

This idea that God will establish a house—a temple—is supported in the scroll by a quotation from the Song of the Sea in Exodus 15:17–18: "As it is written in the book of [Moses: 'The sanctuary] of YHWH which your hands have established; YHWH will reign forever and ever'" (4Q174 1–2 i 21 2–3).

Interestingly, this text limits access to this future temple. It excludes Ammonites, Moabites, bastards, foreigners, and even proselytes.

Other texts not written by the Qumran community also mention an eschatological temple.

In the book of Jubilees, the vision of a new creation includes a promise that "the sanctuary of the Lord" will be "created in Jerusalem upon Mount Zion" (Jub. 1:29). God will build this temple. God will "dwell with [the people]" (1:17).

The Temple Scroll does not just envision the gigantic temple that was never built. There is also a divine promise that at "the day of blessing," God "will create" this temple and "establish it . . . for all times" (11QT^a 29:8–10).

Finally, a prophetic dream found in 1 Enoch 85–90 describes a new Jerusalem replacing present-day Jerusalem. It will be built after the eschatological judgment. God will establish a new Jerusalem that is larger and higher (1 En. 90:28–29). And like in the book of Revelation, there will not be a temple in the new city.

Some New Testament Discussions of the Temple

Matthew's Gospel

The Jerusalem temple and its leadership figure prominently in Matthew's Gospel. The Gospel, written after the Romans destroyed the Jerusalem temple in 70 CE, generally aligns with early Jewish texts critical of the temple.

From the outset, Matthew's Gospel sets the temple leadership and Jesus in conflict. The chief priests and their allies, the scribes, are introduced as societal power figures. They are allied with King Herod in his attempt to kill Jesus (Matt. 2:4). The Gospel presents their failings in distinctively Christian terms. They do not understand Micah 5:2 (cited in Matt. 2:5–6) in relation to Jesus. And they do not go to Bethlehem to honor the newborn Jesus.

Their next appearances locate them as a Jerusalem alliance who, with the Roman governor, will crucify Jesus (16:21; 20:18).

The temple comes into view in chapter 21. Jesus enters Jerusalem and goes to the temple. He drives out the buyers and sellers, turns over the tables of money changers, and disrupts those selling doves (21:12). Doves were a sacrifice that the poor could afford. Thereafter, Jesus hangs out in the temple. He teaches and predicts its downfall (21:23; 24:2).

Readers of these scenes involving the temple often think that they are a transcript of an actual event in the life of Jesus. Here, however, we discuss them as scenes in the Gospel narrative, which originated late in the first century CE, after the temple was destroyed.

This timing matters because it establishes the point of view of this scene. The Gospel, written in the 80s or 90s, looks back on the tumultuous events of 70 CE, when Roman troops ended a yearlong siege of Jerusalem and broke into the city. They looted, raped, destroyed, and burned the temple and the city.

Post-70 CE, numerous writings, including Matthew's Gospel, interpreted the significance of the Roman destruction of Jerusalem and the temple.

Josephus interprets it theologically by borrowing a pattern from the book of Deuteronomy (Deut. 27–29). This pattern says good things or blessings happen when the people live faithfully to the divine purposes. Bad things or curses happen when the people have sinned. For Josephus, God appointed the

Romans to punish the sinful people by destroying Jerusalem and the temple in 70 CE (Josephus, *J.W.* 5.411–12; 6.409–11; 7.358–60).

Second Baruch, written sometime in the 80s–90s, also interprets the events of 70 CE as divine punishment of Israel for disobeying God's commandments (2 Bar. 1:1–5; 4:1). More specifically, it targets priests as "false stewards" of God's house (10:18).

Matthew's Gospel also interprets the temple's destruction as divine punishment by means of the Romans. The Gospel offers three reasons for this punishment of Jerusalem and the temple-based leaders.

Matthew's Jesus announces the first explanation for the temple's destruction in 70 CE in 21:13a by citing Isaiah 56:7: "My house shall be called a house of prayer." The verse evokes Isaiah 56, in which the prophet urges Sabbath observance, prayer, justice-based living, and a society that welcomes outsiders such as foreigners and eunuchs. Matthew's Jesus claims that the temple was destroyed because the sociopolitical temple leaders, priests and scribes, failed to enact the societal vision and practices.

The second explanation in 21:13b cites another prophetic passage, the condemnation of the temple leaders in Jeremiah 7: "You are making [the temple] a hideout for terrorists and bandits" (Jer. 7:11, authors' trans.). Jeremiah's sermon explains Babylon's destruction of Jerusalem and the temple in 587 BCE as divine punishment. The leaders were responsible for unfaithful worship practices; societal injustices; oppression of aliens, orphans, and widows; and disobedience to the Ten Commandments. By analogy, Matthew's Gospel claims that the Roman destruction of Jerusalem in 70 CE punished similar societal injustices committed by the temple priestly and scribal leaders as societal leaders. Ironically, in quoting from Jeremiah 7:11, the Gospel labels the temple leaders as terrorists destroying the temple over which they preside.

The third explanation comes in the next chapter. In Matthew 22:1–11, Jesus tells a parable against the socioreligious leaders, the chief priests and Pharisees (21:45–46). In the parable, the king invites guests to the wedding feast of his son. He sends slaves to bring them to the feast, but they resist, even killing the slaves. The enraged king sends troops, burns their city, and kills the murderers. Then he invites the common folk to the banquet.

The parable is an allegory. The king is God. The guests are elite leaders like the chief priests and scribes. The son is Jesus. The troops are the Romans. The burned, destroyed city is Jerusalem and its temple in 70 CE.

This allegorical parable offers the third explanation for Rome's destruction of the temple. The Jerusalem leaders have failed to respond to God's invitation to receive Jesus as God's agent and to accept his teaching (Matt. 26–27). The temple's destruction is divine punishment for not receiving Jesus.

The Way Ahead

What happened, post-70, to functions that were particularly associated with the destroyed temple? Under Roman control, there was no rebuilding. How was divine presence to be encountered? And atonement for or forgiveness of sins? And revelation of the divine will and purposes?

Matthew's Gospel offers a one-word, pragmatic, confessional answer: Jesus! In the post-70, temple-free world, Matthew's Gospel declares that Jesus is greater than the temple (Matt. 12:6). He takes over the temple's functions when there is no temple. Jesus makes known God's presence (1:23; 28:20). Jesus forgives sins (1:21; 9:2–8; 26:28). Jesus reveals the divine will (chaps. 5–7; 10; 13; 18; 23–25). Commitment to Jesus provides the way ahead.

Clearly those who were not part of the Jesus-movement did not find this advocacy of Jesus to be a convincing solution.

It should be observed that the Gospel does not attack abuses that Christians have often attributed to the temple. Christians who are suspicious of religious rituals often claim that temple worship was inauthentic, going through the motions without commitment of the heart, a failing to encounter God. Such complaints are often projections of regrettable Protestant prejudices against Jewish and Catholic forms of worship.

Paul

The references to temples in Paul are much less numerous than in Matthew's Gospel. He does not specifically evoke the Jerusalem temple. He does not refer to priests. Rather, his references to temples evoke the many temples with which Paul's gentile recipients would be familiar across the Roman Empire. In Corinth, for example, many who became Jesus converts had previously frequented the city's temples dedicated to various gods and goddesses (1 Cor. 6:9; chaps. 8–10).

Paul refers to temples in three ways in 1 and 2 Corinthians.

First, just as the Qumran community identified itself as a temple, so also Paul describes the community of Jesus-believers in Corinth as a temple. In 1 Corinthians 3:9 he identifies them as God's building, constructed by God. In verse 16 he is more specific: "You are God's temple." The defining identity marker is that "God's Spirit dwells in you" (3:16). God dwells among the community of believers.

Perhaps this claim, as in Qumran's Temple Scroll, reflects Ezekiel's vision of a restored temple (Ezek. 37:26–27). It is certainly consistent with Paul's conviction that God's Spirit lives in believers (Rom. 8:9–11).

First Corinthians 3:17 underscores the importance of this identity by issuing a warning against those who would destroy God's temple. In chapters 1–3,

Paul is aware that among the Corinthian believers there is division, quarreling, jealousy, and boasting by which some claim spiritual superiority (1 Cor. 1:10–17, 26–29; 3:1–8). Paul warns against this threat from within. Their quarreling behaviors betray—indeed are destroying—their identity as God's temple. His harsh, attention-getting warning is that God will destroy such destroyers in the judgment.

He reminds them in 3:17 that as God's temple they are to be "holy." To be holy primarily means to be set apart for divine service. It can include a moral quality, but fundamentally it is a statement of identity and orientation. They are to stop bickering and live to serve God in the city of Corinth.

Paul's second use of "temple" defines individual Jesus-followers as temples. He foregrounds a contrast between culturally sanctioned behavior and the behavior that he deems appropriate to their Christian identity (1 Cor. 6:19). In chapters 5–6 Paul rebukes behavior that he thinks is inconsistent with their identity as God's temple (6:9–11). He rejects sexual immorality and the Corinthians' indifference to it. He is appalled that members are taking other members to court. And in 6:12–20 he protests that some men think it is acceptable to have sex with prostitutes.

As we have seen, various texts from Early Judaism protest immoral behavior associated with the Jerusalem temple. Here, Paul argues against immoral behavior as unworthy of the Corinthian believers' identity as God's temple. He says that their bodies are "meant not for fornication but for the Lord," that their bodies are "members of Christ," and that they must not "take the members of Christ and make them members of a prostitute" (1 Cor. 6:13–15). This argument assumes that believers are joined to and united with Christ.

In forbidding immorality, Paul emphasizes that their individual bodies, their lives, belong to God (1 Cor. 6:18–20). How they use their bodies matters. Their lives are to be controlled by the Spirit. "Your body is a temple of the Holy Spirit" (6:19) affirms that the Spirit is both "within" them and comes "from God." Here Paul's emphasis is not on the Christian community in general but on the bodies, the lives, of these particular and individual believers.

Because they are temples controlled by the Spirit, their bodily existence—relationships, activities, participations—is to join with the divine purposes and serve God.

Paul's third use of "temple" engages another instance of forbidden cultural interaction (2 Cor. 6:16–18). This time, the interaction concerns idols. Idolatry was pervasive in the ancient world, and recognition of gods and goddesses by honoring idols was expected in numerous domestic and public contexts. Paul's argument to abandon idol observance concerns both affirmations of identity and demands for appropriate practice.

With a rhetorical question Paul problematizes any relationship between the temple of God and idols: "What agreement has the temple of God with idols?" (2 Cor. 6:16a). Drawing on a long Hebrew Bible tradition, Paul asserts that commitment to God is antithetical to any involvement with idols. As in 1 Corinthians 3, the community of Christ-followers is "the temple of the living God."

Paul follows this assertion against idols with a "testimonia" comprising scriptural texts. The texts are cited as words of God ("as God said").

The first text cited in 2 Corinthians 6:16 comes from Leviticus 26:12. God promises to be present with ("walk among") the people and to be their God. This is covenant language. Paul adds to Leviticus, "I will live in them." This addition emphasizes the presence of the living God among the people. Idols of wood and stone can't compete.

Verse 17 introduces a threefold exhortation shaped by Isaiah 52:11. The exhortations follow from God's promises in verse 16. The Corinthian community is to reciprocate the divine commitment by living faithfully. This living involves separation from cultural practices like idolatry. They are to "come out from them," to "be separate," and to "touch nothing unclean." God promises to "welcome" such faithful adherents.

Verse 18 continues the divine promises that accompany faithful living. We have seen above various writings from Early Judaism using the text in 2 Samuel 7:13 about God's "house" to refer to both a building and a people. Originally the promise of a parent-child relationship was made to David concerning God's relationship with David's descendants (2 Sam. 7:14). God would be a father to Solomon, and Solomon would be God's son. Here Paul reinterprets the promise to apply to the Corinthian believers, who are to be faithful to God alone. God will be their father, and their identity will be God's "sons and daughters."

This collection of texts, promises, and exhortations in 2 Corinthians 6:16–18 closes with another declaration that God speaks: "Says the Lord Almighty." The adjective "almighty" (*pantokratōr*) emphasizes God's authority and power in underlining the blessing of the promises and the responsibility of the recipients to live faithfully in separation from idols.

Revelation

After the explanations for the temple's destruction in 70 CE offered in Matthew's Gospel and Paul's borrowing of the term to identify Christian communities, Revelation offers a further use of temple traditions familiar from Early Judaism.

We have noted above traditions in early Jewish texts concerning a heavenly or celestial temple imitated in the earthly Jerusalem temple. And we have observed traditions about an eschatological temple that God will create when God establishes the new world. The book of Revelation aligns with these traditions with an interesting twist.

Interpreting Revelation is a challenge. Here our discussion is guided by the question, What does Revelation reveal? In brief, Revelation addresses the issue of how Jesus-followers might engage Roman imperial culture. Roman power is presented as idolatrous and demonic. The letters to the seven churches urge distancing (chaps. 2–3). The Roman Empire is revealed to require false, idolatrous worship (chaps. 4–5). It is under God's judgment already (6:1–8:5), though it has a chance to repent (chaps. 8–11). It is under the devil's control (chaps. 12–14). It faces destruction and judgment (chaps. 15–18).

The final chapters reveal the coming triumph of God's reign/empire, which will replace Rome's (chaps. 19–22). This reign is visioned as a new heaven and new earth. A new Jerusalem descends from God (21:1–2). This vision represents God's dwelling with and presence among humans in a new world without pain, injustice, mourning, and death (21:3–4). The city is incredibly large.

Yet the author sees "no temple in the city" (21:22). No temple is present, and no priests are mentioned. Is this a protest against temples as places of empty ritual? Probably not. More likely, the absence of a temple protests temples that in Rome's empire promoted idolatry, false worship, and misdirected allegiance to the empire and emperor.

More positively, however, a temple is not needed to facilitate an encounter with God and Jesus the Lamb: "For its temple is the Lord God the Almighty and the Lamb" (21:22b). God's presence is the temple. God dwells among people and is with them (22:3). The vision emphasizes direct, face-to-face interactions between humans and God.

Matters for Reflections

1. This chapter has identified the numerous functions of temples as well as numerous examples and types of temples. Let's take those two emphases separately.
    a. What functions did temples perform?
    b. Identify the various types of temples (real, communities, and envisioned) mentioned in the chapter.
2. Which early Jewish traditions about temples do New Testament writings pick up and elaborate on? Why do you think the New Testament texts were interested in these traditions and not others?

CHAPTER 4

Groups

Christians often imagine that Judaism in New Testament times was monolithic: All Jews thought the same, talked the same, believed the same. Unnuanced language such as "The Jews believed . . ." or "The Jews practiced . . ." expresses this misunderstanding.

We engage this troubling misunderstanding by recognizing that as with Christianity or any society, Early Judaism was not a monolithic entity. It was diverse, vibrant, multivalent. There were numerous groups, different understandings and practices, creative ideas and spiritualities, diverse quests for faithfulness. Some Jews were members of the small, ruling, wealthy, powerful elite. Others knew various degrees of poverty and struggled for survival. Some lived in Judea and Galilee. Others lived outside the land of Judea and Galilee throughout the Roman Empire. And the Jewish writings that survived and that make up the Dead Sea Scrolls, the Apocrypha, the Pseudepigrapha, and the New Testament come from a wide span of centuries and sociopolitical experiences.

While the existence of these groups attests the vibrancy of Early Judaism, it also points to another reality: There was conflict and competition among some groups. Much, though not all, of the time period in view in this study was dominated by imperial powers. In societies under imperial domination, conflict—both verbal and physical—among local groups increases. This phenomenon, called horizontal violence, arises because oppressed people recognize that open confrontation with the ruling power is frequently futile. Groups direct their resentment and aggression toward other groups. Horizontal violence commonly marks interactions among groups in imperially dominated situations.

In this chapter we discuss some of the diverse groups that constituted Early Judaism. Some of these are familiar to readers of the New Testament. Often

New Testament writings present them in negative light unfairly. Yet there are also groups not mentioned in the New Testament.

Early Judaism

One example of this vibrancy and diversity is exhibited in the life of the Jewish historian Josephus, who lived in the first century CE.

According to his autobiography, Josephus came from a prominent priestly family. He received an excellent education, and some, including himself, considered him a prodigy. At the age of sixteen, he says, he decided to get a firsthand experience of three Jewish groups: the Pharisees, Sadducees, and Essenes (*Life* 1–10).

Josephus names these groups with the Greek word *hairesis*, which has been translated variously as "groups," "sects," and "parties." Literally the word means "a choice." Indeed, Josephus's account suggests that the three groups were voluntary associations that members chose to join (*Life* 10–11).

As we will see, these and other groups had different views on a wide variety of topics. Each group created boundaries that set its members apart, but some boundaries were more porous than others. Their stances toward Jewish society varied too. Some strove to influence it, while others turned inward to focus on their own members.

Josephus spent the last years of his life writing several voluminous books. He offers two overviews of Pharisees, Sadducees, and Essenes. One appears in his account of the Jewish war against Rome (*J.W.* 2.120–61), while the other appears in his all-encompassing history of the Jewish people (*Ant.* 18.12–17). Otherwise, the three groups do not figure much in his writings. For a New Testament reader, this might come as a surprise, as Pharisees loom large in the Gospels. Apparently, their influence on the course of events from Josephus's point of view was rather limited.

When Josephus does speak about the three groups, he presents them as Jewish "philosophies," like the famous Greek philosophical schools (*J.W.* 2.120; *Ant.* 18.11). He presents these Jewish groups as respectable and ancient (*Ant.* 18.11). Like Greek philosophers, Josephus's Pharisees, Sadducees, and Essenes engaged—and differed on—big questions of fate, free will, and life after death.

Perhaps Josephus's decision to present these groups as resembling Greek philosophies explains why he tells us little about other aspects of their existence. A modern reader would like to know when and how they came into existence, especially since they are absent from the Hebrew Bible. In Josephus's writings, Pharisees, for example, appear out of thin air after the Maccabean revolt, in the days of Jonathan the Hasmonean (152–142 BCE).

A curious reader might also wish to know how they got their names. However, Josephus does not tell us. Scholars conjecture that "Pharisee" comes from the Hebrew verb for "separation" and that "Sadducee" derives from "Zadok," the priestly clan of David's high priest. The name "Essenes" is a complete enigma, though some suggest an Aramaic word for "pious."

Yet from Josephus's surveys of the three groups (*J.W.* 2.120–61; *Ant.* 18.12–17), as well as from his other scattered references to them (*J.W.* 1.110–12; *Ant.* 13.173, 288–98, 373–79; 17.41–45; *Life* 191), some important insights emerge.

Pharisees, says Josephus, held in high esteem the traditions or interpretations of the Jewish ancestors. These traditions were not a part of the written law of Moses but were careful interpretations of it. Josephus claims Pharisees enjoyed support from the people and exercised influence on them. They believed in fate yet insisted that humans had freedom of choice. For Pharisees, the soul was immortal, and it was either rewarded or punished after death. At times they were heavily involved in Judean politics, functioning like a political party.

Sadducees also exercised some societal influence. They considered only what was written in the Torah as binding. They quarreled with the Pharisees' valuing of interpretive traditions. They were part of the wealthy elite. When appointed to an office, they followed Pharisaic policies to please the crowds. Sadducees believed in free will and rejected a belief in an immortal soul and retribution after death.

Josephus describes the Essenes in much greater detail. They settled in towns and were involved in agriculture. They shared possessions and did not own slaves. Some of them were celibate and adopted children to increase their ranks. Others married and had children. They led a highly regulated daily routine of prayer, work, and joint meals. A new member underwent a multistage process of initiation. They scrupulously observed purity regulations and had strict Sabbath practices. Their relationships with the temple were strained. They valued writings of the ancients. Everything was in God's hands. They believed in an immortal soul and reward and punishment after death. Essenes engaged in healing. Some of them, says Josephus, were endowed with the gift of prophecy.

Josephus mentions other groups in his writings. Having described the three philosophical schools of the Jews—Pharisees, Sadducees, and Essenes—he mentions "the fourth philosophy" (*Ant.* 18.23–24). Members of this group followed the customs of the Pharisees, but unlike them, they rejected cooperation with Rome. They claimed that they had no master but God. Josephus held them and their violence responsible for the disastrous revolt against and war for independence from Rome in 66–70 CE (*Ant.* 18.25).

Josephus also mentions some individuals who led groups. When a yearlong sojourn with Pharisees, Sadducees, and Essenes left young Josephus unsatisfied, he became a devoted disciple of Bannus. All we know about this man is that he lived an ascetic life in the desert and practiced frequent purifications in cold water (*Life* 11–12). Josephus also mentions another influential charismatic figure, John the Baptist (*Ant.* 18.116–19).

Only sixty miles north of Jerusalem, on Mount Gerizim, a community known as Samaritans built a temple to the God of Israel. Josephus tells us that it was "modelled on that at Jerusalem" (*J.W.* 1.63). Its high priest was a brother of the Jerusalem high priest (*Ant.* 11.306–12; 13.254–56).

The biblical account in 2 Kings 17:24–41 reports that when Assyria conquered the Northern Kingdom of Israel (722 BCE), they deported the Israelite population and brought in settlers from other places. These newcomers worshiped both the God of Israel and their own gods. Scholars consider this story to be polemical. Josephus recognizes the Samaritans' own account (*Ant.* 9.291), which argues that they are descendants of the Israelite tribes.

Jews and Samaritans clashed over the Gerizim temple. Samaritans kept their ancestors' "way of life and customs" (*Ant.* 12.7–10; 13.74–79). In 128 BCE, the Hasmonean ruler John Hyrcanus I destroyed the temple on Mount Gerizim (*J.W.* 1.62–63; *Ant.* 13.254–56). A small Samaritan community survives to this day. Some reside on Mount Gerizim.

Figure 4.1. Mount Gerizim today.

Other Sources

Josephus (died ca. 100 CE) is not our only source on Jewish groups.

Philo of Alexandria (died ca. 50 CE) describes a group called Therapeutae (*On the Contemplative Life*). Their name, he says, comes from the Greek verb meaning both "to heal" and "to worship." These Jewish philosophers lived in many places, but especially in Egypt.

According to Philo, Therapeutae comprised women and men. They led an ascetic life, mostly in solitude. They prayed twice a day and spent the rest of their time in "spiritual exercise" (*Contempl. Life* 28). They studied "laws and oracles delivered through the mouth of prophets, and psalms" (25). Therapeutae read the Holy Scriptures and interpreted them allegorically. They also read texts of their founders. Therapeutae held communal gatherings that included a meal, an instruction based on the Holy Scriptures, and carefully choreographed dancing and singing.

> Philo was a Jew who lived in first-century CE Alexandria. In his many writings, Philo explains the Torah using tools and ideas borrowed from Hellenistic philosophy.

Further, as we have mentioned in previous chapters, texts found among the Dead Sea Scrolls at Qumran attest a group calling themselves Yahad, "together." One such text, Community Rule (S), features a detailed, multistage initiation for new members. It also describes an annual ceremony for a renewal of the covenant between God and the Yahad. Furthermore, the Community Rule contains rules governing communal life and a roster of punishments for those who break the rules. Several copies of this document exist among the Dead Sea Scrolls. They differ from one another, sometimes substantially.

Another text contains regulations for the community's life. The Damascus Document (CD) differs from the Community Rule. For instance, the Damascus Document allows for marriage and childbirth (CD 7:6–7; 12:22–33), whereas the Community Rule is silent on these matters. Some argue that these differences reflect several different groups of Essenes.

> The Damascus Document (CD) tells about the origins of a sectarian community, its opponents, and its way of life. Several copies of this text were found among the Dead Sea Scrolls.

Group Testimonies

Some of the Dead Sea Scrolls created by the group at Qumran, along with several other early Jewish texts, provide a glimpse of how Jewish groups told their own stories. The key word here is "glimpse" because the references are very vague. They use metaphors for the emergence of a group but without providing much specific information.

Here are three very brief and elusive references. The Animal Apocalypse (1 En. 89–91) narrates that, in the midst of "blind" Israel, an unidentified group of those able "to see" appears (1 En. 89:6–7). In another text, the Apocalypse of Weeks (1 En. 93), during the seventh week, the unspecified "chosen will be chosen." They will be "from the eternal plant of righteousness" and will receive "sevenfold wisdom and knowledge" (1 En. 93:10–11). Or again, in Jubilees 23, when the "fathers" abandon the "covenant" (23:16), God brings the nations to punish the unfaithful (23:22–26). And then "the children . . . begin to study the laws, to seek out the commands, and to return to the right way" (23:26).

These three brief accounts do not identify the groups involved. The accounts have some common features: seeing versus blindness, the unfaithful majority, a chosen minority. Similar features appear in the most detailed story of an emergence of a group that we have from this period—namely, Damascus Document 1:1–11 from Qumran.

According to it, when Israel abandoned God, God wrathfully delivered them to Babylonian invaders, who devastated Jerusalem and its temple in 587 BCE. However, 390 years later, from the divinely preserved remnant, God "caused a plant root to spring." Keenly aware of their sins, this minority group was initially "like the blind." Yet since "they sought" God "with a whole heart," God gave them the Teacher of Righteousness "to guide them in the way of his/His heart." It's possible but uncertain that this group—the Yahad—is related to the three groups mentioned above from 1 Enoch and Jubilees.

The Damascus Document goes on to describe a confrontation between this group and its opponents. The latter are described in negative terms: "those who reject the commandments and the rules" (19:5–6), "the apostates" (7:13), "members of His covenant who do not hold firm to these laws" (19:13–14), "traitors" (1:12), and "those who departed from the way" (1:13). Quite dramatically, the Damascus Document compares the opponents' departure from the group to the split of ancient Israel's kingdom into two: Judah and Israel. The seceding group is compared to Israel, who deserted Judah (7:9–14).

The Damascus Document also accuses the opponents of seeking after "smooth things" (CD 1:18–19). Elsewhere, other scrolls call the enemies of the group "seekers after smooth things." This is a pun on Isaiah 30:10. Through this nickname, the community charges the "seekers" with misinterpreting the laws of Torah. Most likely, the "seekers after smooth things" are the Pharisees (4Q169 [4QpNah] 3–4 i 6–8). This means that the dramatic split referred to in the Damascus Document is probably between the Essenes and the Pharisees.

More importantly, at the heart of the conflict is the interpretation of the commandments of the Torah. A document called Some Precepts of the Law, or Some Works of the Torah (4QMMT), highlights these conflicts. This document was written as a letter to an unnamed (temple?) dignitary. In it, the writers list some seventeen points of interpretive disagreement that led to their separation from the rest of the people.

All these disagreements have to do with observance of the Torah and temple rituals. The "works of the Law/Torah" include regulations regarding sacrifices, exclusion of certain groups from the temple, purity laws, gifts for the priests, and marriage.

For example, one well-preserved passage raises a matter of temple purity not addressed in the Torah. It involves the following possible situation: A priest serving at the temple has a jug full of olive oil. Soon, some of it will be offered on the altar. To have just the right amount of oil, he decides to transfer the rest into another jug. Halfway through the process, he recalls that the jug he grabbed is not empty. Worse—it was declared ritually impure but not disposed of. What should he do? Surely, the impure oil in the receiving jug cannot be offered to God. But what about the oil in the original jug? Since the pouring stream connected the two vessels, could it be that both jugs are now impure?

We can easily imagine dozens of other scenarios, in the temple or in a private setting, in which similar issues would arise on a daily basis. The Torah does not say what to do, but decisions have to be made. The opinion of the writers of 4QMMT is that the "pouring does not separate the impure [from the pure] for the poured liquid and that in the receptacle are alike, one liquid" (4Q394 [4QMMT^a] 4:6–7). In other words, both jugs have now become impure. 4QMMT argues against an alternative view that declares the first vessel and its oil to be pure.

Is this just being picky and pedantic? No. At its heart the argument is a recognition that honoring the divine in worship is a most sacred act and requires the very best.

One of the copies of 4QMMT mentions another highly controversial topic pertaining to faithful worship—the calendar. Many Torah regulations create and are linked to specific times of the year. One obvious example would be the scheduling of the festivals like Passover and Pentecost. It is usually assumed that the temple ran on the lunar calendar of 354 days (see Sir. 43:6–7). First Enoch and Jubilees, however, promote a solar calendar of 364 days. Jubilees argues that those "who carefully observe the moon" are mistaken, because this calendar "is corrupt" and will lead to treating a sacred day as "something worthless and a profane day a festival" (6:36–38). Multiple texts from Qumran follow the solar calendar. So it is not surprising that the calendar of 364 days makes an appearance in 4QMMT.

New Testament

The New Testament writings emerge from and interact with Early Judaism and the Roman Empire. With regard to Jewish groups, particularly at the fore are interactions with Pharisees, Sadducees, scribes, and the elders of the people. We will discuss Paul as a Pharisee and then look at the constructions of various groups in the Gospels.

Paul the Pharisee

In narrating features of his life before he became a Jesus-follower, Paul says that he was a Pharisee. His self-description is the only reference to Pharisees outside the Gospels and Acts in the New Testament. Acts refers to Paul as "Saul" before his commitment to Jesus. For ease of reference, we'll continue to identify him as Paul. He defines himself

> as to the law, a Pharisee; as to zeal, a persecutor of the church; as to righteousness under the law, blameless. (Phil. 3:5–6)

Two references in Acts, written decades after Paul's death, also identify him as a Pharisee.

> "Brothers, I am a Pharisee, a son of Pharisees. I am on trial concerning the hope of the resurrection of the dead." When he said this, a dissension began between the Pharisees and the Sadducees. . . . (The Sadducees say that there is no resurrection or angel or spirit, but the Pharisees acknowledge all three.) (Acts 23:6–8)

> They have known for a long time . . . that I have belonged to the strictest party of our religion and lived as a Pharisee. . . . Why is it thought incredible by any of you that God raises the dead? (Acts 26:5, 8 NRSVUE [modified])

The New Testament identifies two other Pharisees: Nicodemus, a leader who converses with Jesus (John 3:1), and Gamaliel, "a teacher of the law, respected by all the people" (Acts 5:34).

How are Pharisees constructed in these verses? We note five features.

First, Paul as a Pharisee defines himself in relation to the Law/Torah. The Acts 26 reference has Paul describe Pharisees as "the strictest party" in their observance. And in Galatians he describes himself as "far more zealous for the traditions of my ancestors" (Gal. 1:14). We noted above the Pharisaic investment in interpreting the Mosaic teaching.

Some Christians think of Law/Torah negatively and celebrate that it is not binding for Christians. This is a misunderstanding, as we will elaborate in the next chapter. Both Jesus (Matt. 5:17–20) and Paul (Rom. 3:31) uphold the Law/Torah even as they interpret it in particular ways. Torah/Law was a divine gift. It was given in the context of the covenant relationship to guide distinctive Jewish life in relation to God and to other people. It upheld practices of piety and worship (circumcision, Sabbath observance, no idolatry, purity), as well as love and justice in human relationships. We can expect Paul as a Pharisee of "the strictest party" to be observant of Torah/Law's extensive guidelines for a faithful and satisfying life. He describes himself as faithful in this observance and not as one who struggles under a burdensome law.

Second, as a Pharisee, Paul identifies himself as a zealous persecutor of the church. Zeal was the feature of famous men—Phinehas (Num. 25:6–13), Elijah (1 Kings 18), and Mattathias (1 Macc. 2:23–27). They showed zeal in preserving Israel's distinctiveness from the nations and enforcing undefiled covenant loyalty to God. Their zeal involved resistance to and violence against both Jews and gentiles.

Why did Paul zealously persecute the church? Perhaps he was motivated by the Jesus-group's breaking down of boundaries by including gentiles. Perhaps he was motivated by the sense that they were lax in not requiring circumcision or other practices. Their teaching would, then, undermine Pharisaic influence on societal practice. Perhaps he was appalled by their claim that Jesus was raised from the dead. A claim of resurrection belonged to eschatological expectations, but clearly the era of a new heaven and earth had not dawned. The Jesus-folks therefore displayed deception, lies, and blasphemy.

Third, as a Pharisee, Paul describes himself "as to righteousness under the law, blameless" (Phil. 3:6). This claim might be surprising for some Christian readers. A Christian stereotype of the pre-Christian Paul is that he struggled with the burden of obeying Torah/Law. Frustrated, he strove for perfection but always failed because Torah/Law was a burden and impossibly demanding. This misunderstanding of Paul results from Martin Luther's projection of his own preconversion spiritual struggles (informed in part by reading Augustine) onto Paul. And Romans 7's struggle between wanting to live one way but doing the opposite has also been interpreted by some, but not by all, as Paul's experience. Paul's testimony in Philippians 3 is to the contrary. He obeyed Torah/Law and lived faithfully.

Fourth, the Acts passages refer to some Pharisaic distinctives. In contrast to the Sadducees, Pharisees affirmed resurrection. They also recognized, along with others in Early Judaism, the existence of angels (1 En. 1–36; Tobit) and spirits (1 En. 15–16; T. Sol. 18). Assuming that these statements in Acts 23:8 are historically reliable, they offer rare information about both Pharisees and Sadducees.

Fifth, the Acts references attest competition, even conflict, among Jewish groups. In Acts 23, the conflict is between Pharisees and Sadducees. In Acts 26, the identity of the Jewish opponents is not specified.

Given these circumstances, why did Paul become a follower of Jesus? Galatians (1:15–16), Philippians (3:2–7), and the narratives of the Damascus road experience in Acts (9:3–6; 22:6–9; 26:13–16) highlight an encounter with the risen Christ. Knowing the risen Christ changed Paul's mind, identity, and mission.

One further observation. In his mission work, Paul says he supported himself by manual work as an artisan (1 Thess. 2:9; 1 Cor. 9:6). Acts 18:3 identifies him as a leatherworker or tent- or sailmaker. As a manual worker, he was of low status. Perhaps Josephus's claim that Pharisees were high status needs some modifying. Certainly, some—perhaps many—Pharisees were related to the ruling groups as retainers or officials and as advocates of a reform of Jewish society aligned with their particular practices and societal vision.

Matthew's Gospel

Matthew's Gospel takes a mix and match approach to the construction of Jewish groups. Ignoring historical-cultural differences among the groups, the Gospel lumps them all together as an alliance of opponents to Jesus. For example, the Gospel constructs these groupings:

- Pharisees and Sadducees (3:7; 16:1–12)
- Pharisees and scribes (5:20; 12:38; 15:1; 23 [six times], etc.)
- Chief priests and Pharisees (21:45; 27:62)
- Chief priests and scribes (2:4; 20:18; 21:15)
- Pharisees and Herodians (22:15–16)
- Chief priests, scribes, and elders (16:21)
- Chief priests and elders (21:23; 26:3, 47; 27:1–20; 28:12)

In addition, each group—Pharisees (9:11, 14, 34, etc.), Sadducees (22:23–24), scribes (7:29; 8:19; 9:3, etc.), chief priests (26:14; 27:6; 28:11)—appears on its own.

What can we observe?

First, Matthew's Gospel significantly increases the number of references found in Mark's Gospel. Mark's twelve references to Pharisees and one reference to Sadducees, for example, become in Matthew twenty-nine and seven, respectively. Both Gospels feature the scribes in equal numbers.

Second, the consequence of the increased number of references is greater conflict between Jesus and these groups. Polemic and conflict mark Matthew's narrative.

Third, the Sadducees have a comparatively minor role in Matthew. They ally with the Pharisees to oppose John the Baptist (3:7) and Jesus (16:1). Jesus warns about their teaching (16:6, 11–12). They do not accept resurrection (22:23). Jesus dominates them by rhetorically silencing them (22:34).

Fourth, the Pharisees are the dominant group. They interact with Jesus in both Galilee and Jerusalem. Matthew's Gospel constructs their biggest failing as being hypocrites. They seem to observe Torah/Law in great detail but are unethical in their societal leadership and practices (chap. 23).

Fifth, the Pharisees' interactions with Jesus indicate some issues and practices to which they are committed: not associating with undesirables (9:11), fasting (9:14), observing Sabbath (12:1–14), washing hands before eating and maintaining food purity (15:20), teaching (16:12), asserting male power in divorce (19:3), paying taxes to Rome (22:15).

Sixth, often these interactions involve competition with and attacks on Jesus for not valuing or observing these practices in the ways that the Pharisees do. More fundamentally, the Pharisees deny Jesus's identity as God's agent. Twice they accuse him of acting on behalf of the devil (9:34; 12:24).

Seventh, Jesus attacks these groups in multiple ways. He accuses Pharisees and scribes of giving loyalty to "the tradition of the elders" while voiding God's will (15:1–20). He discredits the teaching of the Pharisees and Sadducees (16:12). He exposes the chief priests and Pharisees for not receiving him as God's agent (21:45–46). In the harsh chapter 23, he begins in verse 3 by acknowledging that they *read* Moses's teaching (the NRSV mistranslates the verb as "teach") but curses them for not living it. The scribes and Pharisees impose heavy burdens; love public adulation; live as hypocrites; prevent people from experiencing God; manipulate oaths; emphasize tithing while neglecting societal practices and structures based on justice, mercy, and faithfulness; practice extortion, greed, and lawlessness; and kill God's agents.

Such accusations and name-calling were commonplace in contexts of imperial power and in the rhetoric of conflict in the ancient world. Groups or figures often distinguished themselves from others by defining other groups in negative terms. This discrediting often comprised standard accusations against rival groups of, for example, greed, hypocrisy, and oppressive behaviors.

Eighth, scribes are commonly associated with the power groups of Pharisees and chief priests. Scribes were societally powerful because they were associated with teaching and interpretation of Torah and the traditions. The

Gospel's construction of them as powerful figures coheres with their presentation in the book of Sirach. This writing identifies their prominent status and societal influence as members of town councils, public assemblies, and courts and as advisers to rulers (Sir. 38:24–39:11).

Matthew's Gospel presents their authority among the people as inferior to that of Jesus (7:29). Jesus corrects their teaching about Elijah's coming (17:10–12). They accuse Jesus of blasphemy when he offers forgiveness (9:3). Jesus critiques the scribes' and Pharisees' societal vision, which is marked by self-benefit, greed, and self-indulgence and is devoid of justice, mercy, and faithfulness (23:23–25).

Ninth, the Pharisees ally with the chief priests to execute Jesus. Of the twenty-five references to the chief priests in Matthew, nineteen occur in the passion and resurrection narratives of chapters 26–28, presenting them as opponents of Jesus. The chief priests and Pharisees ally in a way that indicates Pharisaic involvement with the governor Pilate in crucifying Jesus (27:62). Scribes and elders are also allied in this execution (26:57; 27:41). Sadducees are absent.

Tenth, the Gospel of Matthew mocks these leaders. It ridicules the chief priests and scribes for failing to read the Scriptures in relation to the newborn Jesus (2:4–6). Matthew's Pharisees ridiculously lurk in a grainfield to see if anyone snacks on some grain on a Sabbath (12:1–2). They are made to oppose Jesus for healing a man's hand on the Sabbath (12:9–14). And Pharisees and scribes are accused of tithing "mint, dill, and cumin" while ignoring "justice and mercy and faith" (23:23). Mockery is not the same as accurate, factual reporting.

> Scholars have noted that Pharisees are concerned with matters of purity (handwashing, washing or consecrating vessels and utensils, types of food, meal associates, tithing, Sabbath observance; Matt. 15:17–20). Some have interpreted these concerns as extending laws that applied to priests in the temple to the everyday life of Jews. The Pharisees affirmed, so it is claimed, that all Israelites were "a priestly kingdom" (Exod. 19:6). They were to worship God in these everyday activities. This interpretation has considerable value, but we must remember that there is little contemporary evidence for viewing this cluster of practices in this way.

How, then, does Matthew's Gospel construct Pharisees, scribes, and Sadducees?

These groups did not exist in isolation from one another or from other societal leaders. The Gospel positions these groups in alliance with the key sociopolitical figures who ruled the Rome-occupied territories of Galilee and Judea. These figures include the Rome-appointed vassal King Herod (2:3–6), the Roman governor Pontius Pilate (27:1–31), and the Jerusalem-based, Rome-appointed chief priests. Josephus describes the chief priests as the "rulers of Judea" (*Ant.* 20.251).

From the outset of Matthew's Gospel, the chief priests and scribes cooperate with King Herod in seeking Jesus's death as the newborn "king of the Jews" (Matt. 2:2–6). Thereafter, scribes are allied with Pharisees as monitors of society. They come from Jerusalem, the center of power, to confront Jesus (12:38; 15:1). Scribes and chief priests are jealous of Jesus's actions and public acclaim (21:15). Jesus anticipates his death at the hands of the murderous elders, chief priests, and scribes (16:21; 20:18; 21:15).

Because of this alliance with the Rome-sanctioned ruling figures, Matthew's Jesus attacks the elders, chief priests, Pharisees, and scribes for the self-benefiting and hierarchical societal vision and destructive practices that they enact. The Gospel's critique is harsh. The leaders lack concern for societal outsiders and the vulnerable (9:10–13). They observe Sabbath without merciful concern for human need, especially of the poor (12:1–14). They ignore "justice and mercy and faith" (23:23). They are greedy and self-indulgent, which harms the poor, those of low status, and the vulnerable (23:25). Their practice is to be violently murderous toward divine agents (23:31). At heart, Jesus attacks the self-benefiting societal vision and practices that these groups oversee.

This alliance of groups cannot tolerate his attacks, considerable popular following, advocacy of different structures and practices, and identification as king of the Jews. They seek to kill him (12:14; 16:21; 20:18). However, as colonized subjects, they did not have the authority to execute Jesus. Only the Roman governor had the power to execute. Accordingly, the alliance of groups works with the main ruling figure in the Gospel, the Roman governor Pontius Pilate, to crucify Jesus (27:1–2).

In presenting the groups in alliance with one another and with the ruling figures, the Gospel constructs them as retainers in the Roman Empire. One of the ways in which Rome ruled its empires was to make alliances with leading figures and groups in the empire's provinces. These alliances were mutually beneficial. Rome allowed local figures and groups to maintain their societal status, privileges, and power *as long as* they remained loyal to their Roman masters and pursued and protected Rome's interests over non-elites.

Retainers were both accountable to and representative of Roman power. They occupied a difficult, ambivalent location of representing both native traditions and Roman interests. They were the face of the ruling elite among local low-ranked non-elites. Accordingly, the Gospel constructs their conflicts with Jesus as a defense of the ruling elite's self-benefiting societal structure and practices against his threat and disruption.

Informing this narrative construction is the aftermath of the Roman destruction of Jerusalem and its temple. The Pharisees seem to be the group that emerged post-70 in the strongest position to shape post-70 life. Conflict resulted because of the very different societal vision and practices advocated by the Jesus-communities.

John's Gospel

The dominant group present in John's Gospel is the Pharisees. Scribes and Sadducees do not appear in the Gospel. Samaritans play some role (John 4:1–42).

As in Matthew, the Pharisees are constructed as powerful societal leaders. Allied with the ruling chief priests, they seem constantly present, continually monitoring events and being suspiciously watchful over the people. They resent Jesus's influence with the common folks.

The Jerusalem-based Pharisees send priests and Levites to investigate John the Baptist (1:24). They send temple police to arrest Jesus (unsuccessfully; 7:32–52). They conflict with Jesus (8:13). They interrogate the blind man whom Jesus healed and declare Jesus is not from God as God's agent (9:13–16). People report to them that Jesus has raised Lazarus. After meeting with the chief priests and being concerned about Roman retaliation if they lose control, they plan to kill Jesus (11:45–53). They are disturbed that Jesus has considerable public support (12:19). With the chief priests they send temple police to arrest Jesus, which leads to his crucifixion (18:3). The Pharisees play no further role in the passion narrative.

Luke-Acts

Luke's Pharisees are wealthy (Luke 16:14). Appropriate to their wealth and status, they are, as in Matthew's and John's Gospels, politically connected as part of the ruling elite (Luke 13:31; 20:20). They have leadership positions and influence in Jerusalem and villages in Galilee (5:17–26, 29–32). Scribes are often associated with the powerful Pharisees in Luke-Acts but lack a distinctive identity and role.

Some readers have suggested that Luke-Acts offers a "kinder, gentler" presentation of the Pharisees and the scribes. It is true that there are some cooperative moments between these groups and Jesus. For example,

- they invite Jesus to eat with them (Luke 7:36; 11:37; 14:1);
- for whatever reason, they warn Jesus that Herod wants to kill him (Luke 13:31);

- they inquire about the coming kingdom or empire of God (Luke 17:20);
- they are not active in the passion narrative;
- the Pharisee Gamaliel is identified as a teacher of Torah/Law, is respected among the people, and advocates for the apostles (Acts 5:34–39);
- some Pharisees become Jesus-believers (Acts 15:5); and
- Paul identifies as a Pharisee (Acts 23:6–9; 26:5).

Yet, as in Matthew's Gospel, conflict between Jesus and the Pharisees and scribes pervades Luke's Gospel (see 5:17–6:11). The invitations to share meals lead to conflicts. In 11:37–54, for example, Jesus delivers curses or woes on the scribes and Pharisees. This is hardly polite table etiquette, and it increases hostility! The warning about Herod and the apparently genuine inquiry about the kingdom/empire of God express significant misunderstandings. And Luke's Jesus issues harsh condemnations—for example, of their hypocrisy (12:1), love of money (16:14), and societal privilege, arrogance, and contempt toward low-status people like "thieves, rogues, adulterers," and tax collectors (18:9–14).

The Gospel of Luke caricatures the Pharisees and scribes in their opposition to Jesus. It presents them as constantly watching Jesus in order to attack him. Ridiculously, the Gospel constructs them as hanging out in grainfields to see if Jesus's disciples have a healthy snack (6:1–2). They watch Jesus in a synagogue to see if he heals on a Sabbath (6:7). They watch him when he has dinner in a Pharisee's house (14:1). And the chief priests and scribes watch and spy on Jesus (20:20).

The Sadducees have a minimal role. They deny resurrection (Luke 20:27–40) and oppose the disciples for preaching it (Acts 4:1–4; 5:17). Acts 5:17 associates them with the high priest and accuses them of being jealous. In the final scene, the Pharisees and Sadducees divide over resurrection, spirits, and angels. The Sadducees deny these realities that Pharisees affirm (23:6–10). The Pharisees vindicate Paul, who even as a Jesus-follower declares his identity as a Pharisee.

Matters for Reflection

1. What is the phenomenon called "horizontal violence"? How do you see it manifested in the discussion of this chapter?
2. Which matters did early Jewish groups disagree on?
3. From the discussion in this chapter, what are the differences between Pharisees and Sadducees?
4. Josephus, in his accounts of the contemporary Jewish groups, devotes most of his attention to the Essenes. Perhaps he thought his readers might find them especially interesting. Why do you think this might be the case?

CHAPTER 5

Torah/Law

One of the most troubling misunderstandings Christians have about Early Judaism pertains to the Torah or Law.

In some contemporary Christian traditions, Torah/Law is viewed with disparagement and derision. We have heard numerous students declare that the law is bad. Some celebrate that Christians have been "set free" from observing this "terrible" burden. Obedience to Torah/Law is stereotypically regarded as impossible. Yet, it has been claimed, Jews without success tried to obey it in order to earn divine favor.

Christians have commonly claimed that Torah/Law has been superseded. Faith in Christ has replaced Torah/Law. Grace replaces works. The church replaces synagogues. Christians replace Jews. Christianity replaces Judaism in the divine scheme of things.

Of course, some verses in Paul can be read without informed understanding to confirm this view, which has dominated Protestant traditions in particular since the Reformation.

> Christ is the end of the law. (Rom. 10:4 NRSV)

> Christ redeemed us from the curse of the law. (Gal. 3:13)

Likewise Ephesians, written in Paul's name after his death, makes this problematic claim:

> [Christ has] abolish[ed] the law with its commandments and ordinances, that he might create in himself one new humanity in place of the two, thus making peace. (Eph. 2:15)

The abolition of Torah/Law creates one people, according to the author of Ephesians. But it does so by doing away with a distinctive marker of Jewish identity. The "new humanity" is a gentile entity, with Jewish identity, practice, and people disturbingly erased. Christianity replaces Judaism.

However, in troubling misunderstandings about Torah/Law in this chapter, we will demonstrate that reading with "Reformation glasses" distorts Paul's meanings. It produces ill-informed and hateful views that are to be abandoned.

In this chapter we recognize covenant as the important context in which God gave the gift of Torah/Law to Israel. Then we look at some ways in which the gift of Torah/Law was interpreted to constitute faithful covenantal living. We then turn to the New Testament, especially to Paul. Interpretations of Paul's letters have dominated Christian (mis)understandings of the law. We emphasize Paul's affirmation of the continuing place of Jews in the divine purposes and his focus on gentiles, and we highlight the significance of the faithfulness that Jesus demonstrated.

Early Judaism

Covenant and Torah/Law

The Hebrew Bible often speaks of the "children of Israel." In several texts from Qumran, the phrase "children of covenant" appears (e.g., 11QPs[a] [11Q5] 28:11–12). It highlights the special relationship between God and the Jewish contemporaries of and including Jesus and Paul.

After delivering Israel from Egypt, God initiated and established a covenant with Israel at Mount Sinai. Why did God choose Israel? Deuteronomy 7:7–8 explains,

> It was not because you were more numerous than any other people that the LORD . . . chose you. . . . It was because the LORD *loved* you and *kept the oath* that he swore to your ancestors. (emphasis added)

In what follows, Deuteronomy describes God as the keeper of the covenant and *hesed* (7:9). *Hesed* is a Hebrew word for "faithfulness," "graciousness," and "mercy." In the Community Rule from Qumran the word pair of "covenant" and *hesed* morphs into "covenant of *hesed*," or "covenant of mercy" (1QS 1:8).

The covenant that God established with Israel is a bilateral one. Exodus 19:5 sets out the terms:

> Now, therefore, if you obey my voice and keep my covenant, you shall be my treasured possession out of all the peoples.

Keeping the covenant means observing its stipulations. These stipulations are laid out in the Torah of Moses (1 Kings 2:3; Ezra 3:2). The Hebrew word *torah* stands for "teaching" or "instruction." The early translators of the Pentateuch into Greek understood it as "law"—hence the familiar expression "the law of Moses."

The Torah/Law of Moses, as found in the books of Exodus, Leviticus, Numbers, and Deuteronomy, offers a detailed set of teachings for a nation in covenant relationship with God. Torah/Law is God's gift to guide faithful living in the covenant. Specific instructions are called "commandments," "laws" (Exod. 15:26), and "regulations" (Num. 36:13). Two texts from Qumran refer to them as the "works of the Torah/Law" (4Q174 [4QFlorilegium] 1–2 i 21 7; 4Q398 [4QMMT^c] 14–17 ii 3). Jews stayed in the covenant and maintained their status as "children of covenant" by doing the works of Torah/Law.

Keeping the commandments leads to divine blessings, while disobedience results in punishment (Lev. 26; Deut. 28). The biblical narrative tells a story of Israel's repeated failure to follow God's will. And yet, God's covenant with them remained intact.

The book of Jubilees claims in describing the revelation to Moses at Sinai that God foresaw Israel's unfaithfulness. Yet God was not deterred from establishing a covenant with them (Jub. 1:7–25). All this time, "in all their judgements and in all their curses," God has "been with them" (1:6). The day will come, claims the book, when they will not turn away from God "forever." God says, "[They] will know that they are my children and that I am their Father . . . and that I love them" (1:25).

An integral part of the covenant was a provision for atonement. Israelites, both as individuals and as a nation, could atone for their failures to observe God's Torah/Law. One notable element of this provision was the annual Day of Atonement. On this day, the high priest offered special sacrifices that removed the stain of sin and impurity from the people and the sanctuary (Lev. 16).

Valuing Torah/Law

Affirming a context of covenant, early Jewish texts hold Torah/Law in high regard. For them Torah/Law is

- a "legislation . . . believed to come from God" (Josephus, *Ant.* 3.320);
- an embodiment of heavenly wisdom (Sir. 24:23; Bar. 4:1);
- identical to the laws governing nature (Philo, *Moses* 2.52; *Spec. Laws* 2.13);
- the "law for the world" (Philo, *QE* 2.42), not for Jews only (Philo, *Moses* 2.44);

- a comprehensive law (Josephus, *Ag. Ap.* 2.173–74), neither capricious nor random (Let. Aris. 161, 163, 168–69);
- the basis for "the good life" (Let. Aris. 127);
- exhibiting the "dominance of reason" (Josephus, *Ag. Ap.* 1.33–35) and "profound logic" (Let. Aris. 143–47, 150);
- "excellently designed to promote piety, friendly relations with each other, and humanity towards the world at large" (Josephus, *Ag. Ap.* 2.145); and
- "immortal" (Josephus, *Ag. Ap.* 2.277), one that "endures forever" (Bar. 4:1), "as long as the sun and the moon" (Philo, *Moses* 2.13).

In light of these views, one is hardly surprised by Ben Sira's claim that "nothing [is] sweeter than to heed the commandments of the Lord" (Sir. 23:27).

That the Torah/Law was held in high esteem is also attested by two kinds of archaeological evidence.

First, in both Galilee and Judea, numerous ritual baths (*mikveh*) for stipulated washings have been excavated. They serve as a tangible representation of both individual and communal efforts to abide by the Torah regulations regarding ritual purity.

Second, of the 220 biblical manuscripts found among the Dead Sea Scrolls, half are copies of the books outlining Torah.

Figure 5.1. Mikveh or ritual bath near the Western Wall of the Temple Mount, Jerusalem.

One curious feature of these manuscripts is that some take what we might consider "liberties" with the text. For instance, in one scroll, 4Q366 (4QRP[d]) 4 i, a passage from the book of Numbers is unexpectedly followed by a passage from Deuteronomy (Num. 29:32–30:1; Deut. 16:13–14). This rearrangement is not impious tampering with a sacred text. Rather, both passages concern the Festival of Booths. The text is fragmentary. It seems that by juxtaposing the two texts the scribe sought to facilitate a better understanding of the divine commands pertaining to the festival.

The book of Jubilees rewrites the entire book of Genesis and some of Exodus. Strikingly, it claims authority for itself as a book that an angel dictated to Moses when Moses was on Mount Sinai for forty days (Jub. 1:1–5). This authority is the basis for four claims that emphasize the importance of Torah/Law:

- The teaching of the Torah/Law existed before creation (Jub. 1:29).
- God chose Israel at the creation of the world (Jub. 2:19–20).
- The patriarchs observed some of the Torah/Law before it was given to Israel at Sinai (Jub. 6:17).
- Some commandments, such as those concerning the Sabbath (Jub. 2:21, 30), were kept in the heavens before creation.

Observing Sabbath as a Holy Day

As is well known, the commandment to honor the Sabbath belongs to the Decalogue or Ten Commandments. The two slightly different formulations of this commandment prohibit doing "any work" on the Sabbath (Exod. 20:8–11; Deut. 5:12–15). However, there is considerable debate about what this prohibition involves for everyday life and people.

The last chapter of the book of Jubilees provides a long list of specific activities that are to be avoided on the Sabbath (Jub. 50:6–13). The book claims the list comes from the dictating angel (50:6). Banned activities include

- sexual relations;
- speaking about work, traveling, selling, or buying;
- drawing water not prepared ahead of time;
- lifting and carrying loads out of one's dwelling;
- taking a trip;
- working farmland;
- lighting a fire;
- riding an animal;
- traveling by ship;

- beating or killing a living creature;
- catching a wild animal, bird, or fish;
- fasting; and
- waging war.

Where do these prohibitions come from? Most of these prohibitions derive from biblical verses dealing with the Sabbath that are scattered across the Hebrew Bible. This is the case with speaking about one's affairs (Isa. 58:13), drawing water not prepared ahead of time (Exod. 16:22–26), carrying burdens (Jer. 17:21–22; Neh. 13:19), going (or speaking about going) on a trip by land or by sea (Exod. 16:29), riding animals (Exod. 16:29; 20:10, animals rest), working farmland (Exod. 34:21), kindling fire (Exod. 35:3), and fasting (Isa. 58:13, which describes Sabbath as "delight").

Yet a few prohibitions do not have an obvious biblical source: sexual relations (yet see Lev. 15:18), beating or taking the life of an animal, and waging war.

Jubilees states the underlying theological reason for prohibiting these actions on the Sabbath: God appointed Sabbath for Israel as "the day of the holy kingdom" on which "to eat, drink and be filled" (Jub. 50:10). The reference to "the holy kingdom" names Jewish identity and cites covenant language: "If you will . . . keep my covenant, . . . you shall be to me a kingdom of priests and a holy nation" (Exod. 19:5–6 ESV).

Jubilees is not the only early Jewish text that lists works from which one should abstain on the Sabbath. A similar but longer list appears in the Damascus Document (10:14–11:18). These lists demonstrate widespread concern with the proper observance of the Sabbath. While Exodus and Deuteronomy briefly instruct restful observance of the Sabbath, they are not specific for everyday situations. So Jubilees and the Damascus Document fill in the gap as a sincere attempt to guide faithful living in the covenant.

Perhaps the attention to small details seems picky to us. Not just no travel, but no travel on a ship! Yet for one ancient reader—Josephus—that Torah regulated "even the minutest detail" was praiseworthy (*Ag. Ap.* 2.173–74).

Messing Up? Repentance, Atonement, Forgiveness

Jubilees concludes its discussion of the works prohibited on the Sabbath with a statement that one work *is* allowed: offering sacrifices in the temple sanctuary. It emphasizes that under no circumstance should the atoning sacrifices stop "in order that they may atone continuously for Israel" (Jub. 50:11).

Torah/Law provides several means of atonement, repentance, penitence, and forgiveness. Failing to be faithful in living Torah/Law did not mean expulsion from the covenant or the loss of divine favor. Here are a few examples of atonement and forgiveness from documents among the Dead Sea Scrolls written by the group at Qumran.

The Damascus Document describes an emerging group as penitents (see chap. 4 above). They recognize "their iniquity" and acknowledge that they are "guilty" and "blind" (CD 1:8–9). Because of this attitude, God notices them and provides them with a Teacher of Righteousness so they will live faithfully (1:10–11). The Damascus Document claims that God atoned for the sins of this community and set it as a "sure house" (3:18). In chapter 3 we noted that the imagery of "the house" was used to identify the Yahad, or community, as a spiritual temple atoning for its members (1QS 8).

> The Community Rule, or S, as scholars have designated it, regulates the life of a sectarian community and explains its worldview. It was found among the Dead Sea Scrolls. Its best-preserved copy is 1QS.

This was not the only means of atonement. The ceremony of the covenant renewal in the Community Rule includes confession and assurance of God's loving mercies. The priests within the community "shall recite the favors of God manifested in His mighty deeds and shall declare all His merciful grace [a plural of *hesed*] to Israel" (1QS 1:22).

The rest of the community confesses,

> We have strayed! . . . sinned and acted wickedly. . . . [And God has] judged us . . . but He has bestowed His bountiful mercy [*hesed*] on us from everlasting to everlasting. (1QS 1:25–3:1)

There is more! Members of the Qumran community, the Yahad, thought of the physical and spiritual world as two camps: the "Sons of Light" and the "Sons of Darkness." Naturally, the members of the community identified themselves as Sons of Light (1QS 3:13–4:26). But it was possible for a Son of Light to succumb to sin and lose their identity as a Son of Light. A remarkable fragmentary scroll, 11QMelchizedek (11Q13), addresses this question.

Like the book of Jubilees, it draws on the biblical Torah/Law. It employs the Torah legislation about the seventh and fiftieth years. This legislation envisions a just society. Every seventh year, says Deuteronomy 15, debts are to be remitted and Israelite slaves are to be freed. On the fiftieth year, the Jubilee Year, if the land, the family inheritance, has been sold, it has to be returned to its original owner (Lev. 25).

Our text interprets these two sets of laws (citing Lev. 25:13 and Deut. 15:2) by spiritualizing them and presenting an eschatological scenario. As Sons of Light succumb to sin, they go into spiritual debt. They lose their "inheritance" within the camp of light and become "captives," slaves, of the archdemon

Belial. In God's appointed time, a heavenly figure named Melchizedek will proclaim a Jubilee Year during which two things will happen. First, the "debts," sins, of the "captives" will be remitted. Second, the former captives will be able to return to their original inheritance.

Many other texts affirm God's mercy. One example is the apocryphal Prayer of Manasseh. The Hebrew Bible portrays Manasseh as the worst king to have ruled over God's people. He worshiped idols and oppressively spilled innocent blood (2 Kings 21:1–18). In the book of 2 Kings he reigns unpunished. The account in 2 Chronicles 33:1–20 has Manasseh being punished by being taken captive by the Assyrian king. Yet he prays to God, and God answers by returning him "to Jerusalem and to his kingdom" (33:13).

The biblical text does not provide Manasseh's prayer. Someone, though, felt the need to fill the gap. We can imagine this person thinking that a prayer that brought God's forgiveness to the worst sinner of all could benefit others. The apocryphal Prayer of Manasseh fills that gap.

The prayer affirms that God "promised repentance and forgiveness to those who have sinned." It is not for the patriarchs, "who did not sin." But repentance has been appointed for Manasseh the sinner (Pr. Man. 9). This statement is followed by a description of Manasseh's wrongdoings, his lowering himself, and his imploring forgiveness.

The lesson of this prayer is clear: If the wicked Manasseh can gain forgiveness because of his change of heart, others can as well.

Several other "penitentiary" prayers appear in early Jewish writings (Bar. 1:15–3:8; Prayer of Azariah; Tob. 3:1–6; 3 Macc. 2:1–20). Along with the Torah's sacrificial system and the vision of the future remittance of sins, these texts provide a glimpse of different patterns of atonement and forgiveness provided by Torah/Law within the framework of Israel's covenant.

The New Testament

Paul

Among New Testament writers, Paul's letters have been central to Christian interpretations of Torah/Law. Is Paul, a Jew, anti-Jewish in his views of this special Jewish gift? Have interpretations of Paul accurately understood his discussion of Torah/Law? The issues are certainly complex, and our space here is limited. We identify seven key claims that Paul makes.[1]

---

1. For three stimulating and quite different interpretations of Paul's views on the law, see E. P. Sanders, *Paul and Palestinian Judaism: A Comparison of Patterns of Religion* (Philadelphia: Fortress, 1977); J. D. G. Dunn, *The Theology of Paul the Apostle* (Grand Rapids: Eerdmans, 1998); Pamela Eisenbaum, *Paul Was Not a Christian: The Original Message of the Misunderstood Apostle* (New York: HarperOne, 2009).

1. Paul Recognizes Covenant with Israel as the Context for the Gift of Torah/Law to Israel

Paul says, "They are Israelites, and to them belong . . . the covenants, the giving of the law" (Rom. 9:4). He then expresses praise for God's good gifts: "God [be] blessed forever" (Rom. 9:5). He affirms that "the Jews were entrusted with the oracles of God" (Rom. 3:2). Appropriately he declares, "So the law is holy, and the commandment is holy and just and good" (Rom. 7:12).

In these affirmations, Paul evokes God making covenant with Israel (Gen. 17:1–14; Exod. 6:2–9). He recalls God giving the law through Moses (Deut. 4–31). Paul locates himself in the context of the divinely gifted covenant and Torah/Law discussed above.

The important implication of Paul's recognition is that Jews are born into covenant. This privileged identity results from an act of divine grace. Jews "get into" the covenant by birth. They do not need to earn or merit anything. As we have seen, they "stay in" the covenant by living lives guided by the divine gift of Torah/Law. If they mess up, Torah/Law provides means of repentance and forgiveness. Paul is convinced that God remains faithful to God's commitments, even in the face of human unfaithfulness (Rom. 3:1–4).

Given that covenant and law are divine initiatives and good gifts for Israel, there is no *textual* basis for Christian antagonism to Torah/Law.

2. Torah/Law Guides Jews to Live a Distinctive Way of Life Marked by "Works of the Law"

In the context of covenant, the Torah/Law was given to Israel to guide Jews to live a particular way of life. Torah/Law identifies certain ethical expectations that are to mark this way of life. It stipulates general behaviors, such as those named in the Ten Commandments or the Decalogue: no other gods or idols; honor parents; do not murder, nor commit adultery, nor steal, nor bear false witness; and so forth (Exod. 20:1–21).

Early Jewish narratives identify commitment to the provisions of Torah/Law, especially in contexts of conflict when Jewish identity is threatened.

In 1 Maccabees 2, Mattathias appeals to the covenant and its commandments in refusing to sacrifice to the god being imposed by the Hellenistic imperialist Antiochus IV Epiphanes. Subsequently, some seek to honor the Sabbath by refusing to fight on the Sabbath. When they die by not fighting, others, including Mattathias, decide that they must fight on the Sabbath to preserve faithful Jewish identity and way of life.

> In the book of Tobit, Tobit is exiled in Assyria. In this diaspora context, he maintains his covenant identity by living faithfully to Torah/Law. He observes food purity practices, does charitable works, gives food and clothing to the needy, and buries the dead.
>
> In the book of Judith, the Jewish widow Judith rescues her people from the invading Assyrians. She gains access to the camp of the Assyrians to murder their general, Holofernes. She is presented as a faithful and pious Jew in fasting, honoring festivals and Sabbath, praying, and purifying herself. Significantly, when Holofernes invites her to dine with him, she refuses to eat his gentile food and observes food purity practices by eating her own food and drink—before cutting off his head (Jdt. 10–13).

Torah/Law also stipulates some "works of the law" that have a special role in marking Jewish identity: circumcision, Sabbath observance, no idols, no other gods, food purity. These actions signify distinctive and privileged Jewish identity. They do not earn Jews any favor with God, because the gifts of covenant and Torah/Law already constitute the Jewish identity as God's people.

Rather, these "works of the law," as Paul calls them, mark this identity. They distinguish Jews from gentiles. They put a "hedge" around Jews to prevent them from being corrupted by gentile practices such as idolatry, polytheism, sexual practices, and pollution from eating unclean foods (Let. Aris. 128–71, esp. 142). Many gentiles thought circumcision absurd. They thought the nonobservance of idols and multiple gods in order to worship one God was ridiculously risky. They thought Sabbath observance showed Jews to be lazy.

However, for Jews, these acts signified their identity as God's people. They did these works of the law not to be saved but to express an identity already gifted to them and to maintain a distinctive way of life. They did not perform them to earn divine favor, because divine favor was granted in the covenant and the gift of Torah/Law.

3. What About Gentiles? Paul Wrote Letters to Gentile Jesus-Believers

Paul's letters were not general or public writings. The letter Philippians, for example, was not written to the town of Philippi. It was written to a community of Jesus-believers in the town. This is true for all Paul's letters.

More specifically, most of, if not all, the Jesus-believers whom Paul addressed were gentiles. It seems that among the believers in Rome addressed in Romans, there was probably a small number of Jews. Otherwise, gentile believers were Paul's addressees.

Writing to gentile Jesus-believers is consistent with Paul's identity as apostle to the gentiles. He says he seeks to bring about "the obedience of faith among all the nations/gentiles" (Rom. 1:5). In Galatians he narrates that his meeting with church leaders in Jerusalem confirmed "that we should go to the gentiles" (Gal. 2:9). His mission and letter-writing tasks target non-Jews.

4. When Paul Mentions Torah/Law in His Letters, He Addresses Gentiles, Not Jews

Recognizing that the recipients of Paul's letters are gentiles has important implications for understanding what Paul says about Torah/Law. When he talks about Torah/Law, he addresses gentiles and the relationship of gentiles to Torah/Law. He is not concerned with Jewish relations to Torah/Law. He does not speak against Jewish observance of the law as God's gift to guide life in the covenant. His concern is with gentiles. He pursues the question of how gentiles are incorporated into the divine purposes.

Paul is adamant: "Is God the God of Jews only? Is he not the God of gentiles also? Yes, of gentiles also, since God is one" (Rom. 3:29–30). One thing is clear: Gentiles are also included in the divine plans. Paul knows God's promise to Abraham that through him all the families of the earth will be blessed (Gen. 12:1–3).

Paul is also clear that gentiles do not have to become Jews in order to encounter divine favor. Speaking to and about gentiles, he says in Galatians,

> Yet we know that a person is justified not by the works of the law. . . . No one will be justified by the works of the law. (Gal. 2:16)

He is not addressing Jews, who are born into the covenant. "Works of the law" signaled the covenant relationship Jews already enjoyed and the distinctive "works" that signified this divine gift. They were not earning divine favor.

Rather, Paul's concern is to argue that gentiles do not encounter divine favor by doing these works of the law. His particular focus in Galatians is circumcision. Paul argues against gentile circumcision because to be circumcised would be to identify with a marker of Jewish identity. Gentile believers do not need to become Jews (Gal. 5:1–6).

How, then, does God deal with gentiles? As we will see shortly, just as Jews do not earn divine favor but are gifted it, so it is also gifted to gentiles.

5. Yet Torah/Law Is Relevant for Instructing Gentiles

While Torah/Law is God's particular gift to Jews to guide faithful living in the covenant, it also has implications for gentiles.

One role of Torah/Law for gentiles is to educate gentiles about sin. Paul says, "Therefore the law was our teacher" (Gal. 3:24). The law condemns stereotypical gentile failings like idolatry and uncontrolled desires or lusts (Rom. 1:18–25). It identifies behaviors that fail to acknowledge God and the divine will for human living (Rom. 1:28–32). It articulates a curse on gentiles for living in ways that Torah/Law prohibits (Gal. 3:10–13, citing Deut. 27:26).

The famous "struggling" passage in Romans 7 describes what happens when gentiles encounter Torah/Law. This passage identifies the ethical struggle of someone who does not do what they want to do, but does what they do not want to do. Who is this person? Commonly it is claimed that the passage is an autobiographical description of Paul's (or Luther's) pre-Christian experience, which was marked by failure to obey the ultrademanding law. Yet Paul attests he was a faithful and obedient observer of Torah/Law, not one who struggled to perform its teaching (Phil. 3:6; Gal. 1:14).

Rather, given Paul's gentile addressees, Romans 7 is better understood as gentile experience. Paul uses the rhetorical technique of prosopopoeia. This technique creates a character and supplies them with a speech. In Romans 7, the character is a gentile.[2] The passage describes a gentile's encounter with Torah/Law's education about sin:

> Yet, if it had not been for the law, I would not have known sin. I would not have known what it is to covet if the law had not said, "You shall not covet." (Rom. 7:7)

A gentile encountering Torah/Law learns that certain behaviors (idolatry, sexual lust, coveting) are sinful. But while Torah/Law educates gentiles by identifying actions that are sinful toward God, it is not its role to empower a life pleasing to God.

> I can will what is right, but I cannot do it. For I do not do the good I want, but the evil I do not want is what I do. (Rom. 7:18–19)

What are gentiles to do?

6. God Acts Toward Gentiles with Grace Just as God Acts with Grace Toward Jews

Paul's "good news" is that God acts in the death and resurrection of Jesus for gentiles. "Christ is the end [in the sense of the goal] of the law" (Rom.

---

2. Eisenbaum, *Paul Was Not a Christian*, 227–33; Dunn, *Theology of Paul*, 472–77 (the [gentile] believer).

10:4 ESV). The law, which educates about sin, leads gentiles to Christ as the solution for their alienation from God.

Paul uses numerous metaphors to describe God's act of grace for gentiles. These metaphors include reconciliation, adoption, redemption, and atonement. There is space here to discuss only one metaphor: justification or setting right. What does it mean to be justified by faith(fulness) in Christ (Gal. 2:16–21)?

Commonly, the phrase "faith in Christ" is understood to refer to a gentile person exercising faith or trust in Jesus. However, interpreters have argued in recent decades that the construction is better understood as referring to the faithfulness that Jesus exhibited in being "obedient to the point of death" (Phil. 2:8).

There are two significant changes in translation and understanding here. One concerns agency. Instead of a person's faith in Jesus, the focus falls on Jesus's act of faithfulness or faithful obedience. And second, instead of the term "faith," the preferable English translation for the Greek noun *pistis* in Paul's letters, on the basis of its other uses, is "faithfulness."

The phrase "faith/faithfulness in/of Christ" in Greek (*pistis Christou*) can be interpreted in two ways: "faith in Christ" or "the faithfulness of/demonstrated by Christ." One factor that points toward the latter option, Jesus's demonstrated faithfulness, is that Paul uses an almost identical phrase to refer to the faithfulness Abraham exhibited in responding to God's promise (Rom. 4:16). The phrase in Romans 4:16 *could* be translated as "faith in Abraham," but Paul does not exhort anyone to put their trust in Abraham. Rather it makes much more sense to understand the phrase as referring to the faithful obedience displayed by Abraham that enabled God's favor to extend to Israel.

In the same way, Paul commends the faithfulness that Jesus displayed. Jesus faced the deadly consequence of his ministry, which challenged imperial ways in Rome-occupied Galilee and Judea, and he was crucified. Gentiles are to align themselves with this example of courageous faithfulness. Just as Jews were to respond to God's gracious and faithful gift of Torah with obedience and by embodying the way of life it indicates, so gentiles are to respond to God's gracious and faithful gift of Jesus's faithful death by imitating and living the ways of Jesus, by which he confronted the oppressive and unjust structures and practices of Rome's empire. Just as covenant and Torah express God's grace to Jews, so Jesus's death expresses God's grace to gentiles. And God gives the Spirit to assist gentiles in living faithfully.

Paul summarizes God's workings through grace and faithfulness in Romans 3:30–31.

> (God) will justify the circumcised (Jews) on the ground of faithfulness and the uncircumcised (gentiles) through the same faithfulness. Do we then overthrow

the law by this faithfulness? By no means! On the contrary, we uphold the law. (authors' trans.)

So Paul affirms that God justifies the circumcised, Jews, on the basis of God's faithfulness to the covenant. And he affirms that God justifies the uncircumcised, the gentiles, by means of God's faithfulness and the faithfulness of Jesus. These acts of faithfulness do not overthrow the law in any way. The law continues as a gift for Jews.

7. Doing "Works (of the Law)" and Faithfulness Are Partners, Not Opponents

We have noted above that Torah/Law requires a response of active faithfulness expressed in a Jewish way of life. Various deeds are to mark this life: no murder, no idols, no false witness, and so forth. Moreover, Jews undertook a small cluster of very important works of the law that signified Jewish identity: circumcision, food purity, no idols, no other gods, Sabbath observance. Paul does not oppose any such actions of faithful Jewish response to God's faithful expression of grace.

What about gentiles? The old stereotype since the Reformation has been that faith and works are opposed. Faith in Christ replaces doing works because the latter are viewed suspiciously as attempts to earn divine favor. The misunderstanding is that as long as you "believe in Jesus," you can live as you like!

However, if we understand that Paul speaks instead of the faithfulness that Jesus displayed as something that gentiles are to participate in and emulate, works or actions or deeds become not only important but absolutely necessary as expressions of and responses to divine grace. Grace shapes an active and faithful way of life.

Rather than earning anything, good actions or deeds are responses to divine grace and faithfulness. Good deeds or actions, especially works of love and justice, constitute the way of life that comprised Jesus's life of faithfulness. They constitute good societal life.

One clear expression of this expectation for gentile actions is found in Romans 13:8–10.

> Owe no one anything, except to love one another; for the one who loves another has fulfilled the law. The commandments, "You shall not commit adultery; You shall not murder; You shall not steal; You shall not covet"; and any other commandment, are summed up in this word, "Love your neighbor as yourself." Love does no wrong to a neighbor; therefore, love is the fulfilling of the law. (NRSV)

Paul cites four of the Ten Commandments, the ones against adultery, murder, stealing, and coveting. These commandments pertain to societal interactions.

But Paul sees them as examples of a much larger way of life marked by love for the other. This love reflects the love that God shows in the death of Jesus (Rom. 5:8). Of course, Paul does not invent the importance of love. The command to love is also part of Torah/Law (Lev. 19:18). Jews and gentiles are linked by the divine will for this loving way of life.

> Compare the Gospels' presentations of Jesus's summary of the teaching of the law as requiring love for God and for neighbors. Jesus cites Deuteronomy 6:5 and Leviticus 19:18. See Matthew 22:34–40; Mark 12:28–34; Luke 10:25–28.

Significantly, Paul follows this general instruction with specific address to a likely conflict among gentile believers in the churches in Rome. It seems that some gentile believers have adopted Jewish works of the law: food purity (Rom. 14:2, 14, 17, 20–21), Sabbath observance (14:5–6), not drinking wine that may have been offered to idols (14:21). Others have not adopted these practices. Some Jewish believers continue to observe these practices while some may have stopped doing so. Romans 14 shows that the conflict over diverse practices is marked by bad feelings in quarreling, despising, and judging. Paul does not ally with either side but says they are not "walking in love," not pursuing "peace" and "mutual upbuilding" (14:15, 19). What matters, he says, is *how* they interact.

Faithfulness and works or actions or a way of life are not mutually exclusive. God's faithfulness is expressed in actions, the gracious gift of covenant and Torah/Law to Jews and the gracious gift of Jesus's faithful obedience even to death for gentiles. These acts of faithfulness are to be received with lives of faithfulness by both Jews and gentiles.

> The writer of James shares these emphases. In 2:1–13 he emphasizes the necessity of actions of love that embrace the oppressed poor and do not show partiality to the rich and powerful. In 2:14–26 he announces that claims of faithfulness must result in actions or works of love and justice. So those lacking clothes must be clothed, and the hungry must be fed (cf. Matt. 25:31–46). The writer appeals to the examples of active faithfulness exhibited by Abraham in offering Isaac (James 2:21–24) and

by Rahab the prostitute in providing hospitality for and protecting the spies scoping out the land (2:25–26).

Matters for Reflection

1. What in the content of this chapter surprises you? Challenges you? Encourages you? Mystifies you?
2. What is the relationship between covenant and Torah/Law? What does the phrase "works of the law" refer to?
3. How do early Jewish texts portray life and human experience aligned with the Torah/Law?
4. From what you have learned from this chapter, how would you sum up Paul's attitudes to the law?

CHAPTER 6

Messiah/Christ

Preachers in Christian pulpits often make two claims about the Messiah: (1) All Jews were waiting for *the* Messiah; and (2) Jesus didn't fit the profile, so Jews killed him.

Students are vexed to learn that both claims are historically wrong and troubling misunderstandings. After all, they have heard such claims numerous times. Yet there wasn't a fixed, uniform, universal expectation of a messiah among Jews. And only the Roman governor Pontius Pilate had the authority to execute criminals in Judea.

In this chapter we trouble these misunderstandings by recognizing that the extensive texts of Early Judaism that we outlined in chapter 1 use the term "messiah" or "Christ" infrequently. These writings have few references to a messiah, and they say relatively little about this figure. Likewise, Hebrew Bible writings do not use messiah language to name a future figure. Reading with Jesus glasses, Christians have subsequently borrowed language from some passages in order to understand Jesus (e.g., Isa. 53).

Many Jews were not waiting for a messiah. And among those who were, expectations were diverse. There was not a fixed job description.

Messianic expectations were not pervasive but peripheral.
Messianic expectations were not majority but minority.
Messianic expectations were not monolithic but multiple.

At the center of these minority and diverse expectations was the hope for a figure who would shape the world according to divine purposes, ending corruption and unfaithfulness as well as oppressive Roman rule.

New Testament writings aligned with and continued this minority Jewish tradition of a figure anointed by God to carry out the divine will. They made central for the Jesus-movement the claim that Jesus was God's Messiah/Christ. And so the *Christ*ian movement was named (Acts 11:26). We will examine how leading writers—Paul, Mark, John—interpreted this identification.

Two words. Two languages. The English word "messiah" derives from a Hebrew word, *mashiakh*. The English word "Christ" derives from a Greek word, *christos*. Both words mean "anointed." They designate an "anointed person."

In the Hebrew Bible, priests are anointed or "messiahed" (Lev. 4:3, 5). So are kings (Ps. 2:2) and prophets (1 Kings 19:16). That is, anointing signifies a person whom God has commissioned to carry out tasks appropriate to an identity—as a priest, a king, a prophet. God even commissions Cyrus the Persian, a gentile ruler, as God's "anointed one" to return the people home from exile in Babylon (Isa. 44:28–45:1). To be anointed is to perform a role. It does not signify divinity, nor do these references anticipate Jesus.

Messiah Expectations in Early Judaism

In the New Testament, the term "messiah" looms large, yet early Jewish writings rarely address this topic in any detail. The texts that do so reveal a range of views on the nature and role of the Messiah as God's anointed agent. First, we look at some scattered references to messiahs (yes, some expected several messiahs!) in the Dead Sea Scrolls. Then we examine the mere four references found in the large collection of texts known as the Pseudepigrapha.

Dead Sea Scrolls

Within the Dead Sea Scrolls, some writings express an understanding that the divine judgment is just around the corner. Several passages express an expectation of divinely anointed figures, though without much detail.

For example, the Dead Sea Scrolls community anticipated two messiahs: a priestly messiah called the Messiah of Aaron, and a nonpriestly one called the Messiah of Israel. A key text, Community Rule, states that community members will be judged by a certain set of rules "until the coming of . . . the Messiahs of Aaron and Israel" (1QS 9:10–11).

Likewise, in another important text, the Damascus Document, the arrival of the Messiahs of Aaron and Israel ushers in divine judgment, when the unworthy "will be given to a sword" (CD 19:10–11). The Messiah of Aaron, a priestly messiah, is called the Interpreter of the Torah. The nonpriestly messiah is titled Prince of the Whole Congregation. Citing Numbers 24:17, the Damascus Document says that this prince will "smite all the children of Seth" (CD 7:18–20). The biblical "children of Seth" refers to the wicked, whom the nonpriestly messiah will punish.

Another text, Rule of Blessings, elaborates the role of this prince of the congregation in a special blessing dedicated to him (1QSb 5:20–29). God will renew with him the covenant of David in order "to establish the kingdom of His people forever." The prince will judge the lowly ones of the earth with equity—an echo of Isaiah 11:4. He will walk blamelessly before God and establish his covenant. God will extol the prince and make him "a fortified tower upon a high wall."

Relying once again on Isaiah 11:4, the text envisions the prince destroying the earth and the wicked by the might of his mouth and the breath of his lips. God will grant him "everlasting might, the Spirit of knowledge and of the fear of God." The prince will gird himself with righteousness. His might will be like that of a striking bull with iron horns and copper hooves. He will be like a lion, and the peoples—most likely the nations that previously oppressed Israel—will serve him.

The writings referring to the Messiahs of Aaron and Israel mention the priestly Messiah of Aaron first. This order might suggest his greater authority. His supremacy is further highlighted by another text, Rule of the Congregation (1QSa). Outlining the protocol of a banquet that will take place in the end of days, it subordinates the Messiah of Israel to a priest, perhaps a priestly Messiah. The Messiah of Israel enters and partakes of the meal only after the priest has done so (1QSa 2:11–22). The order is important! In this scene, the Messiah of Israel accepts the authority of the priestly figure.

A similar point is made in a commentary on Isaiah 11:3. There the nonpriestly messiah is identified as a Davidic messiah who will arise in the last days. He will be given a throne of glory, a diadem, and a special garment. He will judge nations with his sword. However, when he administers judgment, he cannot "decide by what his ears hear" (Isa. 11:3). Why? He must decide according to what he has been taught by the priests (4Q161 [4QpIsa^a] 8–10 15–29).

In a commentary on 2 Samuel 7:12–13, the nonpriestly messiah is again linked to David and is called a "Branch of David." This phrase comes from Jeremiah 23:5 and 33:15. This Branch of David will stand with the Interpreter of the Law in Zion in the last days. He will "save Israel" (4Q174 [4QFlorilegium] 1–2 i 21 10–13).

The same title is given to a future messiah in a text commenting on Genesis 49:10. There, Jacob's promise to Judah is interpreted with reference to the Davidic dynasty: "until the righteous Messiah branch of David comes" (4Q252 [4QCommGen A] 5:1–4). This messiah will exercise kingly rule.

These Qumran texts construct messiahs who will judge the wicked and nations, establish God's kingdom, and exercise kingly rule.

Pseudepigrapha

Four pseudepigraphic writings offer further glimpses of early Jewish thought about the Messiah, a figure anointed to carry out divine purposes.

Psalms of Solomon

The Psalms of Solomon is a collection of eighteen psalms written in the first century BCE. In Psalm of Solomon 17, the speaker laments that David, a king to whom God made a promise "about his descendants forever," has been replaced (17:4–5). The replacements were the Maccabean or Hasmonean kings, who hailed from the tribe of Levi. In opposition to them, says the psalm, God raised "a man alien to our race" who "hunted down their descendants" (17:7, 9). This man is the Roman general Pompey, who in 63 BCE ended the rule of the Hasmoneans and annexed Judea to the Roman Empire.

The psalmist elaborates the devastation and moral degradation caused by the Roman invasion (Pss. Sol. 17:11–18). In response to these dire conditions, the speaker asks God "to raise up for them their king, the son of David" (17:21). The job description of this anointed king or messiah is to take revenge on the Romans, to "destroy unrighteous rulers," to "purge Jerusalem from gentiles," and to "drive out sinners from the inheritance" (17:22–23). The psalm envisions the Messiah "destroying the unlawful nations with the word of his mouth." He condemns "sinners by the thoughts of their hearts" (17:25, echoing Isa. 11:3–4). Indeed, he relies on God, rejecting the "horse, rider and bow" (Pss. Sol. 17:33).

Having destroyed the Romans, this messiah will be "compassionate to all the nations (who) reverently (stand) before him" (17:34). They will serve him and come "from the ends of the earth to see his glory" (17:30–31). The Messiah will gather the exiles of Israel, rule them, and return them to their tribal lands (17:26–27). During the reign of "the Lord Messiah," "all shall be holy" (17:32), and the Messiah "himself (will be) free from sin" (17:36). God will make him "powerful in the holy Spirit and wise in the counsel of understanding, with strength and righteousness" (17:37, evoking Isa. 11:2). He will shepherd or rule Israel "faithfully and righteously" (17:40).

The Parables of Enoch

Another writing, the Parables of Enoch, is part of a collection of writings known as 1 Enoch (chaps. 37–71). The Messiah is named in 48:10. Throughout these chapters, this messiah is a heavenly, ruling, judging figure. He is also called the Anointed One, the Chosen One, the Righteous One, and the Son of Man (not a reference to Jesus!).

This last title, Son of Man, evokes Daniel's vision in Daniel 7:13–14, where a heavenly figure "like a son of man" will appear with the clouds of heaven. God, identified as "the Ancient of Days," gives him an everlasting dominion or rule over all peoples and creation.

Scholars debate the identity of the Son of Man in 1 Enoch 37–71. Toward the end of the book, he is identified with Enoch (Gen. 5:21–24) and transformed into an angel (1 En. 71:14). However, this identification with Enoch might be a later addition to the text.

In the Parables of Enoch, the Son of Man dwells among the angels "beneath the wings of the Lord of the Spirits" (39:6–7), a common identifier for God in 1 Enoch 37–71. The Son of Man is described as having the appearance of a man, though his face is full of graciousness like that of the holy angels (46:1). This Son of Man existed before the world was created, hidden from all by God's will (48:3–5; 62:7). He is God's chief agent for the eschatological or final judgment. He condemns the agents of oppression, "the kings of the earth and the mighty landowners" (48:7–8) and "the kings, the governors, the high officials, and the landlords" (62:1).

Describing him as a judge, the text also evokes Isaiah 11:4: "And the word of his mouth will slay all the sinners, and all the unrighteous will perish from his presence" (1 En. 62:2). The actual punishment of the unworthy with a sword, however, comes from God: God's "sword is drunk with them" (62:12).

At the same time, the Son of Man advocates for the righteous. He is "a staff for the righteous" and "a hope for those who grieve in their hearts" (48:4). "In his name they are saved" (48:7).

The Son of Man also judges angels who sinned (69:28). Moreover, the text envisions a universal resurrection (51:1; 61:5). "All who dwell on the earth will fall down and worship before him, and they will glorify and bless and sing hymns to the name of the Lord of Spirits" (48:5).

These early Jewish messianic expectations often engage passages from the Hebrew Bible, even though the Hebrew Bible texts they engage do not use the term "messiah" or "Christ" or make any explicit messianic identification. Among these texts are Jacob's promise to Judah (Gen.

49:10), Balaam's prophecy (Num. 24:17), Nathan's oracle to David (2 Sam. 7:5–16), Isaiah's prophecy in 11:1–10, and Daniel 7:13–14.

4 Ezra and 2 Baruch

Two post-70 CE texts—4 Ezra and 2 Baruch—also mention a messiah. These texts were written shortly after the war for independence from Roman rule ended with the Roman destruction of Jerusalem and the temple in 70 CE. This event caused a massive crisis of identity and debates about the way forward among Jews.

In 4 Ezra, "messiah" appears in several passages that do not present a neatly coherent scenario. After numerous events that lead to the end of this age (4:40–5:13), the Messiah is revealed (7:28). The Messiah rules "for four hundred years" (7:28), after which he and "all who draw human breath" die (7:29). A general resurrection and judgment follow, though the Messiah has no role.

Another more detailed description appears in 4 Ezra 12–13. The Messiah is described as preexistent and hidden for ages (12:32; 13:26). He is from the line of David (12:32). His role is to reprove, judge, and destroy the ungodly, first and foremost the Roman Empire (12:32–33). He delivers the "remnant" of Israel and "makes them joyful until the end comes, the day of judgment" (12:34).

In yet another vision, Ezra depicts the Messiah as a "figure of a man" who comes out of the sea, flying "with the clouds of heaven" (13:1, 3). This allusion to Daniel 7:13–14 indicates that the Messiah is the agent of God's reign. A great horde gathers against him to wage war.

The Messiah "neither [lifts] his hand nor [holds] a sword nor any weapon of war" (4 Ezra 13:9). Rather, he stands atop Mount Zion (13:35). He sends "forth from his mouth as it were a stream of fire, and from his lips a flaming breath, and from his tongue he [shoots] forth a storm of fiery coals," burning the "nations who gathered against him" (13:10). Ezra learns that all this fiery imagery stands for reproof, reproach, torment, and destruction "by the law (which was symbolized by the fire)" (13:37–38).

Yet another multitude gathers around the Messiah: "Some [are] joyful and some sorrowful" (13:13). These are the lost tribes who return to the land (13:40–47). Indeed, all those who are found within the borders of Judea will be saved (13:48).

In 2 Baruch, as in 4 Ezra, the Messiah appears several times. The book elaborates the "many tribulations" that will lead to the end of this age (2 Bar.

25:2–29:2). These tribulations include earthquakes, sword, and famine. These will befall all the living, but those dwelling in Judea will enjoy God's protection.

Then "the Messiah will begin to be revealed" (2 Bar. 29:3). This time is marked by an abundance of food and health (29:4–8). The "marvels every day" (29:6) include the reappearance of manna from the exodus wilderness. The "advent of the Messiah will be fulfilled and he will return in glory" (30:1). Next, "all those who have fallen asleep in hope of him will rise" (30:1), but, as in 4 Ezra, the Messiah plays no role in the resurrection and the following judgment.

Elsewhere in 2 Baruch, the Messiah is charged with reproving and slaying the last-standing wicked ruler (40:1) while protecting God's people who dwell in the land (40:2). The wicked ruler is most likely the Roman emperor. The Messiah's "rule will stand forever, until the world of corruption is completed and until the aforementioned times will be fulfilled" (40:3).

In yet another place, 2 Baruch states that the Messiah will slay those nations who oppressed Israel but will spare those who did not (72:2–3). Then the Messiah will sit "in peace forever on the throne of his kingdom" and reveal all kinds of blessings to the world: joy, rest, healing, and gladness and no premature death, vengeance, hatred, or birth pains. Animals and humans will be at peace, and human toil will be greatly alleviated (71:2–74:2).

Thus among all the vast number of texts of Early Judaism, we have references to a messiah in only a few Qumran texts, in one of the Psalms of Solomon, in a couple of chapters in 1 Enoch, and, post-70, in a few passages in 4 Ezra and 2 Baruch. These expectations are minimal and multivalent.

Messiah Expectations in the New Testament

In identifying Jesus as Christ or Messiah, New Testament writings locate Jesus in continuity with this minority Jewish tradition of awaited agents whom God has anointed to bring deliverance from oppressive rule and establish divine purposes. The New Testament writings interpret the term "Christ" in relation to Jesus's life, death, resurrection, and return. Doing so defines what God has anointed or commissioned Jesus as Christ to do.

Paul

Paul uses the term "Christ" more than 260 times in his six genuine letters (Romans, 1–2 Corinthians, Galatians, Philippians, 1 Thessalonians). This is about half of the New Testament uses of the word. Paul acknowledges Jewish messiah traditions. Among the privileges of Israelites are "the patriarchs, and from them, according to the flesh, comes the Christ" (Rom. 9:5).

Paul does not write the confession "Jesus is the Christ," but commonly he assumes that the term "Christ" refers to Jesus. So he writes "Jesus Christ," "Christ Jesus," "Lord Jesus Christ," to whom he declares his loyalty as an apostle and slave (Rom. 1:1; 15:16; 1 Cor. 1:1; Gal. 1:1, 3). Using "Christ" as a name rather than a confession makes sense since the audiences for Paul's letters are gentiles who were not especially familiar with minority Jewish traditions.

Paul's use of "Christ" identifies Jesus as God's anointed agent. Jesus Christ provides benefits of salvation, establishes a bond with believers, constitutes a community, and shapes a particular way of life.

Paul commonly links "Christ" with Jesus's death. He preaches "Christ crucified, a stumbling block to Jews and folly to gentiles" (1 Cor. 1:23 ESV). He often declares that "Christ died for you/us," thereby identifying Jesus's death as a noble death in providing the benefit of salvation for believers (Rom. 15:6, 8; 14:15; 1 Cor. 8:11; 1 Thess. 5:9–10). Less commonly, Paul uses "Christ" with reference to resurrection (1 Cor. 15:12–22); more commonly, he uses it to refer to Jesus's death and resurrection together (1 Cor. 15:3–5; Rom. 6:3–11 [baptism]; 8:34). Rare are uses of "Christ" in relation to Jesus's life or future return (Phil. 1:6 ["the day of Jesus Christ"], 1:10; 2:16).

Paul identifies the various benefits that Jesus, as Christ, brings to believers and that they experience through faithfulness (Gal. 2:16). Christ's grace has called believers through the preaching of the gospel of Christ (Gal. 1:6; Rom. 10:17). Christ has welcomed believers (Rom. 15:7), redeemed them (Rom. 3:24), justified or rendered them righteous (Gal. 2:16; Phil. 3:9), made them alive (1 Cor. 15:22), and promised them reward (or punishment) in the judgment (2 Cor. 5:10). To know Christ (Phil. 3:8) is to experience love from which one cannot be separated (Rom. 8:35–39). It is to be devoted to Christ (2 Cor. 11:3). Christ lives in believers (Gal. 2:20; Rom. 8:10) and is being formed in them (Gal. 4:19). Christ brings salvation (1 Thess. 5:9) and frees from condemnation (Rom. 8:1). He ensures believers' participation in the future resurrection (1 Cor. 15:20–22) and in the final victory in which Christ will establish the divine purposes (1 Cor. 15:23–28).

These benefits are experienced in communities of Christ's followers. Paul understands that these communities are constituted by Christ's death and resurrection and that they live toward the final establishment of the divine will. In baptism, we "who were baptized into Christ Jesus were baptized into his death, . . . [and] we will certainly be united with him in a resurrection like his" (Rom. 6:3, 5; cf. 1 Cor. 12:12–13). In this mystical union, Paul declares that he has been "crucified with Christ" and that "Christ lives in" him (Gal. 2:19–20) and speaks in him (2 Cor. 13:3). Until the resurrection, believers are to "walk [live] in newness of life" (Rom. 6:4).

This uniting with Christ constitutes a fundamental identity. Community members are "of" and "in" Christ (1 Cor. 1:12; 15:23; Gal. 3:29). Paul says, "You are Christ's" (1 Cor. 3:23). He insists that this identity of being of or in Christ, of belonging to Christ, creates unity among believers and overrides the defining power of all other identity markers, whether of ethnicity, social status, or gender:

> For in Christ Jesus you are all children of God through faith. As many of you as were baptized into Christ have clothed yourselves with Christ. There is no longer Jew or Greek; . . . slave or free; . . . male and female, for all of you are one in Christ Jesus. And if you belong to Christ, then you are Abraham's offspring. (Gal. 3:26–29)

Believers create and belong to "one body in Christ" (Rom. 12:5). Unity, though, does not mean uniformity. Members have diverse strengths, gifts, and functions, for "the body does not consist of one member but of many" (1 Cor. 12:14). In this one body in Christ, "not all the members have the same function," but every member is graced with gifts or roles to be exercised for the benefit of all (Rom. 12:4–8; 1 Cor. 12:12–31).

Finally, for Paul, to be in or of Christ constitutes ethical living. Christ's life is to shape how believers live. Members are to have the "mind" of Christ Jesus in furthering the interests of others (Phil. 2:4–5). They are to imitate Christ and Paul (1 Cor. 11:1). Just as Christ did not look out for only his own interests, members are to seek to benefit their neighbors (Rom. 15:2–3). "Welcome one another, therefore, just as Christ has welcomed you" (Rom. 15:7). The "love of Christ" is to control us (2 Cor. 5:14–15). Bearing "one another's burdens . . . will fulfill the law of Christ" (Gal. 6:2). Belonging to Christ Jesus means to "have crucified the flesh with its passions and desires" (Gal. 5:24), thereby enabling new life. To sin against your brothers and sisters is to sin against Christ (1 Cor. 8:12).

Mark's Gospel

In contrast with Paul's letters, the Gospels use the term "Christ" much less frequently. Mark, the first written Gospel, uses it only seven times. Elaborating Mark as a source, Matthew uses it sixteen times, and Luke twelve times. Acts, the second part of the two-part work Luke-Acts, uses it twenty-six times. Because of space limitations, we will focus on Mark's Gospel as the shortest Gospel.

Mark's Gospel opens with a declaration of Jesus's identity as "Jesus Christ" (1:1). In continuity with the Jewish traditions identified above of a figure anointed to carry out the divine purposes, this opening statement identifies Jesus as God's anointed agent. But the affirmation does not identify *what* Jesus is anointed to do. Since there is not a fixed job description for a messiah, the only way to answer this question is to read on in the Gospel.

Accordingly, in chapters 1–8, readers come to understand that Jesus is anointed to proclaim God's reign or kingdom or empire, which seeks to transform the injustices and oppression of the Roman-ruled world. He calls followers; heals sick people; casts out demons; conflicts with the Rome-allied, Jerusalem-based leaders over societal structures and practices; and performs nature miracles. In these chapters, Jesus displays much transformative power.

In 8:27–30, Mark's Jesus asks his disciples, "Who do people say that I am?" Peter confesses, "You are the Messiah." This is the second of the Gospel's seven uses. Interestingly, Jesus does not congratulate Peter on naming Jesus's identity correctly. Rather, Jesus commands his disciples not to tell anyone.

Why? Jesus explains that a consequence of his conflict with the Rome-sanctioned and allied Judean leadership will be his death and resurrection. This suffering and humiliating death are part of his identity as Christ. For disciples to understand Jesus's identity accurately, they must hold together his suffering and his power.

The next three uses of "Christ" are diverse. The first links disciples with Christ: "Whoever gives you a cup of water to drink because you bear the name of Christ will by no means lose the reward" (9:41). Hospitality for those identified with Christ will be rewarded.

The next reference (12:35) introduces a theological dispute concerning links between "Christ" and "son of David." Subsequently Jesus warns that in the time approaching his return and the establishment of God's purposes, some will mistakenly identify the Christ (13:21).

The last two references occur in the narrative of Jesus's death. After his arrest, Jesus is questioned by "the chief priests, the elders, and the scribes" (14:53). They accuse him of threatening to destroy the temple (14:58–61). The chief priest then asks him if he is the Messiah (14:61). Jesus answers,

> I am, and "you will see the Son of Man seated at the right hand of the Power," and "coming with the clouds of heaven." (Mark 14:62)

Significantly, Jesus's answer evokes the vision in Daniel 7:13–14, which we have seen is important in the Dead Sea Scrolls and 1 Enoch. He identifies himself with a figure not called "Christ" but "like a son of man" (ESV). This figure is an agent of God's power and will rule over all creation and people. He will displace all current structures of power.

Mark's Jesus defines his identity as Christ in terms of agency, power, and rule. This vision threatens the Jerusalem leaders' power and status. Jesus's claim to exercise future power and rule is, in their view, politically threatening to Roman rule, and his claim to be God's agent is religiously blasphemous. He deserves to die as a popular, unsanctioned "king of the Jews."

The last of Mark's seven uses occurs as Jesus dies on the cross. Passersby and those crucified with him mock him. The chief priests and scribes taunt him:

> Let the Messiah, the King of Israel, come down from the cross now, so that we may see and believe. (15:32)

The taunt is interesting in that, like Jesus's response in 14:62, it associates the title "Messiah" with rule and power by calling Jesus "King of Israel." Their taunt is ironic in the Gospel's point of view; they identify Jesus as Christ and king by speaking more accurately than they know. As the Gospel declared in its opening verse, Jesus *is* the Christ, anointed by God. Here in the passion narrative, it is clarified that he is anointed to return in power and glory to manifest God's rule over all people and creation.

Luke's Gospel expands Mark's use of "Christ/Messiah." An angel identifies the newborn Jesus as "the Messiah, the Lord" (Luke 2:11). Subsequently, Jesus is confessed by Peter (9:20) and mocked on the cross as "the Messiah of God" (23:35). Luke's Gospel elaborates on what God has anointed Jesus to do by quoting Isaiah 61:1–2:

> The Spirit of the Lord is upon me, because he has *anointed* me to bring good news to the poor. He has sent me to proclaim release to the captives and recovery of sight to the blind, to let the oppressed go free, to proclaim the year of the Lord's favor. (Luke 4:18–19 NRSV, emphasis added)

The verb "anointed" could be translated "christed": "because he [the Lord] has *christed* me to bring good news." Placing this passage at the beginning of Jesus's public activity frames and defines what Jesus as Christ is anointed or commissioned by God to do. Subsequently, the meaning of "Christ" expands to include Jesus's ascension (Luke 22:67–69), kingship (23:2–3), and suffering (23:39; 24:26, 46).

John's Gospel

John's Gospel also locates Jesus in this Jewish tradition of a figure anointed to carry out the divine purposes.

While Mark's Gospel assumes that "Christ" means "anointed one," the characters in John's Gospel have to discern and confess Jesus's identity as Christ/Messiah, as well as understand what Jesus is "christed" or anointed to do. The Gospel uses "Christ" or "Messiah" nineteen times. Two uses identify Jesus as "Jesus Christ" (1:17; 17:3). The remainder come in contexts concerned with making and understanding the confession that Jesus is the Christ, commissioned by and originating from God to reveal God's will. This is the purpose of the Gospel story about Jesus:

> But these are written so that you may come to believe that Jesus is the Messiah, the Son of God, and that through believing you may have life in his name. (John 20:31 NRSV)

Throughout the Gospel, characters must identify and define the Christ/Messiah.

- Authorities from Jerusalem ask John the Baptist if he is the Christ. He denies it (1:20, 25; 3:28).
- Andrew and Simon Peter encounter Jesus and confess, "We have found the Messiah." The author adds "which means Christ" to explain the Hebrew term with its Greek equivalent (1:41; also 4:25).
- In her conversation with Jesus, the unnamed Samaritan woman declares that when the Messiah/Christ comes, "he will show us all things" (4:25, authors' trans.; cf. 4:29). She affirms a key element of what Jesus is anointed to do—namely, to reveal the divine will. Shortly after, Jesus confirms that his task as Messiah/Christ is to do "the will of him who sent me and to complete his work" (4:34).
- In 7:25–31 people from Jerusalem speculate on Jesus's identity. Is he the Christ? Some think so because the authorities have not silenced him (yet!) (7:26). Others do not claim to know Jesus's origin but posit that no one will know the Christ's origin (7:27). Others suggest he is Christ because no one can perform more signs than Jesus (7:31). In the middle of these speculations, Jesus identifies what defines him as the Christ/Messiah—namely, his origin. He has been sent from God (7:28–29).
- More speculation and debate follow in 7:40–44. Some say Jesus is the Christ. Others are dubious because the Christ does not come from Galilee. They argue that the Christ is to descend from David and come from David's village, Bethlehem. Jesus's consistent claim that he comes

from God to do God's will names the Gospel's definition for Jesus to be called Christ (4:34; 5:19–20, 36–37; 6:38).
- Knowing Jesus's origin (from God), task (to reveal and do God's will), and identity as Christ or anointed by God functions as an identity marker separating the community of Jesus-followers (9:22) from the synagogue. The Jerusalem-based leaders do not recognize Jesus as one who has come from God (9:29).
- In 10:24 the leaders ask Jesus to tell them plainly if he is the Christ. Jesus's response defines his identity as the Christ: He is one with God his Father (10:30), has been commissioned and sent into the world by God to make known and do the works of God (10:37–38), and is in intimate relationship with God (10:38).
- In response to Jesus's declaration that he is the resurrection who brings new life in the new era, Martha confesses Jesus to be the Christ/Messiah (11:27). Her confession is consistent with the purpose of the Gospel narrative stated in 20:31.

In John's Gospel, unlike in Mark's, Jesus's identity as Christ is not assumed. It is continually debated. The narrative includes wrong answers that function as foils for determining the right confession and content for the term. As the Christ, Jesus is anointed or sent by God to make known God's will and works. Some confess, others resist this inconvenient and powerful claim, even to the point of putting Jesus to death.

Conclusion

Only a few early Jewish texts express an expectation for a messiah, a figure anointed to carry out the divine purposes. Among those that do, there is not a lot of detail. Expectations are few, marginal, and diverse. At their heart, these expectations were for a figure commissioned or anointed by God to deliver people from ungodly circumstances and Roman rule and to accomplish God's purposes. In continuity with this minority tradition, the early Jesus-movement identified Jesus as anointed or commissioned by God as Christ/Messiah. New Testament writers, especially Paul and the Gospel writers, elaborated in various ways what Jesus was anointed to perform.

Matters for Reflection

1. How does the Hebrew Bible use the term "anointed"? Which other texts in the Hebrew Bible contribute to the expectation of a special messianic figure, even though they do not use the term "messiah"?
2. It can be difficult for Christians to understand that not all Jews were waiting for a messiah and that references to a messiah are comparatively few among the large number of texts from Early Judaism. Review the mentioned texts from Qumran, the Psalms of Solomon, 1 Enoch, 4 Ezra, and 2 Baruch. What roles do they attribute to a messiah?
3. The New Testament texts do not hesitate to call Jesus "Messiah" or "Christ." Choose Paul or Mark's Gospel or John's Gospel. How does the author construct the Messiah? What alternative or opposing views emerge?

CHAPTER 7

Demons and Angels

Demons and angels are very common in contemporary forms of entertainment. Video games, movies, and TV programs, for example, frequently feature them. So do Halloween parties and costumes.

In some Christian circles, talk of demons and angels is common and troubling. Demons get blamed for all sorts of human foibles and failings, thereby removing human responsibility. Guardian angels get credited with protective and beneficial acts. Other Christian circles are uncomfortable with any talk of demons and psychologize Gospel references to demons and exorcisms as mental illnesses. Demons have also featured in polemical attacks on opponents. For millennia, in an appalling display of bigotry and hatred, Christians have referred to Jews as children or agents of the devil (so John 8:44). This is a troubling misunderstanding that must be rejected. There is no place in the human family for such talk.

In this chapter we investigate the roles of angels and demons in some of the writings of Early Judaism. And then we turn to investigate their construction in some New Testament writings.

Early Judaism

The Hebrew Bible mentions other heavenly beings besides God. However, it says surprisingly little about them. Early Jewish writings, on the other hand, reveal that heaven is a very populated place. These texts preserve rich and diverse traditions about angels, angels who sinned, and demons. Here we can discuss only some references.

Angels

According to the book of Jubilees, God created angels on the first day of creation (Jub. 2:2). Jubilees identifies seven kinds of angels. Five control various natural phenomena: clouds and winds, dew and snow, thunder and seasons. The remaining two kinds, the "angels of the presence" and the "angels of holiness," have cultic roles. Unlike other angels, these two groups were created circumcised (15:27). They keep Sabbath (2:18, 21, 30) and officiate in the heavenly temple (30:18; 31:14; see chap. 3 above).

> The book of Jubilees presents itself as a book dictated by an angel to Moses on Mount Sinai. It rewrites the book of Genesis and some of the book of Exodus.

Another early Jewish text, 1 Enoch, offers a wealth of information about angels. It refers to them as the "sons of heaven," "holy ones," "spirits," and "watchers"—possibly a reference to their sleepless attending to and praise for God (1 En. 39:12–13). "Ten thousand times ten thousand" angels are constantly present in God's heavenly temple (14:22–23). Some of 1 Enoch's angels oversee elements of nature (69:20–24). Some are responsible for the stars (82:9–20).

> First Enoch is not really one book but a collection of several early Jewish texts written in Aramaic. Different as they are, they all highlight the biblical figure of Enoch from Genesis 5:21–24.

First Enoch also describes hierarchies of angels. Some angels are in charge of ten angels (1 En. 6:7–8). There are chief angels called archangels: Michael, Sariel, Raphael, and Gabriel (9:1; 40), as well as Uriel, Reuel, and Remiel (chap. 20). These archangels deliver God's messages (10:1–3), impart knowledge (72:1), intercede with God on behalf of humans (chaps. 9–10), punish the wicked, and heal the earth (10:4–22).

> The Qumran community believed that angels were present among them (4Q266 [4QD^a] 8 i 9; 1QSa 2:8–9). While the Angel of Darkness and his hosts sought to lead the Sons of Light astray, God and the "angels of his truth" stood by them (1QS 3:24–25). The community believed that when they prayed, they did so along with angels praising God in heaven (1QS 11:7–9; 1QH^a 11:21–23). In the future eschatological war, they believed that God's angels would fight on the side of the Sons of Light (1QM 7:6; 12:8–9).

Angels Who Sinned

The book of Jubilees says God created angels. An explanation for the origin of evil angels is found in 1 Enoch 6–11. It begins with a tale of two hundred heavenly watchers led by the watcher Shemihazah. These watchers—their chiefs are named in 1 Enoch 6:7–8—conspire to leave heaven. They come down to earth and take the "beautiful and comely" human women as wives (1 En. 6:1–2). Watchers and women conceive children. These children are giants who wreak havoc on earth. They oppress humans by eating everything people produce. And when they devour all there is to eat, the giants begin "to kill people and devour them." Finally, they devour one another (7:4).

This scene in 1 Enoch 6–11 rewrites and interprets an enigmatic passage from Genesis 6:1–4. The "sons of God" of Genesis 6:2 are the "watchers, the sons of heaven" of 1 Enoch. The "Nephilim" and the "heroes of old, men of renown" (NJPS) of Genesis 6:4 are the giants.

What does the word "Satan" mean? "Satan" appears in Job 1–2. This figure is in the heavenly court and challenges God. Accordingly, the Hebrew word *satan* means "opponent" or "accuser" or "adversary." This is a job title, not a personal name. In later Jewish and Christian texts, "Satan" becomes a name that identifies the leader of evil spiritual beings or demons. Early Jewish texts assign other names to this figure: Belial (or Beliar, Hebrew for "wickedness"), Prince Mastema (Hebrew for "hostility"), and Beelzebul ("ruler of demons").

In 1 Enoch 6–11, taking human wives is not the angels' only sin. In these chapters, several traditions about fallen angels merge. According to another strand of this tradition, they teach humans forbidden knowledge and crafts. These include sorcery, spells, astrology, making weapons of war, and cosmetics (7:1; 8:2–3).

God punishes these sinful angels by binding them and casting them into darkness. This is a temporary measure. On the future judgment day, they will be taken "to the fiery abyss, and to the torture, and to the prison where they will be confined forever" (1 En. 10:1–6, 11–14). The evil giants perish too—they kill one another (10:9–10, 15).

In Genesis, the short account about the "sons of God" and "daughters of humans" helps explain God's wrath on humanity and its destruction in the flood. In its rewriting in 1 Enoch 6–11, the stories about the watchers/angels explain how evil came into the world.

Demons

If, as 1 Enoch 10 says, the angels who sinned are locked up until the final judgment, where do the demons and continuing evil come from? First Enoch provides an answer. When the giants die, "the spirits that have gone from the body of their flesh are evil spirits" (1 En. 15:9). Since they "were begotten on the earth, on the earth is their dwelling" (15:10). These evil spirits "lead astray, do violence, make desolate, attack and wrestle and hurl, and cause illness" (15:11). They will continue doing so "until the day of the consummation of the great judgment" (16:1).

Taking this view as a point of departure, the book of Jubilees shows how the evil spirits operate. It reports that after the flood the "impure demons" began targeting Noah's grandchildren (10:1–14). They misled them, made them act foolishly, and destroyed them. Jubilees thus underscores acute human helplessness in the face of demonic attacks.

Seeking a remedy, Noah prays for God's help. He pleads with God to imprison the demons so that they may not rule over the living. Initially, God grants his request. However, Prince Mastema appears. As a heavenly adversary (he is even called "Satan" in Jub. 10:11, echoing Job 1–2), he challenges God's decision. His argument? If all the demons are locked up, he claims, "I shall not be able to exercise the authority of my will among humanity," for "they are meant for (the purposes of) destroying and misleading" (Jub. 10:8). God, surprisingly, concedes, leaving nine-tenths of the demons imprisoned but setting one-tenth free.

Though God acquiesces to Mastema's plea, God is well aware that demons will "neither conduct themselves properly nor contend fairly" (Jub. 10:10). Jubilees assumes that the readers know that demons cause diseases. Therefore, God commands faithful angels to teach Noah "all the medicines for their diseases with their deceptions." The remedies for demon-caused diseases are "earth's plants." Noah records them and gives the book to his son Shem (10:12–14).

This is Jubilees' explanation for the limited demonic presence in the world. Yet Jubilees sees a further role for demons in the divine plan. It claims that all the nations of the world are under the dominion of evil spirits. God made demons to rule the nations "in order to lead them astray" (15:31).

But "no angel or spirit" rules over Israel. God "alone is their ruler" and "will guard them and require them for himself from his angels, his spirits, and everyone" (Jub. 15:31–32).

What Do Demons Do?

First Enoch, Jubilees, and Qumran texts describe ways in which demons exercise destructive power over humankind. This power ranges from leading astray to causing illness, violence, and destruction.

Demons lead humans astray by influencing their thoughts and inclinations. In Jubilees, Abraham prays for divine protection from demonic powers: "Save me from the power of the evil spirits who rule the thoughts of people's minds" (Jub. 12:20). In a Qumran text, the speaker confesses that demonic "spirits of controversy" struggle for control of the speaker's body (4Q444 [4QIncantation] 1–4 i + 5 2). These spirits are referred to as the spirits of wickedness and impurity (1–4 i + 5 4, 8).

Along with the power to control human thoughts, demons have the power to cause illnesses. The Damascus Document claims that a skin disease results from an evil spirit operating in the human body (4Q266 [4QD^a] 6 i 6–8). The Testament of Solomon, written between the first and third centuries CE, catalogs thirty-six demons by name, by their portfolios or job descriptions, and by the formulas that bind them. Artosael damages eyes, Shandor paralyzes limbs, Katrax causes incurable fevers, Rhyx Anatreth causes bowel problems, and Rhyx Axesbuth causes diarrhea and hemorrhoids. In addition, some demons cause domestic conflicts, jealousies and fights among people, and the collapse of houses.

And demons also cause violence and death. In the book of Tobit, one of the protagonists, Sarah, wishes to marry. She has been married seven times. However, the demon Asmodeus killed her seven husbands during the first night after the marriage (Tob. 3:7–8).

Thwarting Demons

Just as early Jewish texts show demons exercising power in various ways, so they show numerous ways to prevent demonic influence or fight back against it.

Referring to the internal somatic strife caused by the "spirits of controversy," a Qumran fragment encourages the reader, "And fortify yourself by the precepts of God, and to fight against the spirits of wickedness" (4Q444 [4QIncantation] 1–4 i + 5 4). Likewise, the Damascus Document argues that when a person vows to return to the Torah of Moses and follows through on their promise, the angel of Mastema will "depart from" them (CD 16:4–6).

In addition to following Torah, there are other preventive measures. Among them are protective or apotropaic prayers. We have already seen Abraham's prayer: "Save me from the power of the evil spirits who rule the thoughts of people's minds" (Jub. 12:20). Another prayer from Qumran pleads, "Let not a satan dominate me, nor an unclean spirit" (11QPs^a [11Q5] 19:15–16). That the Qumran community took warding off demonic influence very seriously is indicated by the task assigned to one of its chief officials. His task was "to frighten and te[rrify] all the spirits of the destroying angels and the spirits of the bastards"—a reference to demons who originated from the union of angels with women. He accomplished this protective role by "proclaiming the majesty of his [God's] beauty." Apparently, he recited the hymns that follow in this text (4Q510 [4QSong of the Sage^a] 1 4–5).

There are also examples of freeing or exorcising those under demonic influence. Methods of exorcism vary. In the book of Tobit, when Sarah is afflicted by the demon Asmodeus, the archangel Raphael instructs Tobias to expel the demon by burning a heart and a liver of a fish (Tob. 8:1–3). When the demon flees, Raphael binds him.

When Genesis Apocryphon rewrites the story of Sarah's abduction by Pharaoh, it says that God "sent . . . an evil spirit . . . and it scourged him and all his household" (20:16–17). When Pharaoh finally asks Abraham for help, Abraham exorcises the spirit by praying for Pharaoh and laying hands upon his head (20:20, 21, 28, 29).

The Jewish historian Josephus reports a scene in which Eleazar successfully exorcises a demon. He uses a ring containing a root that King Solomon prescribed, mentions Solomon's name, and recites incantations that Solomon wrote (*Ant.* 8.42–49). This story illustrates Josephus's discussion of Solomon's great wisdom. Solomon had a "knowledge of the art used against demons for the benefit and healing of people. He also composed incantations by which illnesses are relieved."

Qumran texts also attest early Jewish incantations against demons. One incantation is found in a badly damaged scroll, 11QapocrPs (11Q11) 5 4–13. It begins by claiming that it was composed by King David. The choice of David is by no means accidental. In the Hebrew Bible, David makes the evil spirit tormenting Saul go away (2 Sam. 16:23). Then the text provides

> [an incanta]tion in the name of YHW[H. Call an]y time on heav[en], for he will come to you in the nig[ht] . . .

The incantation has not survived in full, but what remains of it has two parts. First, the person attacked by a demon needs to identify the demon:

> . . . [and] you will say to him, "Who are you, [one born of] man and of the seed of the ho[ly one]s? Your face is a face of [delu]sion and your horns are horns of dream. You are darkness and not light, injustice and not righteousness."

Second, the afflicted person threatens the demon with divine power. The chief of God's army will imprison the demon behind "[the ga]tes of bronze through [which n]o light [passes] and [the] sun wh[ich rises on the] righteous [will] not [shine]."

Another fragmentary incantation from Qumran, this time in Aramaic, targets a specific disease. The illness is unclear—probably malaria—but what is remarkable is that the text seeks to exorcise not one but two demons, male and female, who caused the illness. The badly damaged text addresses the demons with the phrase "I adjure you, O spirit" and makes a possible connection between illness and sin (4Q560 [4QExorcism ar]).

Demons in the New Testament

Imperializing Contexts

Demons are common in the New Testament. Sixty-two references appear in nine New Testament writings. Exorcisms are common, as is the nasty accusation that someone is possessed by a demon:

> For John came neither eating nor drinking, and they say, "He has a demon." (Matt. 11:18)

> They said, "It is only by Beelzebul, the ruler of the demons, that this man casts out the demons." (Matt. 12:24)

Why were demons so common and exorcisms so pervasive in texts of Early Judaism and the New Testament? What was happening to impact these writings from the third century BCE to the first century CE?

Studies of instances of demonic possession and exorcisms in particular societies have shown that demonic activity often occurs in distinct historical, societal, political, and economic contexts. Studies have particularly drawn attention to situations marked by insertions of imperial power. Demonic activity is common in contexts of invasive colonizing powers.[1]

In contexts of colonizing power, subjugated peoples often invoke demons to represent the invasion of their people and land. They commonly borrow features of the invading forces to name the demons. So in Mark 5, the demons are called "Legion." This is the name of the foundational unit of the Roman army that had invaded the territory of the Gerasenes. With this naming, the spirits or demons are understood to represent the destructive evil of the invading forces.

Yet the appeal to demons in these contexts can divert attention away from the actual invading forces. Diverting attention to demons has the benefit of

---

1. See, e.g., Richard Horsley, *Jesus and the Politics of Roman Palestine* (Columbia: University of South Carolina Press, 2014), 80–107.

preventing people from openly confronting the various strategies of imperial power, which would not go well for dominated locals. The focus on demons strangely creates a process of mystification that disguises and masks the imperial situation and its strategies and practices.

These dynamics are evident in early Jewish and New Testament texts. From the 300s BCE to around 100 CE, Judeans were subject to imperial forces. As we have seen, 1 Enoch 6–15 tells of the oppressive giants born from the union of angels and women. These giants "were devouring the labor of all the sons of men, and men were not able to supply them" (1 En. 7:3). They taught humans how to make weapons of war and taught them "all iniquity on the earth" (9:6). The giants became "evil spirits" who "do violence, make desolate, and attack and wrestle and hurl upon the earth and cause illnesses" (15:8–11). The giants-become-evil-spirits represent the imperialism of various Hellenistic political powers whose rule across these centuries was experienced as oppressive and exploitative.

From Qumran, the War Scroll envisions a final battle between the Sons of Light and the Sons of Darkness. The "Prince of Light" and his spiritual forces will fight the "spirits of destruction," the "host of Belial." The latter categories correspond to and represent the imperializing and demonic Romans. The Romans are identified as the "Kittim" and will be defeated.

The New Testament writings emerge in this context of the assertion of Roman imperial power. Not surprisingly demons are common. Their presence is contextualized by and expressive of Roman invading power.

Gospels of Matthew and Luke

The Gospels of Matthew and Luke introduce the devil as the opponent of God's purposes and agent, Jesus. In the temptation scenes of both Gospels, the devil offers Jesus all the empires of the world on the condition that Jesus worship the devil (Matt. 4:8–9; Luke 4:5–7). The devil's offer discloses the Gospels' analysis of and verdict on the contemporary imperial world. It reveals the Roman Empire to be under the control of the devil. The devil is the power behind the throne. The empire is antithetical to God's ways.

After the devil is identified as the power behind the throne of the Roman Empire, another scene links the devil and demons. Members of the Jewish societal leadership (Pharisees, scribes, and "people") give their verdict on Jesus's exorcisms of demons. They declare that Jesus carries out his exorcisms not by God's power but by "Beelzebul, the ruler of the demons" (Matt. 12:24; Mark 3:22; cf. Matt. 9:34; Luke 11:15). As mentioned previously, Beelzebul is another name for the devil or Satan. Here, demons are presented as agents ruled by the devil and at work in Rome's empire. Jesus responds by explaining that he carries out his exorcisms "by the Spirit of God" and that in his exorcisms "the empire of God has come" (Matt. 12:28, authors' trans.). He asserts God's empire against the devil-controlled Roman Empire.

Revelation

The book of Revelation also links demons and imperial domination. This writing focuses on how Jesus-followers are to live faithfully in Rome's devil-controlled, demon-infested empire.

Revelation 12 identifies an aggressive "great red dragon" that is defeated in a heavenly battle by the archangel Michael and his angels. The dragon is expelled from heaven and is thrown down to earth. The dragon is identified as "the devil and Satan, the deceiver of the whole world" (12:1–9).

In the next chapter, a beast appears. The dragon/Satan has given it "his power and his throne and great authority" (Rev. 13:2). People worship the dragon/Satan and the beast. The beast represents the Roman emperor, who has authority over "every tribe and people and language and nation" (13:8). The scene reveals that the devil has set the Roman emperor, the beast, in power. The empire is shown to be controlled by the devil. Worship of the emperor is worship of the devil.

In 13:11–18 a second beast appears. This beast participates in the power of the first beast and promotes its worship. This second beast probably represents elite persons and rulers in cities throughout the empire. They allied with Roman governors to enhance their own status and express loyalty to the first beast, the emperor, by using their wealth and power to fund games, feasts, temples, rituals, and processions that were occasions for honoring the emperor.

As in the Gospels, the emperor was installed and authorized by the devil, who is the power behind the throne. Revelation issues its verdict on the Roman Empire: It is under the control of the devil. And participation in worshiping the emperor means worshiping the devil.

Accordingly, Revelation shows that demons, the devil's agents, are active in the imperial world. In 16:12–16 demons, described as "foul spirits," propel the "kings from the east" (Rome's enemy, the Parthians) along with "the kings of the whole world" to gather for battle "on the great day of God the Almighty." The scene depicts the demon-controlled Roman Empire and all other kings aligned with it in hostile rebellion against God. They fight to rule the world.

They are not successful. Chapter 18 envisions God's condemnation and destruction of Babylon/Rome and its empire. The detailed fantasy exposes Babylon/Rome as a "dwelling place of demons, a haunt of every foul spirit" (18:2). The chapter identifies the empire's exploitative economic and trade activities that the demons have controlled. And chapter 18, along with chapters

19–22, reveals that the demons and the Roman order are under God's final judgment.

Paul

Paul warns the Corinthian Jesus-believers about the dangers of another means of participation in the demon-controlled Roman Empire (1 Cor. 10:18–22). He speaks against sacrificing to idols because, he claims, doing so is to sacrifice to demons. Participation in the Lord's Supper is antithetical to honoring demon-associated idols with sacrifices.

Paul's protest might be directed against the common cultural practice of honoring household gods. But also, honoring idols and gods in various societal contexts was considered crucial to the well-being of Rome's empire. The gods were to be honored so that they, in turn, would bless and prosper the empire. Fundamental to this understanding was the notion that the gods had chosen Rome as their agent to rule the world (Virgil, *Aeneid* 1.236, 278–83). Paul claims that this practice honors demons that are allied with the empire.

Elsewhere, Paul recognizes the existence of these powers, but he maintains their limited power cannot separate believers from the love of God (Rom. 8:38–39).

Mark's Gospel

Mark 5:1–20 provides a good example of demons possessing a person, destroying their life, and representing invasive, imperial (military) strategy. And it establishes Jesus as a powerful exorcist.

The scene takes place in Gerasa (Mark 5:1). The Hebrew root of the name Gerasa means "drive or cast out" or "banish." Gerasa is a land in need of exorcism. Why? Because in 68 CE, a few years before Mark's Gospel was written, Roman troops attacked Gerasa. They killed young men, captured families, burned houses, attacked nearby villages, and occupied the land. Not surprisingly, the demons are named Legion (5:9). A legion was the basic unit of the Roman military, comprising around five thousand troops. The demon's name represents Rome's invading, occupying, military force.

The possessed man, dominated by demons, represents the damage and destruction wrought by Rome's military conquest of Gerasa. He lives in the tombs, a place of death and social alienation. His behavior is crazy and out of control. Shackles and chains have not restrained him. He howls and damages himself with stones (5:2–5).

The demon encounters Jesus with apparent submission in 5:6 but quickly becomes resistant (5:7–13). Recognizing Jesus's greater power, it tries to ward off Jesus. It begs to stay in the country, thereby maintaining control of the conquered and occupied land (5:10). As a second resort, the demon begs to occupy the pigs, to control the land's production that belongs to local residents (5:12).

Significantly, the boar was the mascot of the Roman tenth Fretensis legion. This legion played a key role in occupying and destroying Jerusalem in 70 CE. Sending the demons named Legion into the pigs closely aligns Roman military power and demonic power. Other indications of military power are evident in language of "send" and "enter." Jesus the exorcist is constructed as a superior military commander.

The locals are not happy with Jesus sending the demon-possessed pigs into the sea. The act destroys an important component of their local economy. Perhaps they fear that they won't be able to pay tribute and taxes if Jesus does more damage. They want Jesus gone (5:17).

In the meantime, the man is "clothed and in his right mind" (5:15). He wants to bear witness to Jesus's transforming, powerful mercy (5:19–20). This exorcism, as with all of Jesus's exorcisms, has rolled back and repaired the damage of Roman occupation. The scene presents a fantasy of freedom from imperial oppression from the perspective of dominated peoples.

Other scenes involve demons possessing people. They throw people to the ground and cause them to exhibit nonsocial behaviors (Mark 1:26; 9:20; Luke 4:31–37; 9:37–43).

Demons and Disciples

Jesus is not the only exorcist. He commissions his disciples to continue his work of exorcism (Matt. 10:8; Mark 3:15). In this task, disciples are both successful (Mark 6:13; Luke 10:17–19) and unsuccessful (Mark 9:14–19). Jesus reminds them that powers of exorcism are no substitute for faithful obedience to Jesus's teaching (Matt. 7:22). And he instructs them not to stop other exorcists at work: "For whoever is not against you is for you" (Luke 9:49–50; cf. Mark 9:38).

Demons and Disease

Consistent with other texts in Early Judaism, the Gospels commonly recognize that demons make people sick. Demons cause people to be unable to speak (Matt. 9:32), to be blind (12:22), to suffer badly (15:22), to suffer from fits such as throwing oneself into fire and water (17:14–15). In the scene of this last example, the boy's behavior is often translated as "epilepsy." The Greek word literally means "moonstruck," whereby the moon was understood as a hostile power or demon (17:18).

The Gospels also provide summaries of Jesus's exorcisms of the demons that cause people to be sick (Matt. 4:24; 8:16; Mark 1:34; Luke 4:40–41; 8:2). Sometimes the exorcisms are quick and instant, effected by Jesus's word. Other times, demons try to resist Jesus's power in verbal confrontations (Mark 1:24, 34; 5:7; Luke 4:33–35, 41). In these exorcisms, Jesus repairs the damage that the Rome-representative demons have created.

The construction of demons as the cause of disease provides another example of the mystification of imperial practices that damaged people's lives. Diseases can result from poverty, stress, unhygienic living conditions, ignorance of basic hygiene, and food insecurity. Imperial practices imposed taxes and tributes on conquered peoples. Taxes and tributes were often paid in kind, such as a percentage of harvests and of other resources. This practice, along with trading activity, removed vital food production and resources from low-status and poor provincials. It transferred resources to ruling elites to sustain their wealthy lifestyles, which were marked by conspicuous consumption (see Rev. 18:11–13).

In addition to taxes and tributes, poor soil, bad weather, and poor harvests meant that many folks in the Roman Empire lived near, at, or under subsistence level in rural contexts. As we know, food insecurity and inadequate nutrition have devastating impacts on human lives. Diseases of contagion result from low immunity, from deprivation of nutrition, from poor hygiene, and from high levels of stress associated with the struggle to procure adequate food. Short lifespans are a consequence.

An appeal to demons as the cause of disease masks the impact of these imperial structures and practices. A cultural focus on demons diverts attention from the damaging and destructive strategies of imperial power. Instead of explicitly identifying imperial practices that remove adequate nutrition and increase stress as causes of disease, blame is directed to demons.

Demons and Polemic

In the bitter exchanges between Jesus and the Rome-allied Jewish leaders, each party accuses the other of being possessed by demons. The leaders attribute Jesus's exorcising power not to God but to demons (Matt. 9:34; 12:24; Mark 3:22–27; Luke 11:14–20). John the Baptist is also accused of having a demon (Matt. 11:18).

In John's Gospel, a crowd accuses Jesus of being demon possessed (John 7:20). Jesus accuses the Jewish leaders of being from and belonging to the devil (8:44). They respond by twice accusing Jesus of being demon possessed (8:48, 52; 10:20–21), which he denies (8:49).

The point of this nasty polemic is to discredit the other. It functions by aligning the other with demonic forces and thereby removing God's sanction from their authority and teaching. The same dynamics are in play in Revelation's aligning of the Roman Empire with demons and the devil.

Angels in the New Testament

The Greek word *angelos* means "messenger." Conventionally, we think of angels as heavenly beings with wings, but the word "angel" can also refer to a human messenger or agent (Luke 7:24, 27; 9:52). Are the angels that are linked to the seven churches in Revelation 2–3 heavenly figures guiding and protecting churches, or are they human leaders and God's representatives in the churches?

Conventionally, we also think of angels as good creatures. Yet the devil has angels or messengers called "demons." They will be condemned in the judgment (Matt. 25:41).

Our focus in the brief space remaining in this chapter is on angels as messengers of the divine will.

Gospels

In the Gospels, angels play a number of roles.

Angels dwell in the heavens with God (Luke 1:19; 2:15; 15:10; Matt. 18:10). There are many angels; Jesus says he can claim twelve legions to fight on his behalf (Matt. 26:53)—as mentioned above, a legion in the Roman Empire comprised around five thousand troops. Angels do not marry (Matt. 22:30). They are very active as agents of God's will in Jesus's conception and birth (Luke 1:11–38; Matt. 1:18–25). They praise God (Luke 2:13–14). They have some roles in Jesus's ministry (guiding Joseph to Egypt, Matt. 2:13, 19; after the temptation, Matt. 4:11). They are messengers of Jesus's resurrection (Luke 24:23; Matt. 28:2, 5). They are presented as being active in Jesus's return (Luke 9:26; 12:8–9) and involved in the judgment of human beings (Matt. 13:39, 41, 49; 24:31; 25:31). They do not know all the divine plans (Matt. 24:36).

Paul

Paul's letters make a few passing references to angels.

Paul describes himself as a messenger or "angel" of God when referring to his reception among the Galatians (4:14). Here the word "angel" refers to a person who is a messenger. He also links angels and Satan. He acknowledges Satan's ability to deceive by disguising himself as "an angel of light" (2 Cor. 11:14). And he identifies his unspecified thorn in the flesh as a "messenger" or angel of Satan (2 Cor. 12:7).

He also makes some claims that seem somewhat unusual. Humans will judge angels in the final judgment (1 Cor. 6:3). Angels speak in their own language (1 Cor. 13:1). And "the law was ordained [ordered] through angels by a mediator" (Gal. 3:19). The passive verb indicates God is the one who ordered the law; the mediator refers to Moses on Mount Sinai. The role of angels in giving the law is recognized in both Hebrew Bible (Deut. 33:2) and New Testament texts (Acts 7:38, 53).

Revelation

Of the 176 references to angels in the New Testament, nearly 70 occur in Revelation. By far, this is more than in any other New Testament writing.

Predictably, angels are heavenly figures in Revelation (Rev. 5:2; 8:2). Their dominant activity in heaven is worship. Consistently, as in 1 Enoch, they praise God.

> Then I looked, and I heard the voice of many angels surrounding the throne . . . , singing with full voice, "Worthy is the Lamb that was slaughtered to receive power and wealth and wisdom and might and honor and glory and blessing!" (Rev. 5:11–12)

> And all the angels stood around the throne . . . , and they fell on their faces before the throne and worshiped God, singing, "Amen! Blessing and glory and wisdom and thanksgiving and honor and power and might be to our God forever and ever! Amen." (Rev. 7:11–12)

Revelation's angels are also active in revealing the divine purposes for the world ruled unjustly by the Roman Empire. For example, angels hold back the winds so they do not damage the earth (Rev. 7:1–3). In chapters 8–9, trumpet-blowing angels reveal the divine judgments that are intended to bring the empire's inhabitants to repentance (8:6–9:21). Angels reveal God's plan by unrolling a scroll (10:1–2) and proclaim "an eternal gospel" that will allow inhabitants to escape divine judgment on the empire (14:6–12). In chapter 16, angels pour out bowls of God's wrath on the earth. In chapter 17, an angel reveals judgment on "the great whore," the city and empire of Rome. In chapter 18, an angel declares Rome's destruction. In 20:1–3, an angel seizes the dragon that is the devil and Satan and confines it to a pit for a thousand years. In 21:10, an angel reveals the new Jerusalem, which descends from heaven and represents the divine will for a world of justice and societal harmony.

The confining of the devil to the pit for a thousand years (20:1–3) is a consequence of a previous scene involving angels. Back in chapter 12, war broke out in heaven; Michael and his angels fought against the dragon. The dragon and his angels fought back, but they were defeated, and there was no longer any place for them in heaven. The great dragon was thrown down, that ancient serpent, who is called the devil and Satan, the deceiver of the whole world—he was thrown down to the earth, and his angels were thrown down with him. (Rev. 12:7–9)

This scene explains the origin of oppressive and violent evil in the world. Heaven is a place of conflict and war. But Michael and his angels restore it as a place where the divine will is done. They defeat and expel the devil and his angels/demons, who are thrown down to earth, where they continue to resist the divine purposes. In chapter 13, the devil and his angels/demons are especially aligned with Rome's empire as a devilish and demonic structure. Revelation ends with visions of the destruction of the demonic Roman Empire, the confining of the devil, and the establishment of God's empire (chaps. 17–22).

Matters for Reflection

1. The texts of Early Judaism and the New Testament take demons very seriously. How do they understand their origins? How do they understand their functions and roles? What is their relationship to invading, imperializing powers like the Roman Empire?
2. According to early Jewish texts, how can humans defend themselves against demons?
3. Was Jesus unique in performing exorcisms?
4. What are angels' job descriptions? Draw up a list of their duties from the discussion in this chapter.

CHAPTER 8

Crucifixion

"Christ killers." "The Jews murdered Jesus." We have heard students and preachers make these claims often. And there are numerous examples just one Google search away.[1]

In this chapter we consider this very troubling misunderstanding and charge that Christians have made against Jews for two thousand years. Christians have charged Jews with being "Christ killers" in crucifying Jesus.

It's important, albeit very uncomfortable for some readers, to recognize that the New Testament writers start and sustain this tradition. Paul says to the church in Thessalonica,

> For you suffered the same things from your own compatriots as they did from the Jews who killed both the Lord Jesus and the prophets and drove us out; they displease God and oppose everyone. (1 Thess. 2:14–15)

And around the year 100 CE, the writer of Acts has Peter accuse his Jewish audience:

> But you rejected the holy and righteous one and asked to have a murderer given to you, and you killed the author of life, whom God raised from the dead. To this we are witnesses. (Acts 3:14–15)

One way that this charge by Jesus-followers against Jews functions is to define the Jesus-community not only as a distinct group but as a superior

---

[1] See Jeremy Cohen, *Christ Killers: The Jews and the Passion from the Bible to the Big Screen* (Oxford: Oxford University Press, 2007).

group. The definition is by contrast. Jesus-groups are defined as devoted to Jesus Christ, whereas Jewish communities are defined as Christ killers. Another way it functions is by using the Bible's authority to define Jews as Christ killers forever, as generation after generation reads these accusations and agrees with them because they are in the Bible and carry the weight of the Bible's authority.

Despite the long-standing nature of the charge, historically it is false. It lacks nuance. It fails to identify which Jews were involved (clue: not *all* Jews) in Jesus's crucifixion. And it fails to recognize the central role of the (gentile!) Roman governor Pontius Pilate as the only character with the power to sentence Jesus to death.

In this chapter we consider historical factors concerning crucifixion, identify the important role of the Roman governor Pilate, and interpret the highly problematic verse in Matthew 27:25: "Then the people as a whole answered, 'His blood be on us and on our children.'" The Gospel accounts, when read from a particular perspective, lay the foundation for this hateful view, which has had disastrous consequences across the last two thousand years. We finish with some expressions of this pernicious charge from the early church.

Crucifixion: Historical Factors

The Romans did not invent the practice of crucifixion, but they used it effectively and extensively as a means of social control, deterrence, and punishment across their empire.

> According to Josephus, punishment by crucifixion in Judea preceded Roman rule. Around the 160s BCE, the Seleucid king Antiochus IV Epiphanes proscribed Judaism. Josephus claims that Antiochus crucified Jews who remained faithful to ancestral customs such as circumcision and Sabbath and festival observances (*Ant.* 12.256).

Rome commonly reserved crucifixion as the death penalty for non-elites. It was a punishment for low-status and marginal figures, such as violent criminals, terrorists or brigands, enemies of or rebels against Roman power, and rebellious slaves. References attest the crucifixion of both men and women. The Jewish historian Josephus calls crucifixion "the most pitiable of deaths" (*J.W.* 7.202–3). In only the most unusual circumstances—such as treason or serious corruption or to humiliate provincial leaders—were elite citizens crucified.

Crucifixion was preceded by torture, often in the form of whipping, along with verbal abuse and social shaming. Victims were publicly displayed as they were marched to the site of crucifixion. It was carried out not in private spaces but in the public gaze. Busy, well-traveled roads, intersections, and public squares were common locations for crosses so that "the greatest number of people [could] look and be seized by this fear" (Quintilian, *Lesser Declamations* 27.4.13). Crucifixion not only punished an offender but also persuasively intimidated populations to comply with Roman rule and order.

There does not seem to have been a standard form for crosses (capital *T*, lowercase *t*, an *X*, a post). Nor was there a standard position for crucified victims. Josephus comments that on at least one occasion Roman soldiers "amused themselves" by crucifying people in differing positions (*J.W.* 5.451). It is not clear whether victims died of asphyxiation and suffocation, shock from the violent process, stress, whipping, exhaustion, or being nailed or fastened with ropes to a cross.

The Hasmonean king Alexander Jannaeus (103–76 BCE) resorted to crucifixion to punish political opponents. Josephus says that he crucified eight hundred men who conspired with the Seleucid king Demetrius III (*J.W.* 1.92–98; *Ant.* 13.376–80). This episode is reflected in Pesher Nahum from Qumran. It identifies the crucified as Pharisees (4Q169 3–4 i). These events may also explain the view taken by another Qumran text, the Temple Scroll. There, someone who betrays his people to foreigners or deserts to a foreign nation and curses Israel is to be "hanged on the tree so that he will die" (11QT^a 64:2–6). Both texts evoke Deuteronomy 21:22–23, the very passage Paul uses in Galatians 3:13 with reference to Jesus's crucifixion.

Why Was Jesus Crucified?

This information about Roman practices of crucifixion enables us to understand why Jesus was crucified. He was not crucified as a religious figure. He was not crucified because he was too spiritual or heavenly minded. He was not crucified for saying his prayers. He was not crucified for being Messiah or claiming to have a close relationship with God or committing some sort of blasphemy. None of these factors resulted in crucifixion.

Rather, Jesus was crucified as a political rebel who posed a threat to Roman rule and the elite-controlled status quo. According to the Gospels, he proclaimed the appearance of the reign or kingdom of God, the empire of God, in the midst of Rome's empire. Talk of another empire by a figure who had popular support was a threat to imperial leaders and could provoke them to remove such a threat. Moreover, Jesus attacked the temple and the Jerusalem-centered provincial leadership, who were allies and agents of Rome and responsible for securing Rome's interests in the province (Mark 11–15). And Jesus declared that he would return in power at a future date and destroy the Roman Empire. He would carry out a kingly role in establishing God's reign in full (Matt. 24–25). He envisioned a different world and future.

These emphases constructed Jesus as a threat to the Roman status quo and its Jerusalem-based provincial allies. Three indicators in the crucifixion stories point to Jesus's crucifixion specifically as a wannabe rebel king.

First, the Gospels narrate that Jesus's cross featured a notice that named his crime.

> Over his head they put the charge against him, which read, "This is Jesus, the King of the Jews." (Matt. 27:37; cf. Mark 15:26; Luke 23:38)

John's Gospel is similar. The Jewish leaders remind Pilate that "everyone who claims to be a king sets himself against the emperor" (John 19:12 NRSV).

> Pilate also had an inscription written and put on the cross. It read, "Jesus of Nazareth, the King of the Jews." . . . It was written in Hebrew, in Latin, and in Greek. Then the chief priests of the Jews said to Pilate, "Do not write, 'The King of the Jews,' but, 'This man said, I am King of the Jews.'" Pilate answered, "What I have written I have written." (John 19:19–22)

Why might being "king of the Jews" get Jesus crucified?

First, it was a matter of authorization. The only way to become a king in a province of the Roman Empire was to be appointed to that role by Rome. Herod was a Rome-appointed king (Matt. 2). To claim to be, or to be understood to be, a king without Rome's sanction was considered treason. One of the leaders of the rebellion against Rome in 66–70 CE, Simon, was executed for claiming to be king without Rome's sanction (Josephus, *J.W.* 4.510; 7.29, 154).

Second, Jesus was crucified along with two insurrectionists or terrorists (Matt. 27:38; Mark 15:27). The common translation of the Greek term *lēstēs*, "bandit," is too vague. In Josephus the Greek word refers to violent terrorists or freedom fighters or rebels or insurrectionists who fought against Roman rule and its representatives. When these rebellious figures were caught, they were killed by troops or crucified.

> The Romans used crucifixion to punish rebels in Judea. During the unrest after King Herod's death, Varus, the Roman governor of Syria, crucified two thousand rebels (Josephus, *Ant.* 17.295–96). Josephus reports that during the siege of Jerusalem in 70 CE, Romans crucified five hundred Jews daily. "So great was their number, that space could not be found for the crosses nor crosses for the bodies" (*J.W.* 5.451).

Third, in these accounts of Jesus's death, there is a prisoner called Barabbas. Pilate offers him to the crowd as an alternative to crucifying Jesus and releases him. John's Gospel identifies Barabbas as a *lēstēs*, a rebel, terrorist, or insurrectionist. Mark's Gospel similarly identifies Barabbas: "Now a man called Barabbas was in prison with the insurrectionists who had committed murder during the insurrection" (Mark 15:7). Two of the Gospels narrate Jesus as being crucified with terrorists or insurrectionists (*lēstēs*) (Matt. 27:38, 44; Mark 15:27).

We must remember that there is no historical evidence for this practice of releasing a prisoner at the festival of Passover. And the prospect of a Roman governor releasing one of "the insurrectionists who had committed murder during the insurrection" seems most unlikely, especially during the risky season of Passover, which celebrated the people's liberation from slavery in Egypt. Pilate was much smarter than that.

How does the motif of releasing a prisoner function as a feature of the narrative? At one level it is important for presenting Pilate as powerfully in control of the administration of "justice." He is able to do something that his Jerusalem allies cannot do. He can release a prisoner.

Second, when Pilate introduces Barabbas into the conversation (Matt. 27:16–17), he requires the Jerusalem leaders to choose between Barabbas and Jesus. They choose Jesus and beg for his execution. Pilate has forced them into a subordinate position whereby they are dependent on his will.

The Role of the Roman Governor Pilate

One of the reasons that the Jews have been blamed for Jesus's crucifixion is the failure to recognize the leading role of the Roman governor Pilate in crucifying Jesus. Pilate was governor from 26 CE to early 37 CE, when he was recalled to Rome just before the emperor Tiberius died.

Roman governors were appointed to be the face of Roman power in the province of Judea. A governor's job description involved representing Roman interests, keeping law and order, administering "justice," and collecting taxes. The office of governor required toughness, loyalty to Roman interests, and political skills in advancing those interests. Governors, of course, enjoyed numerous perks and privileges, including the ability to enrich themselves at the expense of provincials.

We don't know a lot about Pilate's life in particular, but we do have some idea how Roman governors were appointed and who was appointed to rule provinces. Typically, Pilate's family probably would have been among the elites and present in the circles of the emperors Augustus and Tiberius. Most likely, in addition to these family connections, Pilate had both administrative experience (perhaps on a governor's staff) and military experience before being appointed governor.

Pilate ruled his province with a small military force and staff. In addition, he ruled in alliance with the local Jerusalem-based leadership of chief priests, scribes, and leading Pharisees and Sadducees. Rome typically maintained local ruling structures and personnel as allies as long as the local figures were willing to uphold Roman interests.

Pilate's alliance with the Jerusalem-based leadership required Pilate's consideration of and attention to their interests to maintain cooperative interactions. Yet always the governor retained the ultimate exercise of power, that of the death penalty (Josephus, *J.W.* 2.117). Local Jewish leaders could execute anyone who violated the space of the temple sanctuary (*J.W.* 6.126), but otherwise, the death penalty was the preserve of the governor.

These gubernatorial realities must inform our interpretation of the Gospels' presentations of the scenes involving Pilate and Jesus. So often, interpreters misinterpret these interactions because they lack any informed understanding of Pilate as a governor. The stereotype of Pilate as a weak character manipulated by the nasty Jewish leaders, for example, is repeated constantly by interpreters and preachers to sustain the "blame the Jews" fiction. But one thing is clear: Roman governors were not weak—sometimes corrupt and cruel, but not weak.

Also common is the misunderstanding that Jesus was innocent and Pilate was reluctant to crucify the "nice" Jesus until he was bullied into doing so. Jesus, king of the Jews, was not innocent in the eyes of Rome, as the above discussion has shown. These stereotypes are historically impossible and create blatant misreadings of the Gospel narratives.

Pilate was not a weak character who was coerced by the Jewish leaders into crucifying Jesus. To be appointed a governor, he had to have demonstrated strength, courage, some skill in the arts of governance, and undoubted loyalty to Rome's interests. He was not the weak, wimpy character that the "blame the Jews" scenarios assume.

When Pilate's allies brought Jesus to Pilate for crucifixion, it expressed their commitment to, investment in, cooperation with, and defense of the Roman imperial order. Pilate knew their commitments; accordingly, Pilate had to take their concerns seriously to maintain the alliance with them as local leaders. He needed their support to secure order and Rome's control. This recognition of the importance of the alliance, of the Jerusalem leaders' commitments, and of his own role in maintaining law and order meant that Jesus's fate was already sealed. Matthew 27:3 recognizes this reality. Matthew 27:2 narrates Jesus's transfer from the Jerusalem leaders to governor Pilate: "They bound him, led him away, and handed him over to Pilate the governor." Verse 3 does not narrate the encounter between Jesus and Pilate that readers are expecting. Rather, it switches immediately to Judas's perspective: "When Judas, his betrayer, saw that Jesus was condemned . . ." Judas provides commentary on the transfer. Even though Jesus has not appeared before Pilate yet, Judas knows what the outcome will be when one sector of the ruling alliance transfers a prisoner known as "king of the Jews" to the Roman governor. Jesus is condemned. His fate is already sealed. He will be crucified.

While the outcome is certain, the process toward this goal requires some governing skill. The decision to crucify is Pilate's, but the governor cannot ignore the two parties impacted by this decision to secure this outcome. One party consists of his allies, the Jerusalem leaders. He needs them if he is to rule successfully, so he must satisfy their demands. If they present Jesus as a threat, Pilate must respond accordingly. Yet Pilate is the governor. He has the greater power in the alliance. He cannot be dictated to by his allies. He must balance their expectations while showing he is not their lackey. He will assert his dominance.

There is a second interested party that Pilate must consider—namely, the crowd. This is a local crowd gathered in Jerusalem, not all Jews in the first-century world and not all Jews for all time. What will be the fallout when Pilate crucifies a popular "king of the Jews"? Will there be riots? How many followers does Jesus have? How popular is he? How much support does he have? Will Pilate have a large-scale rebellion on his hands?

Pilate negotiates both parties with two skillful strategies. With his elite allies, he plays hard to convince, which positions him as superior and maneuvers the Jerusalem leaders into a subordinate position, whereby they beg for Pilate to act. Second, with the crowd, Pilate orchestrates a poll to see how much support Jesus has and what impact his crucifixion might have on public order. Both strategies secure Pilate's dominance.

First, in polling the localized Jerusalem crowd, he plays Barabbas and Jesus off each other:

> So the crowd came and began to ask Pilate to do for them according to his custom [of releasing a prisoner]. Then he answered them, "Do you want me to release for you the King of the Jews?" (Mark 15:8–9)

The crowd reminds Pilate of the custom of releasing a prisoner. Pilate offers Jesus and seeks the crowd's will. How popular is Jesus, whom he identifies as "king of the Jews"? The question asserts Pilate's control of the situation by polling the crowd to assess how much support Jesus has.

> But the chief priests stirred up the crowd to have him release Barabbas for them instead. (Mark 15:11)

The crowd, manipulated by the chief priests, votes for Barabbas's release, not Jesus's release. This preference for Barabbas and rejection of Jesus tells Pilate that Jesus, "the king of the Jews," does not have much support.

Second, Pilate continues his polling.

> Pilate spoke to them again, "Then what do you wish me to do with the man you call the King of the Jews?" (Mark 15:12)

His question continues to probe levels of support for Jesus. Again, he identifies Jesus as a popular king. And again he positions himself astutely as willing to do the will of the crowd and of the alliance of elite leaders. This is, of course, a ruse. It is an act, made possible because the Jerusalem leaders have already shown their preference. Jesus's fate is sealed. Again, Pilate's polling produces positive results.

> They shouted back, "Crucify him!" (Mark 15:13)

The response of the "they" is quick and united in demanding crucifixion. This call aligns the provincials with the Roman provincial policy that Pilate represents and enacts. Pilate has secured the provincials' support for the governing practice of executing unsanctioned popular kings.

Third, by continuing to poll "them" and press the issue, Pilate further forces his allies into a subordinate position. He makes them beg for Pilate to act. He wants them to name Jesus's crime. He is not weak and trying to release the "nice" Jesus. He is astutely asserting his control of the situation. Jesus's crucifixion is inevitable.

> Pilate asked them, "Why, what evil has he done?" (Mark 15:14)

The question seeks a very obvious answer that would make explicit their rejection of Jesus as "king of the Jews." By prolonging the polling, Pilate continues to subjugate his allies. "They" race over the answer, moving beyond the rationale to the outcome.

> But they shouted all the more, "Crucify him!" So Pilate, wishing to satisfy the crowd, released Barabbas for them, and after flogging Jesus he handed him over to be crucified. (Mark 15:14–15)

Pilate has completed a skilled piece of governing. He has established his dominance over his ruling allies and has presented himself as doing the crowd's will. He has astutely maneuvered the leaders into pleading that the governor do what he would do anyway in dispatching a populist "king of the Jews." His polling has required them to beg, whereby they subordinate themselves to him and are reminded starkly of their dependence on him. Likewise, he has sought the crowd's will, knowing that the leaders are manipulating them and are aligned with them. Pilate has secured his position as the dominant ruling male.

The import of this analysis is that Pilate is responsible for Jesus's death and has accomplished his goals of securing his alliance with the freshly subordinated Jerusalem elites and of securing the compliance of the Jerusalem crowd in doing its bidding. Of course, he has disguised the fact that their will is his will.

Our attention to Pilate's role as the one who made the decision to crucify Jesus has several consequences.

First, it means that not all Jews in the first century were responsible for Jesus's death. Accusing all first-century Jews of being "Christ killers" is a ridiculous charge fed by prejudice and hatred.

Second, it means that not all Jews across the last two millennia, from the first century up to the present, were responsible for Jesus's death. Accusing all Jews of all time of being "Christ killers" is also a ridiculous charge fed by prejudice and hatred.

Third, this analysis has shown that a few Jews were involved in Jesus's crucifixion. The Jerusalem elite, allies of Pilate and beneficiaries of Roman power, sought Jesus's crucifixion by Pilate because they did not have the power to crucify him. They wanted Jesus crucified because he threatened the status quo of Roman rule, with which they had aligned themselves and from which they benefited. They manipulated a small Jerusalem crowd to sustain their demand. Yet it remained Pilate's decision, and he played power games in subjugating them as he forced them to beg him to act.

Fourth, beyond these personalities was a much larger entity that is responsible for Jesus's death. Pilate was an agent of the Roman Empire. This domination system protected the interests of the ruling elites across the empire at all costs.[2] There was no place for a vision or practices of an alternative world such as Jesus offered. The empire knew it could not allow such imaginings and visions. It could not allow a figure to attract crowds of people who might align with another empire, the reign of God. It could not allow a figure whom people proclaimed to be their king. The opinion that "it does not have to be this way, and there is an alternative" is dangerous for any oppressive regime. Long before it was a movie, the (Roman) empire strikes back against a perceived threat.

His Blood Be on Us and on Our Children (Matt. 27:25)

Matthew's account includes an extra scene that has fed the accusation that all Jews for all time are to blame for crucifying Jesus.

As with Mark's account, Matthew's Pilate, in polling mode, responds to the cries of the leaders and crowd to crucify Jesus by asking, "'Why, what evil has he done?' But they shouted all the more, 'Let him be crucified!'" (Matt. 27:23).

Matthew's account constructs Pilate's response: "And when Pilate saw he was *gaining or benefiting* nothing but rather a riot was happening . . ." (27:24, authors' trans.). "Gaining or benefiting nothing" is a literal translation of the verb *ōpheleō*, which is much to be preferred to the NRSVUE translation: "When Pilate saw that he could do nothing . . ." The unsupported translation "do nothing" is influenced by the fiction that Pilate was weak and trying to save Jesus. The more literal translation indicates that Pilate's polling accomplished his purpose of measuring minimal support for Jesus and of subordinating his allies. Pilate would not benefit any further from playing hard to get or continuing to poll the crowd. He accomplished his purposes as "they" shouted for Jesus's crucifixion.

Then, as one unconvincing translation puts it, Pilate "took some water and washed his hands before the crowd, saying, 'I am innocent of this man's blood; see to it yourselves'" (NRSVUE). Commentators quote Hebrew Bible passages such as Deuteronomy 21:7 ("Our hands did not shed this blood . . .") to emphasize Pilate's innocence and to reinforce the "blame the Jews" fiction.

There are two problems with this appeal to Hebrew Bible texts. First, it interprets Pilate's action in a Hebrew Bible context as though Pilate were a Torah-observant Jew. He was not. Pilate was a gentile. It would seem preferable, then, to interpret his action not in relation to Jewish traditions but in relation to Roman traditions.

---

2. Ellis Rivkin, *What Crucified Jesus? Messianism, Pharisaism, and the Development of Christianity* (New York: UAHC, 1997).

And second, Pilate was not innocent. He exercised his power to enact the death penalty to crucify Jesus. Jesus was a dead man because of Pilate's decision.

So what might the handwashing of a Roman governor represent? In Virgil's epic poem *The Aeneid*, Aeneas asks his father to carry "the sacred emblems of our country's household gods." Aeneas himself does not handle them because he has returned from "fierce battle and recent slaughter." He declares that it would be "sinful to handle them" until he has washed himself (Virgil, *Aeneid* 2.717–19 [Loeb Classical Library]). In his act of washing, Aeneas admits he is guilty of causing death and needs to cleanse himself in washing. Likewise, Pilate's washing is a recognition of his responsibility in causing death and is a ritual whereby one is cleansed from responsibility.

What do we make of his following statement: "I am innocent of this man's blood" (Matt. 27:24)? The conventional interpretation takes the statement at face value and understands it as reinforcing the "blame the Jews" scenario. But we have seen that Pilate was not innocent; he as Roman governor sentenced Jesus to be crucified.

Two alternative interpretations present themselves. One is that Pilate was being ironic. He continued his stance from earlier by presenting himself as doing the will of the elite leaders and the local crowd. This approach was not cowardice, as some claim. Rather, he astutely garnered their "buy-in" for an action he himself was inevitably going to carry out. His final comment, "See to it" (Matt. 27:24), enacts the same strategy of disguising his decision as the will of the locals.

In the context of and subsequent to Pilate's handwashing, a second interpretation is likely. The Greek word commonly translated "innocent" can also be translated as "unpunished" or "not paying a penalty." Having washed his hands as an admission of responsibility for causing Jesus's death and of being cleansed of responsibility for doing so, Pilate has declared he now has no penalty to pay. His handwashing ritual has secured his status as now being without penalty.

Pilate disguised his own responsibility by passing it on to the Jerusalem participants. He gave his permission to them to carry out his will: "See to it." The Jerusalem participants accepted it by declaring, "His blood be on us and on our children" (27:25). How do we interpret?

First, we are not reading a historical transcript of an event that occurred around 30 CE. This declaration appears only in Matthew's Gospel. It is missing from the other three Gospels. So there is no other attestation for it as a historical moment. What, then, does it contribute to this Gospel's narrative, which was written in the 80s or 90s CE? How does it function?

One function of the people's declaration is to confirm Pilate's control of the situation. Astutely he has disguised the Roman policy of executing threats to Roman rule as the will of the locals. He authorizes Jesus's crucifixion. Their declaration confirms they have internalized the will of their colonizing masters.

Informing this interaction are the dynamics of the assertion of Rome's power as the conqueror and occupier of Judea. In the narrative setting of the Gospel scene, there have been some ninety years of Roman domination since 63 BCE. More to the point, the Gospel was written in the 80s–90s of the first century CE, just a couple of decades after the Jewish war of independence that ended in 70 CE in devastating style with the defeat and destruction of Jerusalem and its temple.

The Gospel, along with other late first-century Jewish writings, looks back on this defeat and interprets the event as punishment. The Gospel employs a Deuteronomic framework in which obedience and faithfulness are rewarded while sins are punished through devastating historical events (Deut. 28–29). The Gospel interprets Rome's defeat of Jerusalem as punishment on its leaders for crucifying Jesus (Matt. 22:7). It constructs Rome's victory not as a military act of domination over rebellious locals resisting Roman rule, but rather in theological terms. Rome is God's agent, chosen to inflict punishment on those who rejected God's agent, Jesus. The declaration of 27:25 expresses this interpretive perspective.

The scene creates a contrast. Pilate acknowledges after his handwashing that he is now without penalty for crucifying an insurrectionist. The Jerusalem participants do not express responsibility and are punished in the events of 70 CE.

Understanding the historical, narrative, societal, and theological dimensions of this verse makes one thing very clear. Matthew 27:25 addresses a particular context and expresses a particular perspective. It does not hold all Jews either in the first century or for all time accountable for Jesus's death. The verse does not express the rejection of Jews from God's favor and purposes. While interpretations of Jesus's death have commonly emphasized ethnicity, this discussion has demonstrated that alliances of elite power are more relevant.

Early Church Traditions

While historical, narrative, societal, and theological factors work against hateful anti-Jewish readings of these Gospel accounts, they have often not been able to override prejudices and the efforts of subsequent Christian writers to define the Jesus-movement over against and as superior to Jewish groups.

From the second century on, Christian writers regularly repeated the charge that Jews killed Jesus and often accompanied the charge with the assertion that the Roman destruction of Jerusalem and its temple in 70 CE was divine punishment for doing so. The following are a few brief examples of this claim:

> [This] was a prediction, as I said before, of the death to which the synagogue of the wicked would condemn Him. . . . [Christ exhorted] you to repent of your wicked deeds at least after He rose again from the dead, and to mourn before God . . . in order that your nation and city might not be taken and destroyed, as they have been destroyed; yet you . . . have not repented, after you learned that He rose from the dead. . . . Besides this, even when your city is captured, and your land ravaged, you do not repent. (Justin Martyr, *Dialogue with Trypho* 104, 108; second-century Judea and Rome)[3]

> It is he that has been murdered. And where has he been murdered? In the middle of Jerusalem. By whom? By Israel. (Melito of Sardis, *On Pascha* 72; second-century Anatolia, present-day Turkey)[4]

> [Celsus charges Christians with saying that] "the Jews having chastised Jesus, and given him gall to drink, have brought upon themselves the divine wrath." And any one who likes may convict this statement of falsehood, if it be not the case that the whole Jewish nation was overthrown within one single generation after Jesus had undergone these sufferings at their hands. For forty and two years, I think, after the date of the crucifixion of Jesus, did the destruction of Jerusalem take place. (Origen, *Against Celsus* 4.22; third-century Alexandria, Egypt)[5]

> Endeavour therefore never to leave the Church of God; [don't go] either into a polluted temple of the heathens, or into a synagogue of the Jews or heretics . . . into an house of demons, or into a synagogue of the murderers of Christ, or the congregation of the wicked. (Apostolic Constitutions and Canons 2.61.1; fourth century, perhaps Antioch in Syria)[6]

> You Jews did crucify him. But after he died on the cross, he then destroyed your city [the Roman destruction of Jerusalem and temple, 70 CE]; it was then that he dispersed your people; it was then that he scattered your nation over the face

---

3. *Ante-Nicene Fathers*, ed. Alexander Roberts, James Donaldson, and A. Cleveland Coxe (Buffalo, NY: Christian Literature Publishing, 1885), 1:251, 253.
4. Melito of Sardis, *"On Pascha" and Fragments*, trans. Stuart George Hall, Oxford Early Christian Texts (Oxford: Clarendon, 1979), 39.
5. *Ante-Nicene Fathers*, ed. Alexander Roberts, James Donaldson, and A. Cleveland Coxe (Buffalo, NY: Christian Literature Publishing, 1885), 4:506.
6. *Ante-Nicene Fathers*, ed. Alexander Roberts, James Donaldson, and A. Cleveland Coxe (Buffalo, NY: Christian Literature Publishing, 1886), 7:423.

of the earth. In doing this, he teaches us that he is risen, alive, and in heaven. (John Chrysostom, *Adversus Judaeos* 5.1.6–7; fourth-century Antioch in Syria)[7]

There are, regrettably, many more examples.

Just under two thousand years after the crucifixion of Jesus, after two thousand years of endless repetition of the trope that the Jews were Christ killers, a change of perspective emerged.

In October 1965, originating from the Vatican II council, the Catholic Church issued a declaration titled *Nostra aetate* (In our time). This document recognized that as human beings were increasingly being drawn together, it was appropriate for the church to consider its relationships with non-Christian religions, including Judaism. Accordingly, taking a more conciliatory approach, the church walked back its condemnation of Jews as Christ killers. In its place, the document declared that all Jews in the first century were not responsible for Jesus's crucifixion, and all Jews for all time are not responsible for it. Subsequently, numerous Protestant denominations issued statements along similar lines.

Unfortunately, two millennia of bigotry and hatred are not that easily dispelled.

Matters for Reflection

1. Use the chapter's argument to answer the question, Why was Jesus crucified?
2. Recognizing that "the Jews" did not crucify Jesus involves understanding several dynamics that constitute imperial situations. Discuss the importance of the role of the Roman governor and his alliance with the Jerusalem elites, the danger of identifying Jesus as "king of the Jews," and the function of crucifixion.
3. The declaration "His [Jesus's] blood be on us and on our children" is found only in the Gospel of Matthew (27:25). This Gospel was written after the destruction of Jerusalem and the temple in 70 CE. What is the importance of this context for interpreting this declaration?
4. What are your reactions to the extracts from the early Christian writers quoted at the end of this chapter?

---

7. Robert Wilken, *John Chrysostom and the Jews: Rhetoric and Reality in the Late 4th Century* (Berkeley: University of California Press, 1983), 126.

CHAPTER 9

Resurrection

Some Christians have claimed that resurrection is a Christian distinctive, something that Christians believe but Jews do not. Some students are very surprised to learn that some Jews anticipated a future resurrection. They had heard preachers quote Luke 20:27, that Sadducees did not believe in resurrection and so were "sad." They had generalized that statement to all Jews.

This is a troubling misunderstanding that is not true. As we demonstrate in this chapter, there were diverse and developing understandings of resurrection and the afterlife in Early Judaism. The New Testament writers draw on these diverse traditions in interpreting Jesus and the future resurrection of Jesus-believers.

Early Judaism: Resurrection and Afterlife

In his accounts of the Jewish groups (see chap. 4), Josephus reports differences in their views on the afterlife.

Pharisees, he says, believed that the souls of the sinners are imprisoned forever, while those of the righteous "receive an easy passage to a new life" (*Ant*. 18.14; cf. *J.W.* 2.163).

Essenes held that the soul is immortal (*Ant*. 18.16), bound to a mortal body. When death sets it free, virtuous souls reside in "an abode beyond the ocean," while those of the wicked suffer eternal punishment. Facing suffering and death, Essenes "cheerfully resigned their souls, confident that they would receive them back again" (*J.W.* 2.152–58).

Unlike these two groups, the Sadducees, claims Josephus, posited that the soul perishes with the body. They rejected the idea of any postmortem punishment and reward (*J.W.* 2.165; *Ant.* 18.16).

Even though it is not comprehensive, Josephus's report reveals a wide spectrum of ideas about the afterlife. These range from an utter denial of the afterlife to a full-fledged belief in an immortal soul. Josephus's mention of some souls' "easy passage to a new life" (*Ant.* 18.15) "into another body" (*J.W.* 2.163) may even suggest reincarnation.

The variety of views on the afterlife in Early Judaism were shaped by several factors. One was that various biblical references to soul, spirit, and the realm of the dead, or Sheol, led to speculations on the subject. And during the Second Temple period, Judeans experienced considerable suffering and oppression as one imperial power after another occupied their land.

Various beliefs in the afterlife offered plausible answers to the seeming absence of divine justice in everyday life. Was God too weak to resist oppressive nations occupying the land and subjugating the people? Had God abandoned the people? Did God not care that wicked people seemed to prosper and that faithful people suffered unjustly because of them? Was there any benefit in living faithfully? Did God's purposes for justice extend through and beyond death to be experienced in various expressions of the afterlife?

Understandings of resurrection developed in the second century BCE and following as the people navigated oppressive rule and pervasive evildoers. The only explicit reference to the belief in resurrection in the Hebrew Bible, found in Daniel 12:2–3, 13, emerged from these circumstances. This text responds to the persecution of Judaism instigated by the Hellenistic king Antiochus IV Epiphanes in the 160s BCE:

> Many of those who sleep in the dust of the earth shall awake, some to everlasting life and some to shame and everlasting contempt. Those who are wise shall shine like the brightness of the sky, and those who lead the many to righteousness, like the stars forever and ever. . . . But you [Daniel], go your way, and rest; you shall rise for your reward at the end of the days. (Dan. 12:2–3, 13)

This is an enigmatic passage. Yet several elements of this description recur in other early Jewish descriptions of resurrection. First, not all but "many" are resurrected. Second, both the righteous and sinners are raised to life. Third, these two groups have distinctly different destinies. Some will experience "everlasting life" while some will experience "shame and everlasting contempt." Fourth, the fate of the "wise" and "those who lead the many to righteousness" is described with celestial metaphors. They will "shine like the brightness of the sky, . . . like the stars forever and ever." Fifth, resurrection will take place at the "end of the days."

The link between a belief in resurrection and Antiochus's anti-Jewish policies is further highlighted in 2 Maccabees. The Syrian tyrant Antiochus had banned the observance of Jewish practices that were integral to Jewish identity: sacrifices in the temple, observance of the Sabbath and festivals like Passover, observance of Torah requirements for purity, circumcision. He also required the honoring of altars and idols. What were Jews to do? Some complied. Some took up arms to fight him. Some waited for God to act to destroy him. Some openly defied the tyrant's orders and were executed as martyrs in the expectation that they would experience God's justice in the resurrection of their bodies.

The account in 2 Maccabees 7 tells a story of some Jews who defied Antiochus's ban in order to be faithful to God. A mother and seven sons are captured and tortured to death on the king's orders. Their executioners demand they eat pork, which is forbidden by the Torah. All of them refuse. As they die horrible deaths as martyrs, they confess a belief that God will honor their faithfulness in a resurrection that is both bodily and societal.

> They tore off the skin of his head with the hair and asked him, "Will you eat rather than have your body punished limb by limb?" . . . And when he was at his last breath, he said, "You accursed wretch, you dismiss us from this present life, but the King of the universe will raise us up to a renewal of everlasting life, because we have died for his laws."
>
> After him, the third was the victim of their sport. When it was demanded, he quickly put out his tongue and courageously stretched forth his hands and said nobly, "I got these from heaven, and because of his laws I disdain them, and from him I hope to get them back again." (2 Macc. 7:7–11)

They mock the king and the torturers:

> But do not think that God has forsaken our people. . . . But do not think that you will go unpunished for having tried to fight against God! (2 Macc. 7:16, 19)

The mother witnesses the torture and deaths of her seven sons with courage and trust that God will raise them in resurrection and restore their battered bodies:

> The mother was especially admirable and worthy of honorable memory. . . . She encouraged each of them . . . , "Therefore the Creator of the world . . . in his mercy gives life and breath back to you again, since you now forget yourselves for the sake of his laws." (2 Macc. 7:20–23)

She encourages her seventh son with reassurances that the family will be reunited and healed in the resurrection:

> Do not fear this butcher but prove worthy of your brothers. Accept death, so that in God's mercy I may get you back again along with your brothers. (2 Macc. 7:29)

The passage, written around 100 BCE, attests an understanding of resurrection that is somatic and societal, as well as an act of divine justice.

A similar hope for a divine restoration of the body seems to underlie one of the texts from Qumran. The text reinterprets Ezekiel's famous vision of the dry bones (Ezek. 37:1–14). Ezekiel's vision promises not individual resurrection but the restoration of the nation. But in this text from Qumran, the vision is read as a description of the decayed human body parts coming to life in an actual resurrection (4Q385 [4QpsEzek^a] 2 5–8).

In 2 Maccabees 12:39–45, Judas Maccabee, the leader of the uprising against Antiochus IV Epiphanes, sends funds to the temple to provide for an expiatory sacrifice on behalf of soldiers who fell in battle. Second Maccabees claims that they perished because they carried idolatrous amulets. The sacrifice provided atonement for this wrongdoing and ensured their future resurrection from the dead.

While Daniel and 2 Maccabees offer glimpses of early Jewish thought on the resurrection, several texts deal with this topic extensively and with different expectations.

For example, a text incorporated in 1 Enoch, known as the Epistle of Enoch, envisions a resurrection of a soul. In it, the souls of the dead, both the righteous and sinners, are said to descend to Sheol (1 En. 102:4, 11; 103:7). The souls of the wicked are punished immediately in great distress, darkness, a snare, and a flaming fire (103:7). For them, Sheol becomes a fiery hell. When the great judgment takes place, these souls of the sinners "will have no peace" (103:8). Conversely, after the great judgment "the souls of pious who have died" (not their bodies) will come to life, joy, and honor (103:4). Like the "wise" of Daniel 12, these souls will shine as luminaries (104:2). They will experience joy like angels (104:4).

Another part of the Enoch tradition offers a different expectation. In 1 Enoch 22, Enoch travels the earth with an angelic guide. While in the distant regions of the west, he encounters "a great and high mountain of hard rock" (1 En. 22:1). In this mountain, there are four hollow spaces, deep and smooth. Three of them are dark, while one is illuminated.

The angel explains to Enoch that these spaces hold spirits/souls of the deceased until the great judgment. One is for sinners who did not receive retribution in their lifetime. They are tormented in anticipation of the final judgment, when they will be bound and tortured forever. Recognizing pervasive injustice, the text states the second space is for spirits who were unjustly destroyed by the sinners. The text explicitly names the spirit of Abel. The third dark space is for spirits who were sinners and kept company with the lawless.

> First Enoch is not really one book but a collection of several early Jewish texts written in Aramaic. Different as they are, they all highlight the biblical figure of Enoch from Genesis 5:21–24.

The text says that they will not be punished or raised during the great judgment. One possible explanation for this is that these are sinners who received their retribution during their lifetime. This is the only indication in the text that the other groups of spirits will be "raised" or resurrected during the future judgment. The only lighted compartment is for the spirits of the righteous.

This account suggests that the dead are judged twice. The first and universal judgment occurs at the moment of death and determines to which of the four groups a given spirit is assigned. The punishment of the souls of the sinners begins immediately. The second, selective judgment is an eschatological one. The resurrection is part of this scheme.

Several centuries later, 4 Ezra provides another detailed treatment. Again it is a work that emerges from circumstances of foreign oppression. It was composed in the aftermath of the destruction of Jerusalem by the Romans in 70 CE. It, too, focuses on the condition of the dead between their actual death and the future judgment.

Yet it also offers a fairly detailed description of a resurrection in which God's justice will prevail over the wicked and oppressive. Fourth Ezra describes the human body as a "mortal vessel," from which the soul is separated at death (7:88, 100). The soul first "adores the glory of the Most High" (7:79). For seven days it is allowed to be free, seeing things that were predicted (7:101). Then, the wicked and the righteous souls are separated. The wicked souls "immediately wander about in torments, ever grieving and sad" (7:80), "consumed by shame," and "wither[ing] with fear" (7:87). At the same time, the souls of the righteous go into "treasuries" where angels guard them as they rest "in profound quiet" (7:85, 88–98). The souls await their final judgment in the last days (7:88, 95).

Leading to this judgment in 4 Ezra 7:29–32 is the Messiah's four-hundred-year rule as the agent of God's purposes. At the end of this period he dies, and all corruptible things perish too. Then, those who are asleep in the earth are raised up, and their bodies are united with their souls. The judgment consigns sinners to Gehenna and the righteous to a paradise of delight.

> First Enoch 90:26 describes a fiery abyss where the sinners will burn after the great judgment. It is located in Jerusalem. First Enoch 26:4–27:4 calls this place a "deep and dry valley." This valley, remembered in 2 Kings 23:10 as a place of child sacrifice, is known in Hebrew as *ge-hinnom* (Valley of Hinnom; Neh. 11:30), or Gehenna. In 4 Ezra 7:36, after the resurrected bodies and souls are united in a general resurrection, Gehenna appears. It is no longer a specific place in Jerusalem but a general name for the place of torment for sinners. Indeed, in Matthew 10:28 Jesus warns that God can destroy both soul and body in Gehenna.

Second Baruch was written around the same period as 4 Ezra, after the Roman destruction of Jerusalem in 70 CE. It, too, includes resurrection in its vision of God's just future, free of Roman rule. It claims that the resurrection will bring to life the very bodies that humans enjoyed before they died (2 Bar. 50:2–51:6). The purpose of this arrangement is for all to see that God's promises are true. When the resurrected ones recognize one another, the great judgment begins. At that moment, their bodies change. The wicked ones are transformed into "startling apparitions" whose lot is torment (51:5–6). The righteous ones are transformed into "the splendor of the angels" (51:5) and are "deemed equal to the stars" (51:10). Second Baruch says that they can transform into "any shape they wish." Moreover, when they are placed in the heavenly paradise, these righteous ones become "more excellent" than angels (51:12).

> When ancient translators rendered the phrase "garden of Eden" into Greek, they translated the Hebrew word for "garden" as *paradeisos*. This is how we got our word "paradise." In the Book of the Watchers, the oldest work included in 1 Enoch, paradise is situated on earth. When Enoch travels in the eastern regions, he is reported to pass by it (1 En. 32:3). He sees its magnificent trees, including the tree of wisdom, from which Adam and Eve ate. In 2 Baruch, composed around 100 CE, paradise is located in heaven. It is where the righteous who are transformed into the likeness of angels reside (2 Bar. 51:11). This heavenly paradise recalls Paul's experience of being "caught up to the third heaven . . . into paradise" in 2 Corinthians 12:2–4.

New Testament

As with early Jewish texts, New Testament statements of resurrection express a claim of justice in which the oppression of the Roman imperial world, which was experienced in Jesus's crucifixion and in the daily lives of Jesus-followers, is overcome. Roman power is not the final word, nor will the Roman-ruled world last forever. New Testament texts employ resurrection to relativize Roman power, to make sense of Jesus's presence with Jesus-followers, and to understand the present and the future in the divine purposes for a just and life-giving world for all. Given limits of space, we discuss resurrection narratives in Paul and the Gospels.

Paul

Paul offers a lengthy reflection on the significance of resurrection in 1 Corinthians 15. He makes the following points:

- 15:1–11: The resurrected Jesus appeared to many people: Cephas/Peter, the Twelve, more than five hundred brothers and sisters, James, all the apostles, Paul himself. Rome could not keep Jesus dead.
- 15:12–19: Jesus's resurrection counters claims by some that there is no resurrection of the dead. Jesus's resurrection is foundational for the faith that Paul has proclaimed and the Corinthians have embraced.
- 15:20–34: Jesus's resurrection is eschatological. That means it has set in motion a cluster of events that will result in the full establishment of God's just and life-giving rule, which will replace Roman oppression. Jesus's resurrection guarantees the yet-future, general resurrection of the dead (15:20–22). Jesus's resurrection is the "first fruits," an image that comes from the Hebrew Bible practice of consecrating the first fruits of the harvest to God in thanksgiving and in complete confidence of the full harvest (Lev. 23:9–14). Here it constructs Jesus's resurrection as the beginning of the yet-future, guaranteed, inevitable, certain, general resurrection. This general resurrection, though, will not occur until Jesus's return or second coming to establish God's rule (15:23). *Now* the divine purposes are in motion but *not yet* is the divine goal accomplished. Verses 24–28 outline the culmination of those purposes, when "all things," including Roman power, will be "subjected to" God's reign.

Paul's insistence on the "now" of Jesus's resurrection and the "not yet" of the general resurrection may be intended to counter the claims of

> some among the Corinthians that the general resurrection that Paul says belongs to the future divine purposes has "already" taken place (1 Cor. 4:8). Subsequently, similar claims that resurrection has already taken place are made in Ephesians, written after Paul's death, that "God, who is rich in mercy, out of the great love with which he loved us . . . [*has*] raised us up with him and seated us with him in the heavenly places in Christ Jesus" (Eph. 2:4–6).

- 15:35–44: The general resurrection, like Jesus's resurrection, is somatic. Verse 35 introduces the topic: "How are the dead raised? With what kind of body do they come?" Verses 36–44 make the argument that God has created different kinds of bodies for different creatures and contexts. So it is with the resurrection body; it is appropriate to the new age of the full establishment of God's reign. Yet while there is continuity of body between the present and future, Paul recognizes some discontinuity. The seed dies in order to produce a different form of plant. So the resurrection body is "sown a physical body; it is raised a spiritual body" (15:44). In light of these analogies from creation, the notion of a transformed resurrection body appears to be quite reasonable (15:43–44).
- 15:45–49: Verses 45–49 argue further that just as all have shared the existence of human beings represented by Adam ("the first man, Adam"; "man . . . made of dust"), so all will share the eschatological existence of the last Adam, Jesus (the "man . . . from heaven"; "a life-giving spirit"). A resurrection body under the control of the Spirit is inevitable and certain on the basis of Jesus's heavenly body.
- 15:50–57: Verses 50–57 emphasize the transformation that is necessary to participate in the fullness of God's reign (15:50). This transformation applies to all, both the living and the dead (15:51–54). What is currently perishable will become imperishable. This transformation will happen at the parousia, the return of Jesus to end Roman rule and to establish God's reign ("at the last trumpet"). This is the final defeat of death and sin in all its oppressive and destructive expressions (15:55–57).
- 15:58: Paul ends with an exhortation to the Corinthian Jesus-believers to continue their "work of the Lord" (15:58).

This final exhortation in 15:58 returns focus to daily life and service to God in mid-first-century Corinth. This suggests not only that chapter 15 is theological teaching about resurrection in the future but also that it has important practical implications for present living.

This possibility gains support from another observation—namely, that 1 Corinthians 1–14 is very practical in offering teaching about the daily living of followers of Jesus in Corinth. For example, Paul is concerned that there are divisions and quarrels among the believers (1:10–17); that some think that already God's purposes have been accomplished in full (4:8); that there is sexual immorality among them (chap. 5); that believers are taking other believers to court (chap. 6); that there is uncertainty about marriage, sex, and spirituality (chap. 7), as well as food that has been offered to idols (chaps. 8–10); that there are abuses at the Lord's Supper (chap. 11); and that there is confusion about spiritual gifts (chaps. 12–14).

What holds these matters together is that they are all concerned with relational and societal interactions in the church, the body of Christ, and the body politic (12:27). Paul's instructions seek to redress these wrong interactions. Repeatedly his emphasis is that appropriate somatic interactions are crucial for life in the body of Christ. Chapter 15 contextualizes these dos and don'ts in the big picture of God's future purposes. What one does with one's body in the present is directly connected to one's future destiny in God' reign. That future establishment of the divine purposes involves appropriate bodily existence. There is continuity—as well as discontinuity—in the interaction between the present and the future completion of the divine purposes. Participation in those future somatic purposes, in the just and life-giving reign or empire of God, requires appropriate somatic and societal interactions in the present.

Gospels

Each of the four canonical Gospels ends with a resurrection story. Paul's conceptual instruction gives way to narrative. As the following discussion shows, there is not one story of Jesus's resurrection. Rather, the stories developed significantly in length and content across the three decades that the Gospels were written (ca. 70s–ca. 100). An eight-verse narrative in Mark was followed by twenty verses in Matthew, fifty-three verses in Luke, and fifty-six verses in John's Gospel. These decades were overshadowed by the massive display of Rome's power and domination in the destruction of Jerusalem and its temple in 70 CE.

Mark

The resurrection story in the earliest Gospel, Mark, written around 71–72 CE, perhaps in Rome, comprises only eight verses. Strangely, the resurrected Jesus does not appear. Three women—Mary Magdalene, Mary mother of James, and Salome—take spices to the tomb to anoint Jesus's dead body. They do not expect resurrection, yet they find the tomb empty. They encounter an angel who tells them that Jesus has been raised and that they are to tell the disciples to go to Galilee to meet him there. Rome was not able to keep Jesus dead. The women flee in terror and fear and accordingly do not say anything to anybody. The risen Jesus is absent.

Matthew

Matthew's Gospel, written in the 80s or 90s, ends with a twenty-verse narrative. The author uses Mark's account as a source but gives it several major makeovers that significantly change the tone and content of the narrative.

The first edit or redaction revises the motive for the women coming to the tomb. Gone is a reference to spices for a dead body; the women come to "see" the tomb (Matt. 28:1), a verb that suggests "understanding" elsewhere in the Gospel (13:16). They come expecting resurrection. The angel appears and proclaims that the crucified Jesus has been raised. The angel commissions the women to tell the male disciples to meet the risen Jesus in Galilee (28:1–8).

As the women depart, there's a second major edit. Suddenly the risen Jesus appears to them! They see him and touch him, taking hold of his feet (28:9). The risen Jesus speaks; he tells them not to fear and renews their commission to tell the male disciples to meet him in Galilee.

A third edit inserts a whole new episode (28:11–15). The episode narrates a cover-up scheme devised by the chief priests and elders. To counter the narrative of resurrection, the Jerusalem elite bribe the guards to say that they fell asleep and the disciples stole Jesus's body. They promise to take care of the Roman governor if he discovers the plot and the soldiers' admission to falling asleep on duty.

A fourth edit adds the Gospel's final scene, set in Galilee and involving the risen Jesus and the eleven male disciples (28:16–20). In the context of Roman power, Jesus makes the bold and subversive claim that "all authority in heaven and on earth has been given to me." In imitation of Roman imperialism, he commissions the disciples to a subjugating worldwide mission of making "disciples of all nations" who are loyal to Jesus, not to Rome's empire. He reassures them of his presence with them "to the end of the age."

In Matthew 27, there is another Matthean redaction; this passage is not in the other Gospels:

> The tombs also were opened, and many bodies of the saints who had fallen asleep were raised. After his resurrection they came out of the tombs and entered the holy city and appeared to many. (Matt. 27:52–53)

This reference appears in chapter 27 in relation to Jesus's crucifixion, yet it clearly narrates an effect of Jesus's resurrection. The verses set the strange scene of "saints" who had been dead but are now raised and alive, wandering around Jerusalem and being seen by many. Whatever the scenario, it expresses an understanding that Jesus's resurrection is not just about himself. His resurrection ensures the resurrection of those who have died. In narrative form, this scene presents Paul's claim that Jesus's resurrection is the first fruits of the general resurrection, even though the sequence of events and timeline are confused.

LUKE

Luke's Gospel also uses Mark's resurrection story as its source, but it turns Mark's eight-verse account into fifty-three verses. Again the tone and content change significantly. The first twelve verses follow Mark's account, with the discovery of the empty tomb, the proclamation of (now) two angels that Jesus is risen, and the absence of the risen Jesus. The women tell the unbelieving disciples, and Peter runs to see the empty tomb for himself (24:1–12).

Then the narrative develops with a long and novel addition (24:13–35). Two people, one named Cleopas, are walking from Jerusalem to the village of Emmaus. They are joined by the risen Jesus, though they do not recognize him. They describe their disappointment that their hopes that Jesus might set Israel free from Roman rule have come to nothing with Jesus's crucifixion. They also name their puzzlement about rumors that he might be alive (24:19–24). Then Jesus reveals himself, but the two travelers do not recognize him until Jesus breaks bread at the evening meal. They report their encounter to the disciples in Jerusalem (24:25–35). Nothing like this journey appears in the resurrection stories in the Gospels of Mark and Matthew.

Another new scene follows that emphasizes the somatic nature of Jesus's resurrection (24:36–49). The risen Jesus appears to the startled disciples. He shows them his hands and feet, invites them to touch him, and eats a piece of fish to convince them he is not a ghost. He explains the divine purposes to them and tells them to wait in the city for "power from on high." The Holy Spirit will, in Acts 2, empower the church to a worldwide mission. This mission takes place in the context of Rome's mission to subdue the world to its rule.

The chapter finishes with a further innovation. At Bethany, Jesus blesses the disciples and ascends into heaven to God (24:50–53). Again, neither Mark nor Matthew concludes their resurrection story with an ascension account.

JOHN

John's Gospel, written perhaps in the 90s, ends with two resurrection chapters. Together they are slightly longer than Luke's account. John's resurrection account contains several features absent from the resurrection accounts in the other Gospels.

The account begins with Mary Magdalene, Simon Peter, and the disciple "whom Jesus loved" finding Jesus's tomb empty (20:1–10). Mary remains outside the tomb weeping. Two angels appear and listen to her complain that she does not know where Jesus has been entombed. Suddenly the risen Jesus appears, though she mistakes him for the gardener. He speaks her name, and she recognizes him immediately. Mary reports the encounter to the disciples (20:11–18).

A series of scenes in which the risen Jesus appears to disciples follows (20:19–29). First, Jesus appears to the group of disciples, seeming to pass through a locked door into the room where they are gathered. He shows them his wounded hands and side, which his resurrection has not healed. He gives them a mission command: "As the Father has sent me, so I send you." He then breathes the Holy Spirit on them. In none of the other Gospels does the risen Jesus impart the Spirit to disciples. In Luke's account, Jesus tells them to wait in the city for this "power from on high" (Luke 24:49), but it is not given until the festival of Pentecost (Acts 2).

A second appearance scene involving Thomas follows (John 20:24–29). Thomas does not believe the testimony of the other disciples that they have seen the risen Jesus. He declares he will not believe unless he touches Jesus's wounded hands and side. A week later, the risen Jesus again passes through a locked door to appear to Thomas and meet his requirements. Thomas believes. It is interesting that again Jesus's resurrection body is not perfect. It retains the scars of crucifixion, which establishes continuity between Jesus's crucifixion and his resurrection from Roman death-bringing power.

A third appearance involves seven disciples (21:1–14). They have returned to their previous fishing work but have caught nothing. On the beach at the Sea of Tiberias, named after the Roman emperor who ruled all land and sea in the empire and benefited from it through taxation, is the risen Jesus. Unrecognized by the disciples, he orders them to cast out their nets again. They do so and catch a haul of 153 fish. In pulling in the nets, they recognize Jesus. He cooks them breakfast on the beach.

Jesus addresses Peter (21:15–19). Three times he asks about Peter's love for him, which Peter affirms. The threefold question counters Peter's threefold denial of allegiance to Jesus (13:38; 18:17, 25–27). Three times Jesus instructs Peter to express his love for Jesus by caring for his followers. Jesus also predicts Peter's martyrdom.

Subsequently, Peter asks Jesus about the fate of the mysterious "disciple whom Jesus loved." This disciple's fate is not the same as Peter's. Rather, he is to testify to his love for Jesus by truthfully telling the story of Jesus (21:24).

John 20 and 21 focus on Jesus's resurrection, but elsewhere in John's Gospel, the author asserts an imminent general resurrection that divides humanity:

> The hour is coming when all who are in their graves will hear his voice and will come out: those who have done good to the resurrection of life, and those who have done evil to the resurrection of condemnation. (John 5:28–29)

The term "life" designates the life of the new age in which the divine purposes will be accomplished.

Developments

It is clear from this discussion of the Gospel resurrection narratives that they are not fixed or static. While the emptiness of the tomb, presence of angels, and defiance of and victory over death-bringing Roman power are constants, the narratives expand with subscenes and details that express growing understandings.

For example, after his absence from Mark's account, the risen Jesus appears in the other Gospels. More specifically, these appearances are not of one kind. In the Gospel of Matthew the women recognize the risen Jesus instantly, yet it is not so in the Gospels of Luke and John. In Luke two disciples walk nearly seven miles with the risen Jesus without recognizing him. A group of disciples thinks Jesus is a ghost (Luke 24:36–37). In John 20:15–16 Mary thinks the risen Jesus is the gardener, and in 21:4–6 seven disciples do not recognize him as he instructs them to lower their nets again. Some appearances involve individuals; others involve groups of disciples.

Beyond scenes of recognition and nonrecognition, the narratives give diverse attention to Jesus's resurrection body. One presentation concerns the physicality of Jesus's resurrection body. The women hold Jesus's feet (Matt. 28:9). Jesus walks some miles to Emmaus and breaks bread (Luke 24:30). He shows his wounded and not-yet-healed hands and feet and eats fish (Luke 24:39–42). He cooks breakfast on a beach (John 21:9–14).

Yet a second presentation suggests something different about Jesus's body. Jesus appears as a ghost (Luke 24:36–37). He passes through locked doors and walls (John 20:19, 26). In Luke he ascends into heaven (Luke 24:51) and in John anticipates this ascension (John 20:17). What sort of body accomplished these tasks?

A third presentation highlights the wounded nature of Jesus's resurrected-crucified body. Luke notes that Jesus shows the disciples his hands and feet but does not stipulate that they are scarred (Luke 24:39–40). John, however, makes explicit Jesus's woundedness when Thomas demands to touch Jesus's wounded hands and side (John 20:24–29). These wounds link the crucified and the resurrected Jesus, subject to but victorious over Roman tyranny.

Also increasing across the Gospels are explanations of Jesus's crucifixion and resurrection. Luke offers two such scenes in which the risen Jesus provides explanations of the divine purposes, first to the Emmaus road companions (Luke 24:25–27) and second to the gathered disciples (24:44–49). John includes a statement of the purpose of the Gospel in terms of a confession of Jesus's identity and its benefits in the "life of the age" that is free from Roman rule and marked by God's life-giving and just rule (John 20:30–31).

Related are the words of the risen Jesus that elaborate the future tasks of disciples. Matthew's Jesus specifies worldwide mission (Matt. 28:16–20). Luke's Jesus tells disciples to wait for "power on high" (Luke 24:49). John's Jesus commissions the disciples to continue his mission (John 20:21) and breathes the Holy Spirit on them (20:22). These missions are to transform the imperial world and align it with divine purposes.

Conclusion

This chapter has troubled the misunderstanding that resurrection is an exclusively Christian belief. It has demonstrated that Early Judaism had diverse constructions of the afterlife. Some early Jewish texts affirmed the resurrection of bodies. Some posited the survival of souls. Some did not embrace any notion of the afterlife. Christian claims about the resurrection of Jesus and his followers belong in this mix. Here is another indication of significant continuities between Early Judaism and the early Jesus-movement.

Matters for Reflection

1. What functions do expectations of resurrection and the afterlife perform?
2. What understandings of the afterlife and resurrection appear in texts from Early Judaism?
3. Read 2 Maccabees 7 in the Apocrypha. What is the historical context for this text? What do you think this text contributed to the development of Jewish resurrection beliefs?
4. How are the Gospel stories of resurrection similar and different?

CHAPTER 10

Eschatology

With reference to contemporary events, numerous cartoons over many years have featured a bearded, robed figure with a placard announcing, "The end of the world is nigh." Is talk of the end of the world a joke? Is it fantasy, escapist, simply unreal, something that despite dire warnings and speculation for millennia will never happen? Or is it a real threat, whether from nuclear warfare, global warming, or a worldwide pandemic?

Readers of the New Testament have long had varying attitudes toward and experiences of the book of Revelation. Some can't get enough of it; some want nothing to do with it and think it should be left behind. Whenever we teach a church class on Revelation, people ask whether this type of writing was unique in the ancient world, whether anybody understood it then, and whether it has any relevance today.

Whatever your attitude toward "end of the world" talk, we suggest that there are considerable troubling misunderstandings of the origins and functions of eschatological thinking in the ancient world. We show in this chapter that it was a common way of making sense of the world in Early Judaism and an important feature of New Testament writings, including Paul's letters and the Gospel stories about Jesus. Here is another important continuity along with some differences between Early Judaism and the New Testament.

Eschatological thinking is born in part of sociopolitical crises and the frustrated and despairing perception that the world is not as God intends it to be. It is also born of hope that God might intervene to transform the present world and create God's intended world of life-giving justice for all. Eschatological thinking is not fixed but arranges and speculates with a cluster of events in difficult circumstances to express both despair and hope. Resurrection, discussed in the last chapter, belongs to this cluster.

> The study of eschatological perspectives is also known as "teleology." This word comes from the Greek word *telos*, which means "the goal" or "endgame." Teleology emphasizes the goal or purposes of the divine plans and the acts that work toward establishing a new world. Sometimes "eschatology" can be misunderstood to mean that all existence ends in destruction. We use the term "eschatology" here to indicate visions of the new world that are the purpose or goal of the divine work.

Early Judaism

Early Jewish texts offer a remarkable variety of eschatological scenarios. Here we can review only a few. One recurring feature of these scenarios is an attempt to structure time. This structuring of time—often in numerical patterns and distinct periods or ages—delivers a powerful message: God has a timetable. Moreover, God reveals (some of) it to those who are worthy.

One such scenario is found in 1 Enoch 6–11, which we discussed in chapter 7. These chapters of the Book of the Watchers, the earliest book included in 1 Enoch, rewrite Genesis 6:1–4. The enigmatic passage that opens the Genesis story of the flood tells about the sons of God who mated with the daughters of humans. First Enoch 6–11 takes Genesis 6:1–4 as its starting point and blends into it several traditions about angels (here called "watchers") who violated the divine world order. One such tradition comprises angels who came down to earth and married women (1 En. 6–7). This marriage produced violent giants who devoured everything around them. Another tradition charges angels with teaching people forbidden crafts and sciences. As a result, godlessness increased on earth and "humans were perishing" (8:1–4). As the cries of the victims reached to heaven, the archangels pleaded with God to intervene (chap. 9). That intervention offers a glimpse of this text's eschatology (chaps. 10–11).

The wayward angels were bound up for seventy generations. This is the time that will pass until the great judgment. After the judgment, they will be cast into a fiery abyss, tortured, and confined in prison forever.

The earth was then cleansed from all wickedness by the flood. The flood here serves as an archetype of the future judgment day of the Lord. When 1 Enoch 10:16–11:2 describes the post-flood bliss, it actually reveals its view of the aftermath of the eschatological judgment:

- The righteous will "beget thousands," live till old age, and die in peace.
- Earth will produce an abundance of wine, grain, and oil.

- All people will be righteous and worship God.
- Blessings will pour down from heaven.
- Truth and peace will unite forever.

Several elements of this scenario recur in other early Jewish visions of the time when the divine purposes will be established.

One element is a temporal scheme based on the number seventy. In Jeremiah 25:11–12 the length of Israel's exile in Babylon is seventy years. In Daniel 9:24–27 the archangel Gabriel interprets the number seventy as indicating 490 years, during which God has decreed "to finish the transgression, to put an end to sin, and to atone for iniquity, to bring in everlasting righteousness" (Dan. 9:24).

This temporal scheme is at the center of the so-called Animal Apocalypse, found in yet another book included in 1 Enoch, the Book of Dreams. In 1 Enoch 85:1–90:41, Enoch has a dream vision in which he sees the entire human history depicted with symbols borrowed from the animal kingdom. For example, women and men living before the flood are presented as cows and bulls. The people of Israel are sheep. And the gentile nations are wild animals and birds of prey.

According to this vision, sometime before the destruction of the first temple in 587 BCE, God entrusted the wayward Israel into the hands of seventy wicked angelic shepherds (1 En. 89:59). Each shepherd rules for a time: seventy times in total. In the vision, the abusive rule of the seventy shepherds comes to an end during the Maccabean revolt against the anti-Jewish policies of Antiochus IV Epiphanes in the 160s BCE.

Then 1 Enoch 90:17–37 sets out the events that lead to the establishment of God's purposes:

- God strikes the earth, it splits, and the gentile oppressors of Israel sink in it.
- Israel destroys enemies.
- The divine throne is set in the land of Israel, God sits on it, and the judgment begins.
- Angels who sinned with women and the seventy angelic shepherds are cast into a fiery abyss.
- Wicked Israelites are thrown into a different fiery abyss, the Gehenna, located in Jerusalem.
- The current city of Jerusalem is removed, and a new Jerusalem is installed.
- All nations obey Israel.
- Resurrection of the Israelites takes place, and they are all gathered in Jerusalem.

- A special figure—possibly the Messiah—is born; gentiles fear him.
- All humanity is restored to its primordial righteous and perfect condition. There are no more sheep and predators—all are white bulls.

> The new Jerusalem described in the Animal Apocalypse is "larger and higher" than the old city (1 En. 90:28). It seems that God brings the new Jerusalem from the heavens, but there is no temple in the new city. Perhaps the new Jerusalem as a whole was perceived as a temple. Recall that in Revelation 21, the new Jerusalem descends from heaven and also has no temple (21:22).

Yet another eschatological scenario featuring a time scheme of 490 years emerges from one of the texts composed by the Dead Sea Scrolls community (11QMelchizedek [11Q13]). To understand its eschatological vision, we should remember the common practice in this time period of speaking of sin as debt (cf. Matt. 6:12).

The scroll evokes two biblical laws. One comes from Deuteronomy 15:2. This law provides for a forgiveness of debts every seventh year. The other law is from Leviticus 25:13. It provides that those who have lost their familial plot of land, presumably because of debt, are entitled to receive the land back during the specially designated Year of Jubilee.

In 11QMelchizedek, members of the Dead Sea Scrolls community who repeatedly commit sin accumulate "debts." Eventually, these "Sons of Light," as the community members refer to themselves, forfeit their spiritual "inheritance" in the lot of the Sons of Light led by Melchizedek. In fact, their sin-fueled "debts" make them captives of Belial, the chief of the forces of darkness.

To help these former Sons of Light return to their "inheritance," the scroll envisions a special arrangement. It uses the temporal scheme of 490 years, which consists of ten cycles of Years of Jubilee. For the scroll only the last year of this long period is important. The 490th year is precisely the time when both the seventh year remission of debts and the Jubilee return of the property coalesce. At that time, the debts/sins of the sinners will be remitted. They will be set free from the captivity and will be allowed to return to the "inheritance of Melchizedek."

Another text composed by this group reveals a disappointment caused by what seems to have been a failed attempt to calculate the time of the end. The group's commentary on the book of Habakkuk explains God's words to Habakkuk (2:3) in the following way (1QpHab 7:5–8):

> For there shall be yet another vision concerning the appointed time. It shall tell of the end and shall not lie [Hab. 2:3]. Interpreted, this means that the final age shall be prolonged, and shall exceed all that the Prophets have said; for the mysteries of God are astounding.

Clearly, the end had not come when the community expected it. Then the commentary explains the meaning of Habakkuk's call to wait for the prophecy to come true "even if it tarries, . . . for it will surely come and shall not be late" (1QpHab 7:9–14):

> Interpreted, this concerns the men of truth who keep the Law, whose hands shall not slacken in the service of truth when the final age is prolonged. For all the ages of God reach their appointed end as he determines for them in the mysteries of His wisdom.

Once again, the phrase "when the final age is prolonged" indicates an expectation of the timing of the end that has failed. The scroll, however, offers a recipe for coping with the disappointment. Its solution is to keep oneself busy in "the service of truth" and trust in God's plan.

These passages highlight one of the core beliefs of the Dead Sea Scrolls community. The term "age" points to a worldview in which the entire course of history consists of a sequence of periods fixed or predetermined by God. There is a divine timetable, but it is known to God. These are the "mysteries of His wisdom." Such a deterministic view of history wasn't unique to the Dead Sea Scrolls community; it is found in many texts of Early Judaism.

An intriguing variation on the temporal scheme featuring the numbers seven and ten is found in another text incorporated in 1 Enoch, the Epistle of Enoch. There we find the so-called Apocalypse of Weeks (1 En. 93:3–10; 91:11–17). It is a report of a vision in which Enoch is shown the entire human history as a sequence of ten weeks. The first six weeks encompass the events spanning from the creation to the destruction of the first Jerusalem temple. The seventh week appears to be the period in which this text is composed. At the end of the seventh week, the chosen ones, to which the author of the apocalypse likely belongs, are said to be elected. The events of weeks eight to ten are still in the future:

> Eighth week: The chosen ones execute the wicked. The "temple of the kingdom of the Great One" is built forever.
> Ninth week: The law is revealed to "all the sons of the whole earth." Wicked deeds vanish. All humanity looks to "the path of eternal righteousness."
> Tenth week: The eternal judgment is passed on the angels who sinned. First, heaven passes away, and a new heaven appears.

The text concludes with a vision of an infinite sequence of weeks marked by piety and righteousness.

> Second Baruch presents human history as a sequence of twelve alternating, black and bright, torrents of water descending from a cloud (53:1–12; 55:3–74:2). The darkest black water—the thirteenth—that descends after all these stands for the divine judgment. It is followed by a final torrent of bright water—the rule of the Messiah.

To the temporal schemes based on the numbers seven, ten, and twelve, we must add yet another early Jewish view on the course of history—namely, a succession of gentile kingdoms. Daniel 7 famously presents four such kingdoms emerging one after another. In the end, the fourth kingdom is destroyed, and dominion over the earth is given to the "one like a human being" (7:13–14).

Fourth Ezra adopts Daniel's scheme of four kingdoms but focuses on the fourth kingdom alone (4 Ezra 11:1–12:35). In a dream, Ezra sees an eagle with three heads and twelve wings. This eagle, dominating and oppressing the entire earth, is Rome. Then, a creature like a lion appears and reproves the eagle for judging the earth untruthfully, for afflicting the powerless, for injuring the peaceable. As a result, the eagle is condemned to be burned. In the subsequent interpretation of the dream, Ezra is told that the lion is the Messiah kept by God "until the end of the days" (12:32). The lion reproves the empire and destroys it. He also saves the remnant of Israel and makes them "joyful until the end comes, the day of judgement" (12:34).

New Testament

Paul

Paul belongs to and draws on these traditions, yet with several important modifications involving Jesus and the time frame.[1] As we saw in chapter 9, Paul looks to the future, to God's coming triumph over all powers, structures, practices, and personnel that are enemies of and resist the divine purposes (1 Cor. 15:20–28). He claims that this triumph is already underway in part

---

1. J. Christiaan Beker, *Paul's Apocalyptic Gospel: The Coming Triumph of God* (Philadelphia: Fortress, 1982); Pamela Eisenbaum, *Paul Was Not a Christian: The Original Message of a Misunderstood Apostle* (New York: HarperCollins, 2009), 250–55.

in the resurrection of Jesus. Opposition to the divine purposes resides, for Paul, in the Roman Empire.

Our discussion of 1 Corinthians 15 in chapter 9 emphasized resurrection, both Jesus's resurrection and the future general resurrection. Yet in 1 Corinthians 15 Paul also expresses other aspects of his eschatological thinking.

- The future establishment of the divine purposes involves the coming or return of Jesus to earth (1 Cor. 15:23). Notice that in verse 23 Paul jumps very quickly from Jesus's resurrection to the future general resurrection. He marks the interlude of what is nearly two millennia with nothing but a comma! He supplies no schedule or timetable or agenda to fill this time span. Elsewhere, Paul affirms the same two moments of the present that follows Jesus's resurrection and the future establishment of God's purposes at Jesus's return by using past and future tenses: "For if we *have been* united with him in a death like his, we *will* certainly be united with him in a resurrection like his.... But if *we* [*have*] died with Christ, we believe that *we will* also live with him" (Rom. 6:5, 8, emphasis added). Yet he also offers a general exhortation about how to live in the meantime, "in between" these events: "Therefore we have been buried with him by baptism into death, so that, just as Christ was raised from the dead by the glory of the Father, so we too might walk in newness of life" (Rom. 6:4 NRSV). The verb "walk" is common Bible talk for living according to God's will and law (Deut. 28:9). Paul expects that in the time before the future coming of Jesus and the general resurrection, Jesus-believers will live a new lifestyle faithful to the divine will.
- Jesus's future coming will destroy "every ruler and every authority and power" (1 Cor. 15:24) and every enemy and death (15:25–26). That is, his return will be an act of judgment that condemns all structures and personnel that do not welcome him. The dominant ruler and power belong to Rome's empire.
- Following this judgment, everything will be subjected to God's reign (15:27–28). "Everything" includes the Roman Empire, which does not honor God.

In 1 Thessalonians 4:13–5:11, Paul elaborates the expectation of Jesus's return. This elaboration is necessary because some Jesus-believers have died before Jesus's return and some living Jesus-believers are grieving for them and fear the dead have missed out on participating in the full establishment of God's purposes (1 Thess. 4:13). Paul assures them that Jesus's return will embrace both those who have died and those who are living. The returned Jesus will raise the dead and welcome the living to be with him forever (4:16–17).

Paul goes on to remind the Thessalonians that no one knows when "the day of the Lord" will come. He uses at least three images. It will happen "like a thief in the night," when there is "peace and security," like a woman suddenly experiencing labor pains (5:2–3). The phrase "peace and security" was a slogan of Roman power and rule. Jesus's return will bring "sudden destruction" on them (5:3).

How are Jesus's believers to prepare for this sudden coming? They are to live ethically as children of the light and day, not of darkness and the night (5:4–5). This means living faithfully and with love and hope or expectation for the salvation that comprises living with Jesus at his return (5:8–11).

Who Is Involved in God's New Age?

Here in 1 Thessalonian 5, Paul divides humanity into two groups, those of the day and those of the night. Only the former benefit from Jesus's return. Likewise, in 1 Corinthians 15 the beneficiaries of the general resurrection are those who belong to Christ.

> But each in his own order: Christ the first fruits, then at his coming those who belong to Christ. Then comes the end. (1 Cor. 15:23–24)

This restriction to those who belong to Christ seems, however, to be at odds with the previous verse, where Paul seems to suggest that all benefit from Jesus's resurrection:

> For as all die in Adam, so all will be made alive in Christ. (1 Cor. 15:22)

How might the two verses be reconciled? Does Paul think everyone will become a Christ-believer in the end? That is very possible, but the verse has a particular context. Does Paul move in verse 23 from the general to the particular to focus on the believing recipients of his letter? The common interpretation is to retranslate verse 22 to read, "So all in Christ will be made alive." This retranslation is based on the understanding that resurrection talk for Paul applies only to believers (1 Thess. 4:16).

This retranslation, however, may not be the final word. In Romans 11, Paul discusses the place of Jews/Israel and gentiles in the divine purposes. He says,

> A hardening has come upon part of Israel, until the full number of the Gentiles has come in. And so all Israel will be saved. . . . As regards the gospel they are enemies of God for your sake; but as regards election they are beloved, for the sake of their ancestors; for the gifts and the calling of God are irrevocable. Just as you were once disobedient to God but have now received mercy because of their disobedience, so they have now been disobedient in order that, by the mercy

shown to you, they too may now receive mercy. For God has imprisoned all in disobedience so that he may be merciful to all. (Rom. 11:25–26, 28–32 NRSV)

This statement embraces all people, "the gentiles" and "all Israel." Moreover, it affirms the continuing place of Israel in the divine purposes—namely, its salvation, election, and irrevocable "gifts and the calling of God." Further, the verses identify a divine way of working in the world that involves mercy and disobedience, Israel and gentiles. Paul declares that all are disobedient but that all receive divine mercy (11:30–32). Divine mercy has the final word for all people.

Clearly there are tensions in Paul's thinking that are expressed in his letters, which are addressed to different churches facing different circumstances.

Gospels

The three Synoptic Gospels (Matthew, Mark, and Luke) give attention to eschatological matters. The most concentrated discussion occurs in the so-called eschatological discourse attributed to Jesus (Mark 13; Matt. 24–25; Luke 21:9–38). For reasons of space limitations, we will focus on just one of these discourses, the longest one, in Matthew 24–25.[2]

> John's Gospel expects Jesus's return (14:3) and a general resurrection to either life or condemnation (5:28–29). Yet the Gospel emphasizes a realized eschatology, in which some of the cluster of expected future events are experienced already in the present (e.g., eternal life, vindication, condemnation; 3:16–18; 5:24).

In Matthew's Gospel, Jesus enters Jerusalem in chapter 21. He then conflicts with and curses the Jerusalem leaders (chaps. 21–23). In chapters 24–25 the Matthean Jesus delivers his eschatological discourse before the passion narrative in chapters 26–27.

The discourse begins with Jesus's declaration to his disciples that all the stones of the Jerusalem temple will be "thrown down" (24:2). This statement looks back on Rome's destruction of Jerusalem and the temple in 70 CE.

Verses 3–26 describe the time before Jesus's return in power and glory. The disciples ask, "What will be the sign of your coming and of the end of the age?" (24:3). The Matthean Jesus sets out a catalog of difficulties and

---

2. See Warren Carter, *Matthew and the Margins: A Sociopolitical and Religious Reading* (Maryknoll, NY: Orbis Books, 2000), 466–97.

hostilities that disciples will encounter leading up to Jesus's return. These times will include the following:

- Misleading, false messiahs (24:5).
- Rumors of wars and actual wars among nations (24:6–7a).
- Famines and earthquakes, "the beginning of the birth pangs" (24:7b–8).
- Persecution of Jesus-followers (24:9).
- Apostasies as disciples abandon their faith and betray other disciples (24:10).
- False prophets (24:11).
- An increase in lawlessness while love diminishes (24:12).
- Good news: The disciples who survive all of this will be saved, and the good news of God's kingdom or empire will be proclaimed "throughout the world" before the goal (*telos*) comes (24:14).
- A desolating sacrilege that will be established in the temple; those living in Judea should flee (24:15–20; the troops of the victorious Titus performed sacrifices in the Jerusalem temple in 70 CE, Josephus, *J.W.* 6.316).
- Great, unprecedented suffering (24:21–22).
- False messiahs and false prophets will attract followings with great signs that could have led disciples astray if they had not been warned (24:23–26).

The verses do not set out a timetable or linear schedule of events. Rather, they identify the sorts of events that constitute a world in crisis that requires divine intervention.

The coming or return of Jesus is described in spectacular terms in verses 27–31. The account emphasizes great visibility, glory, and power. Unlike the false messiahs and prophets of verses 3–26, the appearance of Jesus will be unambiguous.

Verse 27 sets the coming of Jesus in a cosmic context and underlines its visibility with images of lightning that flash from the east to the west. In the Hebrew Bible, lightning commonly accompanies occasions that disclose divine presence and sovereignty. For example, lightning accompanies Moses at Mount Sinai (Exod. 19:16) and features in God's call to Ezekiel (Ezek. 1:13). But lightning is also associated with Rome's top god Jupiter/Zeus, whose world order and rule emperors represent. Its association here with Jesus symbolizes God's rule and power, not Rome's. The identification of Jesus as Son of Man points to God's victory and Rome's demise. In Daniel 7:13–14, "one like a son of man" exercises God's "everlasting dominion" and "kingship . . . that shall never be destroyed" over "all peoples, nations, and languages." The Gospel reads this passage in Daniel as a reference to Jesus. Jesus's return will mean the end of Rome's empire.

Matthew 24:28 depicts Jesus's return and judgment on Rome. The brief saying indicates the results of a battle in which Rome has been defeated. "Wherever the corpse is, there the [*aetoi*] will gather." Crucial to understanding the verse is the correct translation of the term *aetoi*. Commonly it has been translated as "vultures," but that translation is inaccurate. There is another Greek term for vultures, and the term *aetoi* commonly denotes eagles. The translation "eagles" changes the verse's scenario from vultures feeding on corpses—something eagles were understood not to do in the ancient world—to eagles gathered with corpses.

The key to this unusual scenario is the symbolism of eagles. In the biblical tradition, eagles represented imperial powers, such as Assyria and Babylon, who functioned as agents of punishment on God's people (Deut. 28:47–53). More particularly, the eagle was a symbol of Roman power, displayed, for example, on buildings, coins, and a standard carried into battle as "the symbol of empire . . . an omen of victory" (Josephus, *J.W.* 3.123; *Ant.* 18.120–21). Here, this verse depicts the eagle not soaring above the corpse but gathering among or with the corpse.

The scene is the aftermath of a cosmic battle. The symbol of Roman military power is humbled and defeated by the returning Jesus, Son of Man. Rome is subjugated to and destroyed by God's power and rule.

> The so-called War Scroll (1QM) from Qumran details an eschatological forty-year war between the Sons of Light and the Sons of Darkness. Not unlike ancient war manuals, it provides a minute description of military tactics and weaponry. Yet it also abounds with prayers and speeches. One remarkable feature of this eschatological war is that the angels of God and the angels of Belial fight alongside humans. In the final seventh battle the forces of light prevail.

Jesus's victory in a cosmic battle over Rome not only overturns the world's political order but also effects cosmic transformation (Matt. 24:29). Light from the sun and moon is extinguished; the stars fall from heaven. These are common features of judgment scenarios in which heavenly deities that guide imperial powers like Babylon are destroyed at "the day of the LORD" (Isa. 13:1, 6–10). Coins associated Roman emperors with solar and lunar gods. The coming of Jesus will be "lights out" for Roman rule. God's sovereignty over the created order will be restored (Gen. 1).

An unspecified sign then appears in the heavens, perhaps the Son of Man, perhaps the restored heavenly powers (Matt. 24:30). The nations mourn, perhaps in repentance, perhaps fearing imminent judgment. The returning Jesus dispatches angels to gather the "elect" from throughout the world and heaven (24:31).

Who are the elect? On what basis are they constituted? We don't get the answers to those questions till the subsequent judgment scene in Matthew 25:31. The forty-nine verses between 24:32 and 25:30 use direct teaching and three parables to repeat, and thereby emphasize, the exhortation to be ready for the returning Jesus, Son of Man.

How are people to get ready for Jesus's return?

The Son of Man, now also called the king, will return to conduct judgment of "all the nations" (Matt. 25:31–46). Judgment will be by separation. The vindicated or blessed, identified as sheep, will be sent to the right side of the king. The condemned or cursed, identified as goats, will be sent to the left side of the king (25:32–34). The vindicated or blessed will be welcomed to God's reign or empire and into eternal life (25:34, 46). The condemned or cursed will be dispatched to "the eternal fire prepared for the devil and his angels," to "eternal punishment" (25:41, 46).

On what basis? The somewhat repetitive passage emphasizes deeds of mercy done by the vindicated to the poor and vulnerable: food for the hungry, drink for the thirsty, welcome for the stranger, clothing for the naked, caring for the sick and imprisoned. Among the poor and vulnerable, the Son of Man is present and also receives these acts of service. "Just as you did it to one of the least of these . . . , you did it to me" (Matt. 25:40). Such service among the poor and marginal continues Jesus's mission and counters the hierarchical, elite world of exploitative and self-benefiting power.

This judgment scene, along with other scenes in Matthew 13 (13:36–43, 47–50), exhibits some disturbing features. It presents readers with a graphic rendition of the judgment that pressures (bullies?) disciples into replicating a faithful way of life. It celebrates the forcible imposition of God's empire on all humanity even as the Gospel attacks Roman imperial strategies and structures. It constructs divine justice in the form of harsh condemnation of those who do not live according to the divine purposes. Absent from the scene are elements of divine mercy (Matt. 5:43–45) and covenant faithfulness to Israel (23:37–39).

Revelation

Word limits permit only a very brief discussion here. Revelation is opposed to the oppressive Roman Empire, anticipates its destruction, and envisions the establishment of God's reign or empire.[3] The seven letters to the seven churches in chapters 2 and 3 warn the churches against involvement in the empire, especially its pervasive idolatry. Thereafter, Revelation reveals that the Roman Empire is under divine judgment.

Revelation 6:1–8:3 reveals that this judgment takes place by means of the various strategies and practices of the empire itself. This disclosure happens as six seals on a scroll are broken. The seals do not predict future events but interpret destructive practices that currently uphold Roman power and harm most of its subjects. The first four seals disclose four differently colored horses that appear as the seal is broken. Each horse represents harmful aspects of Roman rule. The first horse represents victory and conquest as normal practices of Rome's destructive empire. The second horse represents war and bloodshed as dominant imperial strategies. The third represents death that results from economic disruption and disparity of access to food. The fourth represents death from disease and famine.

The point is that these strategies and practices of the empire are self-destructive and are causing it to implode from within. They benefit a few elites but harm most of Rome's inhabitants. There is no need for God to be slinging down thunderbolts of punishment from on high. The empire is destroying itself.

In Revelation 15–18 the perspective changes. God has given the Roman Empire a chance to repent and change its ways, but to no avail (chaps. 8–11). Chapters 15–18 announce that time is up for the empire that Roman rulers claim is eternal. These chapters provide a series of fantasies of judgment on Rome, which is disdainfully personified as a female prostitute (chap. 17). In 18:8 Rome is destroyed by "plagues . . . pestilence and mourning and famine—and she will be burned with fire." The beneficiaries of Roman power—"kings of the earth," the merchants, and "all shipmasters and seafarers, sailors and all whose trade is on the sea"—lament Rome's destruction (18:9–24).

The final chapters of Revelation envision the return of Jesus to rule over the nations, the destruction of all enemies of God, the binding of Satan, the reign of Christ, the destruction of evil, and the final judgment of all humanity, which involves two books, one of human actions and one of life. Those whose names are not written in the book of life are destroyed in the lake of fire along with death and Hades. These chapters do not set out a sequence of events but envision aspects of the establishment of God's rule. That rule is embraced in God's creation of a new heaven and new earth with a new city, not Rome but Jerusalem (Rev. 19–22).

---

3. For more on this topic, see Warren Carter, *What Does Revelation Reveal? Unlocking the Mystery* (Nashville: Abingdon, 2011).

Conclusion

In this chapter we have troubled the misunderstanding that eschatological thinking is a joke or an escape from reality. Rather, it analyzes the nature of the current world and reveals it to be out of shape in relation to the divine purposes. It wrestles with big matters, such as what type of world we want to live in and to whom the world belongs. Human responsibility and agency are to the fore, as is accountability to the divine.

Matters for Reflection

1. What are some factors that influenced the heightened interest in eschatology in early Jewish texts?
2. One of the features of eschatological visions is the use of numbers. Why are numbers so important?
3. Eschatological scenarios envision a new world. What are some of the features of this new world that this chapter has identified? Why are these features so important?

CHAPTER 11

Revealing God: Traditions About Wisdom

Some Christians claim that knowing God, experiencing God's presence, and understanding God's will are possible only through Jesus. Numerous websites and classroom encounters attest such claims. The implication, of course, is the Christian supremacist claim that there can be no encounter with God before or apart from Jesus.

Such a troubling misunderstanding is not sustainable for several reasons. It directly contradicts the Christian Scriptures, which include accounts of people encountering God in historical events, in the teaching of Torah revealed to Moses, in the words of prophets, in worship. And in a multireligious world it expresses a lack of respect for other views and beliefs.

In this chapter we trouble this misunderstanding by discussing traditions that emerged in the Hebrew Bible and developed in texts of Early Judaism and the New Testament. Known as wisdom traditions, these texts engage the quest to know God and reveal God's will and presence. They address questions such as how and where God might be known, revealed, and encountered.

Wisdom traditions unfolded across several centuries.[1] They developed by locating divine presence and revelation variously, as we shall see, in creation (Job 12:7–10), among human society (Prov. 8–9), in the Jerusalem temple (Sir. 24:10), in the Torah or Law of Moses (Sir. 24:23; Bar. 3–4), and according to John's Gospel, in Jesus. In this chapter we trace the continuities and discontinuities in wisdom traditions, which developed from a revelatory presence

---

1. Sharon Ringe, *Wisdom's Friends: Community and Christology in the Fourth Gospel* (Louisville: Westminster John Knox, 1999).

in creation, to a personified female figure, to an alignment with Torah, to the figure of Jesus. These traditions embrace both human questing and divine revelation.

Early Judaism

Scholars identify three main wisdom or sapiential writings in the Jewish and Protestant canons of the Hebrew Bible. These are Job, Proverbs, and Ecclesiastes (or Qohelet). Though all three are labeled "sapiential," their constructions of wisdom vary and develop, as do the ways in which people might gain wisdom.

Job 12:7–10, for example, posits that one can learn about God's ways by contemplating nature:

> But ask the beasts, and they will teach you;
> The birds of the sky, they will tell you,
> Or speak to the earth, it will teach you;
> The fish of the sea, they will inform you.
> Who among all these does not know
> That the hand of the LORD has done this?
> In His hand is every living soul
> And the breath of all mankind. (NJPS)

Subsequently, moving beyond a principle in creation, Wisdom is personified as a woman in Proverbs 8. She moves among people and calls to people from "the topmost heights, by the wayside, at the crossroads," and "near the gates at the city entrance" (Prov. 8:2–3 NJPS). She invites all to come to her to be instructed about God and about how to live in God's ways and will (8:5). "Riches and honor," "wealth and success" await her students, as well as "righteousness" and "justice" (8:18, 20 NJPS).

As Lady Wisdom's speech in Proverbs 8 unfolds, it reveals the basis for Wisdom's trustworthy revelation of God. She was with God in the beginning as God created the world (8:22–31):

> I was there when He set the heavens into place;
> When He fixed the horizon upon the deep;
> . . . .
> When He fixed the foundations of the earth,
> I was with Him as a confidant,
> A source of delight every day,
> Rejoicing before Him at all times,
> Rejoicing in His inhabited world,
> Finding delight with mankind. (8:27, 29–31 NJPS)

From this starting point with God, Wisdom goes among people, where she is able to make a reliable revelation of God's presence and purposes and enable people to encounter God. Not everyone, though, is interested or receptive. She creates a divide among people:

> Now, sons, listen to me;
> Happy [blessed] are they who keep my ways.
> Heed discipline and become wise.
> . . . .
> Happy [blessed] is the man who listens to me,
> Coming early to my gates each day,
> Waiting outside my doors.
> For he who finds me finds life
> And obtains favor from the LORD,
> But he who misses me destroys himself;
> All who hate me love death. (Prov. 8:32–36 NJPS)

Encountering Wisdom's revelation of the divine is a matter of life and death.

Several other early Jewish writings adopt and develop the figure of Lady Wisdom.

Book of Sirach

In a lengthy poem found in the book known as Sirach and written by Ben Sira, Lady Wisdom speaks "in the assembly of the Most High" (Sir. 24:2). She narrates her origin with God and identifies herself as the divine speech, God's word, by which the world was created (evoking Gen. 1). She relates how she traveled across the earth and sea; she "held sway" over both nature and people (Sir. 24:3, 6).

And then Lady Wisdom tells of her quest for "a resting place." She explains that by divine "command" she came to reside with the people Israel (24:7–9). And more specifically, not just anywhere in the land of Israel but in Jerusalem ("Zion"), where she ministered in the tabernacle ("the holy tent"; 24:10), the prototype of the future temple.

Wisdom was established in Jerusalem, and she "took root" in God's people and grew (24:12–17). She invites all to come and eat of her "fruits." Those who choose to come "will not be put to shame," and those who work with her "will not sin" (24:19–22). Wisdom reveals God's presence and guides people how to live.

At this point in chapter 24, Ben Sira makes a striking observation. He identifies this heavenly wisdom that came down from God to dwell in Jerusalem and among God's people with the "book of the covenant," the Torah:

> All this is the book of the covenant of the Most High God,
>   the law that Moses commanded us
>   as an inheritance for the congregations of Jacob. (Sir. 24:23)

Sirach's claim is that God's presence, will, and purposes are revealed ultimately in the Torah, the teaching of Moses. Ben Sira instructs his audience to attend to and obey the Law, the Torah. There they will encounter God and find the revelation of God's will.

Having identified wisdom with the "book of the covenant of the Most High God," Ben Sira goes on to compare this wisdom/Torah to an overflowing and life-giving river (24:23–27). Next, he describes himself, a scribe or interpreter of the Torah by occupation, to "a canal from a river," watering a garden. This canal, too, becomes a river, even a sea (24:30–31). This image of abundant water pouring out "like prophecy" stands for Ben Sira's own scribal teaching and interpretation of Torah, which he intends to leave "to all future generations" (24:32–34).

Given this striking description of Ben Sira's role as a teacher-scribe, it comes as little surprise that he praises the scribes as interpreters of Torah and therefore as teachers of wisdom (38:24–34; 39:1–11). According to Ben Sira, scribes

- study God's law;
- seek out the wisdom of the ancients;
- study prophecies;
- "preserve the sayings of the famous";
- understand the "subtleties of parables," "hidden meanings of proverbs," and "obscurities of parables"; and
- meditate on divine mysteries.

The book of Sirach emphasizes that scribes require time and freedom from manual work to undertake the requisite study of Torah and gain knowledge of the divine will. Ben Sira contrasts the scribe's lot with that of a farmer (38:25–26), with artisans who labor night and day (38:27), with the smith who works with iron (38:28), and with the potter working with clay (38:29–30). He recognizes how hard they work and how important their work is, but

> How different the one who devotes himself
>   to the study of the law of the Most High!
> . . . .
> They set their hearts to rise early
>   to seek the Lord who made them
>   and to petition the Most High;

> they open their mouths in prayer
> > and ask pardon for their sins.
>
> If the great Lord is willing,
> > they will be filled with the spirit of understanding;
> they will pour forth words of wisdom of their own
> > and give thanks to the Lord in prayer.
> The Lord will direct their counsel and knowledge
> > as they meditate on his mysteries.
> They will show the discipline of their training
> > and will glory in the law of the Lord's covenant. (Sir. 38:34; 39:5–8)

From his study of Torah and his devotion to God, the scribe gains great understanding and pours it out to others in teaching and interpretation of Torah. The scribe mediates wisdom to others.

Baruch

Sirach is not the only text to espouse the view that wisdom is encountered in the law of Moses. In Baruch 3:37–4:1 there is a similar claim that associates wisdom with Torah as the place where the divine will and presence are revealed:

> He [God] found the whole way to knowledge
> > and gave her to his servant Jacob
> > and to Israel, whom he loved.
> Afterward she appeared on earth
> > and lived with humankind.
> She is the book of the commandments of God,
> > the law that endures forever.

And a Qumran scroll 4Q525 (4QBeatitudes) 2 ii 3–4 also associates wisdom with the Torah. It declares, "Blessed is the one who attains wisdom, and walks in the law of the Most High." Such a person "meditates on it continually" (2 ii 6). In doing so, a person encounters the divine presence and will.

Other Teachers of Wisdom

Early Jewish texts assign instruction in wisdom not only to scribes but also to priests and Levites. In the Aramaic Levi Document, Levi, the namesake of the tribe of Levi, which was chosen by God to take care of the sanctuary, offers his final testament (chap. 13). Among other things, he commands his sons,

And now, my sons, teach reading and writing and [in the] teaching of wisdom to your children and wisdom be eternal glory for you. . . . [And] do not be lax in the study of wisdom. (ALD 13:4–7, 15)

> The Aramaic Levi Document (ALD) focuses on the life and teachings of the biblical forefather of the tribe of Levi. Copies of this Aramaic work were found among the Dead Sea Scrolls.

In a text from 1 Enoch, the Apocalypse of Weeks, a group of the chosen ones receives "sevenfold wisdom and knowledge" from God (1 En. 93:10).

Wisdom is also especially associated with King Solomon. In the Wisdom of Solomon, King Solomon says that he prayed for Wisdom in order to rule well and received her (7:7). Wisdom, whom he describes as "the fashioner of all things" involved with God in creation, taught him cosmology, physics, astronomy, biology, and botany. From her, he "learned both what is secret and what is manifest" (7:17–22). This leads Solomon to praise Wisdom. The text names no fewer than twenty-one laudable attributes of Wisdom (7:22–23).

> I learned both what is secret and what is manifest,
> for wisdom, the fashioner of all things, taught me.
> There is in her a spirit that is intelligent, holy,
> unique, manifold, subtle,
> agile, clear, unpolluted,
> distinct, invulnerable, loving the good, keen,
> irresistible, beneficent, humane,
> steadfast, sure, free from anxiety,
> all-powerful, overseeing all,
> and penetrating through all spirits
> that are intelligent, pure, and altogether subtle.
> For wisdom is more mobile than any motion;
> because of her pureness she pervades and penetrates all things.
> For she is a breath of the power of God
> and a pure emanation of the glory of the Almighty;
> therefore nothing defiled gains entrance into her.
> For she is a reflection of eternal light,
> a spotless mirror of the working of God,
> and an image of his goodness.
> ....
> In every generation she passes into holy souls
> and makes them friends of God and prophets,
> for God loves nothing so much as the person who lives with wisdom.
> ....
> But against wisdom evil does not prevail. (Wis. 7:21–30)

Blending Jewish traditions with Hellenistic philosophical ideas, this work describes wisdom as both immanent and transcendent (7:22–27).

In Wisdom of Solomon, the personified Wisdom is "an initiate in the knowledge of God, and an associate in his works" (8:4), "a fashioner of what exists" (8:6). She effectively runs the world and does it well (8:1). The work illustrates this by showcasing Wisdom's work as God's intermediary in history from the time of creation to the exodus from Egypt (chap. 10).

A text from the Dead Sea Scrolls community identifies one of the community's members as a recipient of divine revelation and a teacher of wisdom. The commentary on the book of Habakkuk, Pesher Habakkuk (1QpHab 7:1–5), argues that while God told Habakkuk to write down the things that are to come upon the present generation, "He did not make known to him when the time will come to an end."

> Pesher Habakkuk (1QpHab) is a commentary on the book of Habakkuk. Found at Qumran, it reflects the worldview of the sectarian community that preserved the Dead Sea Scrolls.

To whom did God reveal this? The scroll claims that this special knowledge, called here "mysteries," was disclosed to the Teacher of Righteousness:

> Interpreted this concerns the Teacher of Righteousness, to whom God had made known all the mysteries of the words of His servants the Prophets. (1QpHab 7:4–5)

The text goes on to link these "mysteries" with the divine plan:

> All the ages of God reach their appointed end as He determines for them in the mysteries of His wisdom. (7:13–14)

This text emphasizes the Teacher of Righteousness as the recipient and teacher of the divine revelation.

The Dead Sea Scrolls mention yet another figure to whom God has revealed God's mysteries. In the Dead Sea Scrolls community, this person occupied the office of Maskil, "one possessing/imparting knowledge" (1QS 9:18). In the Community Rule, the Maskil teaches that two spirits are waging war in human hearts and in the world in general. These are the spirits of truth and injustice. They will wage war until the end predetermined by God (1QS 3:13–4:26).

Wisdom: A Challenge

The quest for wisdom, the revelation of divine presence and will, requires both human effort and divine revelation. While the texts of Sirach, Wisdom of Solomon, and Baruch seem generally confident about the ability to gain wisdom, wisdom can also be elusive and a mystery.

For example, the Parables of Enoch recognizes that Wisdom came from heaven as a revealer of God and sought to find a dwelling place among people. But instead of finding some who receive her, she experienced overwhelming opposition. She returned to heaven and dwells among the angels.

> Wisdom went forth to dwell among the children of the people,
> but she did not find a dwelling.
> Wisdom returned to her place, and sat down in the midst of angels.
> (1 En. 42:1–2)

With Wisdom's withdrawal, an opposing personified entity called Iniquity went out and found a dwelling place among people. Sin and evil dominate the world when people do not seek and receive Wisdom as the revelation of the divine presence and will.

Several writings found among the Dead Sea Scrolls recognize this elusiveness and the mystical quality of wisdom. One such writing is called 4QInstruction. While in Proverbs, Wisdom is the divine instrument and companion at creation (3:19; 8:22–31), in 4QInstruction, God "spreads out the foundations" with the "mystery of existence" or the "mystery of what is to be" (4Q417 [4QInstruction^c] 1 i 8–9). The addressee in 4QInstruction, called the "understanding one," is called to ponder on this "mystery of existence":

> [Day and] night he meditates on the approaching mystery [of existence] and studies (it) always. Then you will know truth and injustice, wisdom [and folly]. . . . Then you will know the difference between [go]od and evil. (4Q417 1 i 6–7)

Here the quest for understanding of the divine ways is not easy but requires constant meditation "[day and] night." With perseverance and sustained effort, one will be able to distinguish "truth and injustice, wisdom and [folly] . . . [go]od and evil."

Another sapiential text from Qumran, called quite appropriately "Mysteries," links the revelation of Wisdom with the eschatological accomplishment of the divine purposes. It envisions a time when "wickedness shall be banished by righteousness, as darkness is banished by the light." Then "knowledge will fill the world and folly shall exist no longer" (1Q27 [1QMysteries] 1 i 3–4, 5–7).

Folly or foolishness is the antithesis of wisdom. Proverbs presents Lady Folly as an alternative to and opponent of Lady Wisdom. Lady Folly "is ignorant and knows nothing" and tries to subvert and divert followers of Wisdom, "who are going straight on their way" (Prov. 9:13–18). While Wisdom reveals God's presence and ways, followers of Folly, called "fools," have no interest in knowing God: "Fools say in their hearts, 'There is no God'" (Ps. 14:1). This text from Qumran, Mysteries, warns that those who do not "know the mystery that is to be," who do not care about the revelation of the divine purposes (wisdom), will not be able to escape the divine judgment in the eschatological future (1Q27 [1QMysteries] 1 i 3–4, 5–7).

These texts make clear that this mystery of being, or mystery of what is to be, cannot be learned only on one's own accord. It is a revealed mystery. Apparently, the mystery of being consists of God's ethical norms about good and evil as they are revealed in the Torah and of the entire divine scheme for the world, encompassing past, present, and future. God reveals this mystery to various recipients and their task is to ponder on it.

Main Features of Wisdom in Early Jewish Traditions

» Personifies divine power and presence but protects monotheism
» Immanent in creation but distinct from it
» Heavenly female figure active on earth
» Revealer figure, who is also elusive and mysterious
» Mediates life—but death results for some
» Invites and is rejected
» Mediates God's presence among humans
» Is encountered in creation (Job), people (Proverbs), Torah (Sirach, Baruch), and various teachers (Solomon, Teacher of Righteousness, Jesus [John's Gospel])

New Testament

New Testament texts are also very concerned with revelation of the divine ways and purposes. Here we focus on one writing, the Gospel of John, and its use of wisdom traditions. We suggest that the adoption and adaptation of wisdom traditions in John's Gospel explain to a large extent the distinctive ways in which this Gospel tells the story of Jesus.

Central to that telling is the distinctive presentation of Jesus as Wisdom, the definitive Word or revealer of God. Such a presentation involves applying features of Lady Wisdom to the male figure of Jesus.

These Texts Are Not the Same as the Others

John's Gospel differs from the Synoptic Gospels[2] in significant ways. In the Synoptics, Jesus undertakes a lengthy Galilean ministry before going to Jerusalem to be crucified. John's Jesus is in Jerusalem in chapter 2 and back and forth between Galilee and Jerusalem multiple times. In John's Gospel, Jesus gathers his disciples before his crucifixion for farewell instructions that extend across five chapters (John 13–17). Lengthy speeches, rather than short scenes ended by punchy one-liners, mark the speech of John's Jesus. Other features of his speech include seven "I am" sayings, dualisms (above-below, life-death, day-night), extended metaphors (good shepherd, the vine), very few references to the kingdom/empire of God, and no parables. John's Jesus performs no exorcisms and only a few other miracles, including healings, feedings, and storm calming. There are different characters, such as the *Ioudaioi*, the term that often names the Jerusalem-based leaders. Other different characters include Nicodemus, the Samaritan woman, the man at the pool, the man born blind, and the dead and revived Lazarus. Familiar scenes in the Synoptics are absent from John's Gospel: no birth stories, baptism, transfiguration, Last Supper.

Scholars have suggested at least four factors that might explain the distinctive telling of the story of Jesus in John's Gospel:

- Sources: The three Synoptic Gospels share sources for their accounts about Jesus. Both Matthew and Luke use Mark as a source, and probably a collection of sayings (oral? written?) known as "Q." John's Gospel probably does not use any of these sources.[3]
- Author: We do not know the identity of the author of this Gospel. The name John was not linked with the Gospel until late in the second century. We do not know the identity of this "John." Yet what is clear about this author is that she or he was creative and insightful in telling the story of Jesus.[4]
- Circumstances: John's Gospel was written in the 80s–90s of the first century CE. We don't know where it was written. Ephesus has been

---

2. The Synoptic Gospels are the three "look-alike" Gospels of Matthew, Mark, and Luke.
3. Warren Carter, *John: Storyteller, Interpreter, Evangelist* (Peabody, MA: Hendrickson, 2006), 140–51.
4. Carter, *John*, 177–96.

suggested, but there is no sure evidence. It addresses a group of Jesus-followers who seem to be in conflict with other synagogue members after the Roman destruction of Jerusalem and the temple in 70 CE (John 9:22; 12:42; 16:2). This catastrophic event and massive display of Roman military power necessitated a major rethinking of Jewish identity and practices. Debates about the way ahead took place, especially how to know the divine will, purposes, and presence. In these debates, the Jesus-followers in the synagogue advocated for Jesus as the definitive revealer of the divine will, purposes, and presence. They failed to carry the day.[5] These debates and claims shape the Gospel's claims about Jesus.

- Wisdom traditions: In order to persuade others to commit to Jesus as the definitive revealer of God's presence, purposes, and will, the Gospel interprets Jesus as the personification of wisdom. What does this mean?

John's Jesus as Wisdom

The Gospel presents Jesus as the agent and definitive revealer of God. Its presentation of Jesus borrows some fourteen features of wisdom traditions that had developed through the texts of the Hebrew Bible and Early Judaism identified above.[6]

- Origin: Like Wisdom, the Johannine Jesus exists in the beginning with God (John 1:1–2). From the outset, he shares life with God. Being from God, he is the only one to see God (1:18; 6:46). He is one with God (10:30). Being with God from the beginning is the basis for the revelation of God that he makes in his ministry.
- Agent of creation: Like Wisdom, Jesus is present at, and an agent of, creation. "All things came into being through him"—particularly, "what has come into being in him was life" (1:3–4).
- Revealer of God: Like Wisdom, Jesus is authorized to be the definitive revealer of God. Jesus is identified from the outset as the "Word." This image expresses Jesus's identity and role as the communication of God (1:1). As the reliable and definitive revealer of God, Jesus makes God known (1:18). Repeatedly, the Gospel emphasizes the reliability and definitive quality of Jesus's revelation because he comes from God. It describes Jesus as coming down from heaven (6:38, 41, 51). He is the one whom God has sent (6:39, 44, 57). He is the divinely sanctioned revealer.
- Activity among people: Like Wisdom, Jesus carries out his revealing work among people. The Word "became flesh and lived among us"

---

5. Carter, *John*, 158–74.
6. Ringe, *Wisdom's Friends*, 46–92.

(1:14). Like Wisdom, Jesus reveals God among people. Jesus meets people where he is staying (1:39), under a fig tree (1:48–49), at a wedding in the village of Cana (2:1–11), in the Jerusalem temple (2:13–14), in the Judean countryside (3:22–23), at a well (4:5–6), in the portico of the Jerusalem temple (5:2–3), on the other side of the Sea of Galilee/Tiberias on a mountain (6:1–3, 25), and in the house of Mary, Martha, and Lazarus (12:1–8).

- Material gifts: Like Wisdom, Jesus makes bountiful material gifts—of wine (2:1–11), of living water (4:7–15), of good health (4:46–54; 5:1–9), of abundant food (6:1–14).
- Revealer of words: Like Wisdom, Jesus manifests the presence and will of God. He reveals what he has seen of God and speaks words that God gave him to speak. "I declare what I have seen in the Father's presence; as for you, you should do what you have heard from the Father" (8:38). Again, Jesus says, "For I have not spoken on my own, but the Father who sent me has himself given me a commandment about what to say and what to speak. . . . What I speak, therefore, I speak just as the Father has told me" (12:49–50).
- Works: Jesus reveals the presence and will of God in the works he performs. "The works that the Father has given me to complete, the very works that I am doing, testify on my behalf that the Father has sent me. . . . I have shown you many good works from the Father" (5:36; 10:32).
- Knowing God: Jesus's words and works reveal God's presence and will (1:18). Just as to know Wisdom is to know God, so also to know Jesus is to know God (14:7). To have seen Jesus is to have seen God (14:9). To hear Jesus is to hear God (14:10, 24). To have seen Jesus's works is to have seen God's works (14:10). Like Wisdom, Jesus renders God knowable, visible, audible, active.
- Division: Like that of Wisdom, Jesus's ministry divides those whom he encounters (1 En. 42:1–3; Bar. 3). Some receive him; some reject him. "He came to what was his own, and his own people did not accept him. But to all who received him, . . . he gave power to become children of God" (John 1:11–12). To those who receive him, he facilitates relationship with God.
- Revealer of life: Like Wisdom, Jesus facilitates relationship with God marked by *life*. Jesus came to make abundant life available (5:21; 10:10). This life comprises knowing God (17:3). It is not simply biological life, which everyone has. It is eschatological life, which belongs to the coming age when the divine purposes will be established. It is "age-ly" life or "life of the age" (often misleadingly translated as "eternal life"). This phrase, "life of the age," appears in Daniel 12:2 to refer to the future

new age of the resurrected, when they will be free from the deadly tyrant Antiochus IV Epiphanes and subject to God's rule. In the Gospel's time, the phrase refers to an age free from oppressive Roman rule. It is a qualitatively different life marked by the full establishment of God's good purposes. To commit to Jesus in the present is to pass from death to life of the age and not to be under judgment anymore (John 5:24). Everyone who believes in Jesus, whom God sent, does not perish but has life of the age already, at least in part in the present and fully in the future resurrection (3:16; 5:24; 6:47). As the one who reveals God, Jesus himself embodies and mediates this life that consists of knowing God (6:48; 11:25–26).

- Creation of community: Like Wisdom, Jesus creates a community of disciples or learners/followers (1:35–51). This life is societal, lived in relationship with other disciples (1:12). It is marked by love and seeking the good of the other, not by domination and the self-interest of the Roman Empire's ruling elite (13:12–17, 34–35). It is also marked by material and physical benefits (2:1–12; 4:46–54; 6:1–15).
- Friends: Like Wisdom, Jesus identifies this community of followers as "friends" who have received the revelation from God (15:13–15). Wisdom of Solomon uses the same term, "friends," to identify recipients of Wisdom (Wis. 7:27).[7]
- Elusiveness: Like that of Wisdom, Jesus's revelation remains elusive to and rejected by some. The main rejecting groups are "the world" (John 1:10; 14:18–19)[8] and the *Ioudaioi*.[9] This latter term, used over seventy times, is difficult to translate. Some have translated it as "the Jews" or "the Judeans." Sometimes that translation is appropriate, especially when it is used descriptively, as in a phrase such as "the Passover of the Jews" (2:13; cf. 7:2). And there are some positive uses of the term (11:19, 31–33); some *Ioudaioi* received and believed in Jesus (8:31; 11:45). Jesus, too, is a Jew (4:9). But a translation of "the Jews" can be inaccurate and misleading. It does not always refer to all Jews; sometimes it refers to a specific group of Jesus's opponents. A better referent for the term in those cases is "the ruling elite." They first appear as a distinctive, powerful group of Jerusalem-based leaders (priests, Levites, Pharisees) in 1:19. Their opposition to Jesus emerges strongly in chapters 5–12. They seek to kill Jesus (5:16–18; 8:40), resist his teaching (6:41), misunderstand his mission (7:35), intimidate Jesus-followers (7:13; 9:22; 12:42; 19:38), desire to arrest Jesus (7:30–32), seek to stone him (10:31). They

---

7. Ringe, *Wisdom's Friends*, 64–83.
8. Carter, *John*, 91–92.
9. Carter, *John*, 67–73.

do not know his origin from God (6:41–42) or that he is authorized as God's agent and revealer (7:28–30). They successfully arrest Jesus and have Pilate crucify him (18:12; 19:12).

Jesus's conflict with this group is intense. John's Jesus interprets their rejection of him as signifying that they are not able to hear God's voice (5:37), that they do not believe Moses's revelation (5:46–47), that they do not know God (7:28). Jesus's worst interpretation of their rejection of him appears in chapter 8. Jesus asserts his origin "from above" as the revealer from God. By contrast, he declares the resisting *Ioudaioi* to be "from below" (8:23). Subsequently it becomes clear that "from below" means not just "not from God" but from the devil! "You are from your father the devil, and you choose to do your father's desires. He was a murderer from the beginning and does not stand in the truth because there is no truth in him. When he lies, he speaks according to his own nature, for he is a liar and the father of lies" (8:42–44).

The Johannine Jesus employs a dualism of origins to interpret their rejection. Those who receive him share his origin from God; those who do not receive him come from the devil. Of course, the Gospel does not associate all Jews with the devil. It interprets a particular group in particular circumstances. Unfortunately, extending this to Jews as a whole has been a common misinterpretation and hateful accusation among Christians.

- Return to God: Like Wisdom, Jesus returns to God when he has finished his ministry. He is "lifted up" on the cross and through resurrection and ascension (3:14; 8:28; 12:34). He had "come from God and was going to God," from whence he would return to earth (13:3; 14:18). With God, he prepares a place in his Father's house for disciples to be with the Father and himself (14:2–7). In the meantime, like Wisdom, the ascended Jesus sends the Holy Spirit among disciples (Wis. 9:17).[10]

> And I will ask the Father, and he will give you another Advocate, to be with you forever. This is the Spirit of truth, whom the world cannot receive because it neither sees him nor knows him. You know him because he abides with you, and he will be in you. (John 14:16–17)

> Nevertheless, I tell you the truth: it is to your advantage that I go away, for if I do not go away, the Advocate will not come to you, but if I go, I will send him to you. . . . When the Spirit of truth comes, he will guide you into all the truth, for he will not speak on his own but will speak whatever he hears, and he will declare to you the things that are to come. (John 16:7, 13)

---

10. Ringe, *Wisdom's Friends*, 84–92.

Matters for Reflection

1. Wisdom traditions emphasize the revealing or making known of God. From the discussion in this chapter, where and how is Wisdom—the making known of God—encountered?
2. Read some of the passages that celebrate Wisdom: Proverbs 8–9; Wisdom of Solomon 9–10; Sirach 24. What do you notice about Wisdom?
3. Which aspects of Wisdom in these sources facilitated the association between Wisdom and Jesus?

CHAPTER 12

Prayer

Numerous online discussions claim that praying in Jesus's name reflects the confession that access to God is possible only through Jesus.[1] The implication of this claim is that God does not listen to any other prayer, including Jewish prayer. In addition, a long tradition has criticized Jewish worship as being empty ritual, mere formality, never heartfelt, and addressed to a disinterested God. For example, a long-standing view among some scholars is that "Judaism was the antithesis of Christianity. Judaism was a legalistic religion in which God was remote and inaccessible. Christianity is based on faith rather than works and believes in an accessible God."[2] Clearly prayer is futile if the divine is distant, remote, and inaccessible.

In this chapter we critique these troubling misunderstandings of Early Judaism.

These unsustainable claims ignore Hebrew Bible and early Jewish invitations to prayer and assurances of answered prayer made long before Jesus. For example, "Call to me, and I will answer you" (Jer. 33:3). Or Ben Sira's instruction: "But above all pray to the Most High that he may direct your way in truth" (Sir. 37:15). Or the answers to the earnest prayers of Tobit and Sarah: "At that very moment, the prayers of both of them were heard in the glorious presence of God" (Tob. 3:16).

---

1. We refrain from citing specific websites because we are not interested in targeting particular individuals, and the issue is broadly attested.

2. The influential view of F. Weber from the late nineteenth century, summarized and critiqued by E. P. Sanders, *Paul and Palestinian Judaism: A Comparison of Patterns of Religion* (Philadelphia: Fortress, 1977), 33–59, esp. 33.

In this chapter we consider continuities and discontinuities in the practices and contents of prayer across the texts of Early Judaism and the New Testament.

Early Judaism

Early Jewish writings attest both an extensive and varied practice of prayer. We begin with three general observations about prayer in early Jewish writings.

First, many prayers address God directly in the second person. And these writings from Early Judaism also offer a wealth of hymns, psalms, and blessings that do not address God directly. It is possible that these, too, were perceived and functioned as prayers.

Second, the Torah, like the Hebrew Bible in general, does not explicitly mandate praying, either for individuals or for communities. Nor does it regulate the wording of the prayers, set particular times to pray, or require a specific posture or location during praying. The writings of Early Judaism, in part, similarly do not standardize practices for prayer. Yet as we will see, it is during this period that attempts to regulate prayer emerged.

Third, there are hundreds of prayers, hymns, and psalms in the writings of Early Judaism. These early Jewish prayers are marked by an astounding variety of content and custom. In the midst of this variety, some formulations and practices emerged as being preferred more than others.

Though there is an extensive amount and variety of material, we can address only a few examples here. Generally speaking, most of the prayers and prayerlike materials can be divided into two groups. First, there are prayers embedded in a wide variety of writings, especially in narratives. Second, there are texts consisting entirely of prayers, hymns, and psalms.

Prayers Embedded in Narratives

In many early Jewish narratives, the protagonists pray. The sheer volume of these prayers—and some of them are long indeed—suggests that they were viewed as significant. They express the protagonists' piety. They show that praying is important. Readers learn when and how to pray. They also learn central theological content of the tradition. So though we don't know whether these prayers reflect how contemporary Jews actually prayed, they allow us to see how early Jewish writers constructed proper praying.

Here are a few examples.

In the Greek version of Esther, both Esther and Mordecai pray one prayer. The setting is the Babylonian city of Susa. Israel has been defeated by the Babylonians. Numerous Jews, including Mordecai, have been taken in exile to Babylon to serve in the court of the victorious king. Mordecai's cousin, Esther, is married to the king and has become the Persian queen. A court official named Haman deeply resents the king's favor to Mordecai and Esther. He has the king issue a decree authorizing the murder of Jews across the empire. Mordecai prays,

> O Lord, Lord, you rule as King over all things, for the universe is in your power and there is no one who can oppose you when it is your will to save Israel. . . . I will not bow down to anyone but you, who are my Lord; . . . And now, O Lord God and King, God of Abraham, spare your people; for the eyes of our foes are upon us to annihilate us. (Add. Esth. C 13:9–15)

Mordecai's prayer recognizes God's supreme power and favor toward Israel, as well as Mordecai's loyalty to God. He seeks God's intervention against Haman and the king.

Esther prays a similar prayer for God's saving intervention:

> But save us by your hand, and help me, who am alone and have no helper but you, O Lord. . . . O God, whose might is over all, hear the voice of the despairing, and save us from the hands of evildoers. And save me from my fear! (Add. Esth. C 14:14, 19)

God answers the prayers, and Haman's plot is thwarted.

A similar situation arises in the Greek version of Daniel 3 (v. 23), again in the context of exile in Babylon. Three young Jewish men—Shadrach, Meshach, and Abednego—refuse to bow down to the Babylonian gods. The king punishes them by throwing them into a very hot furnace. One of them offers a lengthy prayer, acknowledging that in the exile God is punishing Israel for unfaithfulness. And he asks for deliverance:

> Deliver us in accordance with your marvelous works, and bring glory to your name, O Lord. Let all who do harm to your servants be put to shame; . . . Let them know that you alone are the Lord God, glorious over the whole world. (Pr. Azar. 1:20–22)

When the angel of God saves them, they sing an extensive song of praise to God (Song of the Three).

Another example of prayer being introduced into biblical stories is found in one of the Dead Sea Scrolls, 4Q365 (4QReworked Pentateuch^c). In Exodus 15, after God has led the people through the sea and saved them from the pursuing Egyptian army, Moses leads Israel in a victory song known as the Song of the Sea (Exod. 15:1–19). Right after this song, in Exodus 15:20–21, Moses's sister, Miriam, leads women in a song. In the traditional Hebrew text of verses 20–21, Miriam is identified as "the prophetess," but she merely rehearses Moses's opening words from Exodus 15:1. However, in the scroll 4Q365, Miriam's song is significantly longer. Though the text is damaged, it can be partially restored:[3]

1. daughters [of my people I will sing to YHWH   ]
2. for he has [do]ne glorious things. [Yah is my] **st[rength** and might]
3. You are great, **performing** s[igns   ]
4. The enemy's hope perished and [his memory] is for[gotten   ]
5. perished in the **mighty waters** enemy[   ]
6. **and you shall exalt** to the heights [for] you gave [a cove]nant [to our fathers]
7. [the one do]ing glorious things."[   ]

(4Q365 6a ii + 6c 1–7)

The songs attributed to Moses and Miriam share several similarities. The bold type identifies them. Clearly, the scribes responsible for Miriam's long song used that of Moses as a model. Yet Miriam's song introduces some unparalleled words, such as the reference to God's "covenant."

Other figures pray in early Jewish texts. Baruch, Jeremiah's scribe, offers a lengthy prayer in Baruch 2:11–3:8. King Solomon in the Wisdom of Solomon prays to God to receive wisdom (Wis. 9). In the book of Tobit, Tobit, Sarah, Tobias, and Raguel pray on various occasions (3:1–5, 11–16; 8:5–7, 15–17; 13). Judith offers a lengthy prayer as she prepares to seduce and kill the commander of the Assyrian forces attacking Israel, Holofernes (chap. 9).

In 3 Maccabees, the high priest, Simon, asks God to prevent a Hellenistic king from desecrating the temple (3 Macc. 2:1–20). Simon's prayer is an example of a penitential prayer. Ubiquitous in early Jewish texts, these prayers typically feature a confession of sins, a recollection of God's past merciful dealings, and a renewed appeal for God's mercy. All these elements are present in Simon's prayer (vv. 10–20). The prayer of Azariah from the fiery furnace, mentioned above, also includes a confession of sin, as does Esther's prayer.

Simon's prayer exhibits another common feature of penitential prayers: using the Hebrew Bible to list previous acts of God. In this case (3 Macc. 2:4–7), Simon evokes past events from the Hebrew Bible in which God's righteous judgment was manifested. He names the mighty giants of Genesis 6:1–4, "the people of Sodom," and "the audacious Pharaoh who had enslaved your holy people Israel." Just as God had acted to deliver God's people in the past,

---

3. Ariel Feldman, "Song of the Sea (Exod 15:1–21) in Early Jewish Writings," in *The Torah in Jewish and Christian Imaginations*, ed. Ariel Feldman and Timothy Sandoval, Forschungen zum Alten Testament 171 (Tübingen: Mohr Siebeck, 2023), 67–90.

Simon prays, God would intervene now to prevent the Hellenistic king from desecrating the temple.

The Dead Sea Scrolls include lots of prayers added to biblical narratives. Most of these are highly fragmentary; sometimes we know the speakers, sometimes not. Genesis Apocryphon contains additional prayers of the fallen angels, Abraham, and Melchizedek (1QapGen 0:1–18; 19:7–8; 20:12–16). A fragmentary composition retelling Israel's past features a prayer by Joseph (4QNarrative and Poetic Composition[a] [2Q22; 4Q371–373a]). Multiple prayers are also found in the texts rewriting the books of Joshua (4Q378 [4QapocrJosh[a]] 6 ii 4–8; 13 i; 19 ii; 22 i; 4Q379 [4QapocrJosh[b]] 1; 5; 18), Samuel, and Kings (4Q160 [4QVisSam] 4 i + 5; 4Q382 [4Qpap paraKings] 15 5–8; 23; 30; 38; 49; 105; 110; 111; 115). One fragment mentions "words of a prayer and a suppli[cation]," apparently by "Hezekiah king of [Judah]" (4Q382 46).

In a psalm from Qumran (11Q5 [11QPs[a]] 27), King David is presented as the ultimate author of Jewish liturgy. He is credited with 3,600 psalms, 364 songs to accompany the daily sacrifice in the sanctuary, 52 songs for the Sabbath offerings, and 30 songs to accompany the offerings on the first day of each month and the festivals. He is also credited with composing 4 songs for protection from demonic attacks. In total, David is said to have authored 4,050 pieces of liturgy.

Collections of Prayers and Prayerlike Texts

In addition to prayers embedded in narratives, there are also compositions consisting entirely of prayers and prayerlike materials. Most of these collections emerged from the Dead Sea Scrolls. Here we list only a few of them:

- Hodayot or Thanksgiving Hymns (1QH[a,b]; 4Q427–432). Many of the hymns included in this work open with the phrase "I give thanks to you, O Lord." Some of them (1QH[a] 10–17) relate distinctly personal experiences, including that of communion or fellowship with angels (1QH[a] 11:19–23).
- Songs of the Sage (4Q510–511). These are apotropaic hymns. The term "apotropaic" means they are intended to offer protection from demonic attacks. The refrain "amen, amen" indicates a communal setting for these hymns (5Q511 63–64 iv 3).

- Rule of the Blessings (1QSb). This work is a collection of blessings intended for the end of the days. The addressees include those who fear God, sons of Zadok the priest, a messianic figure (here called the Prince of the Congregation), and the high priest.

These three compositions are closely linked to the Dead Sea Scrolls community. Yet there are also compilations of prayers and prayerlike materials from wider Jewish circles:

- 11QPsalms^a (11Q5). This scroll contains many psalms included in the book of Psalms as we know it from the Jewish and Protestant Bibles. It also features seven other psalm-like compositions. Two of these, a Plea for Deliverance (col. 19) and Syriac Psalm III (or Ps. 154; col. 24) address God directly.
- Scrolls 4Q380 and 4Q381 (4QNon-Canonical Psalms A and B) feature hymns/psalms referring to God in both second and third person. These seem to be ascribed to biblical figures.

One prayer found in 4Q381 is attributed to King Manasseh. In the biblical account, Manasseh, king of Judah, is known as a defiant sinner. No other king sinned as much as he did (2 Chron. 33:1–9). Yet according to 2 Chronicles 33:11–14, when the Assyrian king captured Manasseh and brought him in chains to Babylon, Manasseh entreated the Lord his God and humbled himself greatly before the God of his fathers. Manasseh prayed, and God granted the prayer and returned him to Jerusalem to his kingdom. Then Manasseh knew that the Lord alone was God.

His change of heart is remarkable, and the act of divine mercy is astonishing! If a prayer, prayed by Manasseh of all people, could elicit such divine mercy, other people would surely find it very useful too. However, Chronicles does not supply Manasseh's prayer (2 Chron. 33:18–19). So someone else filled the gap; it is found in 4Q381 (33a, b + 35 8–11). It is a pseudepigraphic prayer, one that was composed by an unknown poet with Manasseh's story in mind.

Once again, the text of the scroll is fragmentary. First comes the ascription, which locates Manasseh's circumstances as captured by the king of Assyria:

Prayer of Manasseh, King of Judah, when the King of Assyria imprisoned him.

In what follows, the speaker, "Manasseh," declares that his salvation is in God's hands. He acknowledges his sins and guilt. He understands that as a result of his actions he will not see the "eternal joy" and his "soul will not see what is good." He also confesses that he did not remember God and did not serve him. This is the entirety of the fragmentary Prayer of Manasseh from Qumran.

Readers of the Apocrypha are, however, familiar with another pseudepigraphic prayer attributed to Manasseh. In this penitential prayer, Manasseh acknowledges divine power as well as immeasurable mercy. He then argues that the righteous have no need for repentance but that repentance has been "appointed" for sinners like himself (Pr. Man. 7). Manasseh's sins are "more in number than the sand of the sea" (v. 9). The speaker declares, "I have sinned, O Lord, I have sinned" (v. 12). He is weighed down by his sins as by iron chains, but he bends "the knee of [his] heart" and implores God's forgiveness (v. 11).

Finally, several compilations of prayers found among the Dead Sea Scrolls create schedules for prayer. These collections reflect attempts to regulate prayer:

- Words of the Luminaries (4Q504–506). This composition offers prayers for one week. These prayers were recited at the change of the luminaries—namely, the sun and the moon. They are communal petitions evoking key biblical events, from creation to the return from the Babylonian exile.
- Daily Prayers (4Q503). This scroll features a routine of daily prayers for the duration of one month. These prayers were to be offered in the morning, the evening, and possibly during the night. Each prayer opens with a blessing of God and concludes by blessing the congregation.
- Prayers for the Festivals (1Q34 + 1Q34bis; 4Q507–509). This highly fragmentary work contains prayers for the festivals. At least one festival is spelled out in full, the Day of Atonement (1Q34 + 1Q34bis 1 + 2 6).
- Songs of the Sabbath Sacrifice (4Q400–407; 11Q17; Mas 1k). This enigmatic composition contains thirteen songs intended for thirteen consecutive Sabbaths. These "songs" are not prayers but rather complex descriptions of the heavenly temple and its angelic priesthood, with a particular emphasis on the angelic praise of God. An underlying idea is that humans can achieve union with angels in worship.

The Dead Sea Scrolls community believed that angels were present in their midst (1QS 11:5–9; 1QSa 2:8–9; 1QM 1:9–12; 7:6; 12:7–9). In the Songs of the Sabbath Sacrifice, the community is envisioned joining the heavenly chorus of angels in praising God (4Q400 2 6–8). Curiously, in this text the community appears to remain silent, as if human speech is inadequate for praising God in the heavenly realms.

Prayer Practices

Early Jewish texts shed light not only on the contents of contemporary prayers but also on a variety of prayer-related practices.

Praying at Specific Times

Several early Jewish writings suggest set times for praying. In the book of Daniel, Daniel prays three times a day (6:10). One of his prayers takes place at the same time as the evening sacrifice in the temple (9:21). A link between an individual prayer and temple sacrifice is suggested also in the book of Judith. Judith prays when the evening incense offering is made in the sanctuary (Jdt. 9:1). Wisdom of Solomon recommends praying at dawn (Wis. 16:28). A custom to bless God after a meal is implied in the book of Jubilees (2:21) and the scroll 4Q370 (4QAdmonFlood 1 1–2).

As to communal prayers, Ben Sira mentions those praying at the temple during the Day of Atonement (Sir. 50:17–19). Baruch refers to "confession" in the temple "on the days of the festivals and at appointed seasons" (1:14). The aforementioned scroll 4Q503 (Daily Prayers) assumes morning and evening prayers (and so also 1QM 14:12–14; 4Q408 [4QapocrMoses^c] 3 + 3a). Several texts from the Dead Sea Scrolls posit a communal prayer before meals (1QS 6:4–6; 10:14–15; 1QSa 2:17–21).

Early Jewish writings also name other circumstances for praying:

- Special days in the Jewish sacred calendar. The prayer routine of the Maskil—an office within the Dead Sea Scrolls community—prescribes prayers on the first day of each season, on the first day of every month, on festival days, and at the beginning of the Sabbatical and Jubilee Years (1QS 10:1–17).
- Protection from demons. In Tobit 8:1–9, Tobias and Sarah seek God's protection from the demon through prayer. Several Dead Sea Scrolls contain apotropaic prayers and incantations against attacks by demons (11Q11 [11QapocrPs]; 4Q444 [4QIncantation]).
- Ritual purification. Several Dead Sea Scrolls outline purification procedures, including prayers for persons who have become ritually impure (4Q284 [4QPurification Liturgy]; 4Q414 [4QRitual of Purification A]; 4Q512 [4QpapRitual of Purification B]).
- Communal rituals. The annual ceremony of renewing the covenant between God and the Dead Sea Scrolls community incorporates a confession and blessings (1QS 1–2). An expulsion of a member from the community also involves a prayer (4Q266 [4QD^a] 11 8–14).

Preparing to Pray

Early Jewish writings name several ways of preparing to pray. Preparations include immersion in water (Jdt. 12:8; ALD 2:4–5), placing ashes on one's head (Jdt. 4:15; 9:1; Add. Esth. C 14:2), wearing sackcloth (Jdt. 4:8–13; 9:1; Bar. 4:20), and fasting (Jdt. 4:9, 13; Bar. 1:5).

Texts also identify various postures for prayer:

- lifting one's face and eyes to heaven (Tob. 3:11–12; ALD 3:1)
- prostration (Sir. 50:17; Jdt. 4:11; 9:1; 2 Macc. 3:15; 10:4; 13:12)
- kneeling (Dan. 6:10; 3 Macc. 2:1)
- stretching hands and fingers to heaven (Sir. 51:19; 2 Macc. 3:20; ALD 3:2; 4Q512 [4QpapRitual of Purification B] 42–44 6)
- directing oneself toward Jerusalem (Dan. 6:10)

New Testament

New Testament writings recognize prayer as a common activity for Jesus-followers. Paul begins six of his seven letters with a prayer of thanksgiving (Rom. 1:8; 1 Cor. 1:4; 2 Cor. 1:3; Phil. 1:3; 1 Thess. 1:2; Philem. 4); the exception is Galatians. Paul is not pleased with the Galatian believers so does not give thanks for them. Elsewhere, he instructs his readers to pray and "with thanksgiving let your requests be made known to God" (Phil. 4:6). He recognizes that prayer can supersede sex "for a set time" (1 Cor. 7:5). He requests prayers for himself from the churches for his safety in his mission work (Rom. 15:30–32; 2 Cor. 1:11).

Elsewhere, New Testament writings urge prayer "at all times" for one another (Eph. 6:18). Jesus-followers are to pray "for one another, so that you may be healed" (James 5:16). Prayer is to be offered with boldness and confidence that God hears petitions according to God's will (1 John 5:14–17). "Prayers, intercessions, and thanksgivings" are to be made "for everyone, for kings and all who are in high positions" (1 Tim. 2:1–2).

New Testament writings also provide teaching about prayer (Mark 11:22–25; Luke 18:1–14; Col. 4:2–4). And Acts regularly presents the church at prayer (2:42): in an upstairs room (1:13–14), in the Jerusalem temple (3:1; 22:17), in houses (9:17; 10:2; 12:12), by a river (16:13, 16), in prison (16:25). Church members pray for divine guidance in selecting a leader (1:24–26; 13:2–3), for divine protection and boldness to speak the good news in a threatening context (4:24–31), for forgiveness of enemies (7:59–60), for healing (9:40; 28:8), for church leaders (14:23), for blessings in departing from a church (20:36; 21:5–6). Evident in these references are prayers of thanksgiving, praise, and petition.

We highlight three New Testament prayers for more detailed discussion.

Mary's Prayer (Luke 1:46–56)

The angel Gabriel has informed Mary of her pregnancy and the identity and roles of her son Jesus (Luke 1:26–38). Her pregnancy is confirmed with her visit to Elizabeth (1:39–45). The forward movement of the plot is now halted with Mary's prayer of praise (1:46–56). Often called the Magnificat, the prayer takes its name from the Latin verb in the first line, "My soul magnifies the Lord." The prayer functions to offer praise to God for God's action, as well as to identify and interpret the nature of that action as a demonstration of God's delivering power.

The prayer aligns with other such expressions of praise for critical divine interventions across the tradition—those of Moses (Exod. 15:1–18), Miriam (Exod. 15:20–21), Deborah and Barak (Judg. 5:1–31), Judith (Jdt. 16:1–17). Especially resonant with Mary's praise is Hannah's prayer in 1 Samuel 2:1–10: "My heart exults in the LORD; / my strength is exalted in my God" (2:1). Both Hannah's prayer and Mary's prayer emphasize the reversal of the sociopolitical status quo and structures that the divine action accomplishes. Hannah prays in language that Mary imitates:

> The bows of the mighty are broken,
>   but the feeble gird on strength.
> ....
> The LORD makes poor and makes rich;
>   he brings low; he also exalts.
> He raises up the poor from the dust,
>   he lifts the needy from the ash heap
> to make them sit with princes
>   and inherit a seat of honor. (1 Sam. 2:4, 7–8)

Mary's praise divides into two halves. Luke 1:47–49 focuses on Mary's circumstances. She sets out two reasons for rejoicing "in God my Savior." First in verse 48, she names God's favor extended to her, on "the lowliness of his servant." The term "lowliness" refers to circumstances of oppression inflicted by foreign powers on Israel. In Mary's context, that oppressive empire is Rome (3:1–2). The liberative nature of the favor will be elaborated in 1:50–55.

Her second reason for rejoicing in God is stated in verse 49. She names God as the "Mighty One," the divine warrior who fights on behalf of Israel against its enemies. Mary's personal circumstances are embedded in and representative of Israel's sociopolitical circumstances.

Verses 50–55 elaborate God's pose toward Israel and, given some undefined language, toward humanity in general. The divine attitude and action are motivated by mercy (1:50). God's action is described as showing "strength with his arm" and takes the form of a societal restructuring in opposing the proud, the powerful, and the wealthy. The corollary of this opposition is the advocacy of a divine reversal of unjust societal and political structures by elevating the lowly and hungry (1:51–53). This action enacts God's merciful commitment to God's covenant with Abraham (1:54–55).

The Lord's Prayer (Matt. 6:9–13)

The New Testament provides two versions of the Lord's Prayer (Matt. 6:9–13; Luke 11:1–4). A comparison of the two versions highlights differences between them. The discussion here focuses on Matthew's account.

The Matthean version of the prayer is part of a discussion of three acts of justice (6:1)—namely, almsgiving, prayer, and fasting (6:2–18). In this section Matthew's Gospel presents how Jesus-followers are to pray by contrasting negative presentations of prayer in synagogues and by gentiles (Greeks, Romans, Syrians, etc.). The verses falsely and nastily accuse Jewish pray-ers in synagogues and on street corners of hypocrisy in praying to be admired by others (6:5). Gentile prayer is disparaged as consisting of "empty phrases" and "many words" (6:7). Neither construction is fair, accurate, or researched. Both are nasty, uncharitable, and self-serving parodies. Their role is to provide contrasts with the supposedly superior prayer practices and identities of Jesus-followers. These followers are to pray in secret, not publicly, and they don't need many words because God already knows what the pray-ers need (6:6, 8).

The Matthean Jesus then instructs his followers how to pray by offering a model prayer. The prayer raises several interpretive questions. *How* is the prayer answered? By God? By those who pray it? Or more likely, by both? And *when* is the prayer answered? In the eschatological future when God establishes the divine purposes in full? Or in the present imperfectly and in part? Or more likely, in both the present and the future?

The prayer begins by addressing God as "our Father in heaven." Addressing God as Father was well established in Early Judaism (Sir. 23:4; 51:10; Tob. 13:4), as was the recognition of heaven as God's dwelling place (Tob. 1:18; 7:12; Jdt. 6:19). Distinctive here is the pronoun "our." The prayer is not that of loyal adherents of father Jupiter/Zeus or of the Roman emperor (known as "father of the fatherland," *pater patriae*), but of adherents of "your Father" (Matt. 6:1) manifested by Jesus (2:15; 3:16). The "our" indicates a communal prayer prayed by a community of God's children. It is an identity-securing address.

The first three petitions request God to act in ways that will transform the imperial world of Roman injustice and establish a world aligned with God's life-giving and just purposes. God's name is hallowed or honored when God acts to free people from oppression (Ezek. 36:22–37). Likewise, when God asserts God's reign or empire, human society is no longer subjugated to oppressive, unjust, and destructive powers and empires. God's will is already established in heaven (Matt. 5:34), so the third petition requests God to extend that reality to earth.

These petitions are answered in both the present and the future and by both God and disciples who live according to Jesus's teaching of the divine will and who enact God's empire or rule in their actions. Yet while the lifestyle of Jesus's followers in the present is crucial as communities manifest the divine purposes, the three petitions have ultimately an eschatological outcome.

After three petitions for God's action, the next four petitions have to do with human concerns (food, forgiveness, testing, evil). The petition for "daily bread" (Matt. 6:11) has provoked much debate. Some have interpreted it as an eschatological reference akin to Isaiah's vision of a celebratory feast for all people (Isa. 25:6–10). But more pressing is the recognition of widespread food insecurity across the Roman Empire, where some 80 percent experienced varying degrees of poverty. The petition seeks the replacement of a system of imperial injustice with one in which the material needs of all are met.

The next petition requests forgiveness for debts. Often the petition is understood as a request for spiritual forgiveness of sins in which personal obligations and commitments have been violated. God's forgiveness mandates and accompanies forgiveness for other people (so also Sir. 28:2).

Yet the language of "forgive" and "debts" also appears in provisions for the Sabbatical Year, when literal debt is to be forgiven (Deut. 15). This intertext suggests societal and economic sin is also in view. Certain economic mechanisms often ensured that poor people were indebted, having to borrow in order to survive. But when crops fail or unemployment happens, loans cannot be repaid. The petition in Matthew seeks divine intervention to end a situation of economic injustice.

The third petition's meaning is similarly debated. The common translation for God not to tempt pray-ers is unconvincing since across the biblical tradition God does allow people to be tempted (Tob. 12:14; Job; Abraham, Gen. 22). A preferable translation is "Do not bring us to the time of trial" (Matt. 6:13). This translation reflects an interpretation shaped by the presence of the language of "time of trial" in the Greek version of Exodus 17:7. In that scene, Israel tests God at Massah by doubting God's presence and ability to deliver the people and supply them with water. The petition in Matthew, then, is a prayer against doubt and despair caused by God's apparent inactivity, powerlessness, absence, and failure to assert God's reign for justice. The petition to not be brought to this time of trial can be answered by divine action.

The final petition in Matthew 6:13 parallels the previous one. God can rescue pray-ers from the evil one by overcoming the strategies, practices, systems, and agents of evil that cause so much injustice and misery among humans. But as long as situations of imperial oppression, domination, and injustice continue, disciples may doubt the divine will and ability to transform the world. The petition is for God to complete God's salvific work.

The prayer constructs a world that recognizes the divine will is not done. Those in the present world lack material needs, are burdened by debts and sin, are dominated by the evil one, and experience doubts and despair about divine inactivity and powerlessness. The pray-ers pray against such a world and seek its transformation. In a world dominated by Roman imperial power—or any hegemony—that benefits ruling elites at the expense of the rest, to pray this prayer is a subversive act. It seeks the demise of all structures and agents of injustice. It constructs the existence and identity of a community of children of God who yearn for a transformation and commit to live accordingly in the meantime and in the hope of the future and full establishment of God's reign.

Jesus Prays (Matt. 27:46)

Just as texts of Early Judaism show key figures like Tobit, Solomon, and Judith praying, so the Gospels present Jesus praying at key moments—at his baptism (Luke 3:21), before choosing his disciples (Luke 6:12), at the transfiguration (Luke 9:28–29), on the Mount of Olives before his arrest and crucifixion (Luke 22:41–46). The Gospels also present several of Jesus's prayers. For example, he gives thanks for God's revelatory work (Matt. 11:25–27) and healing of Lazarus (John 11:41–43). Jesus's longest prayer offers three petitions. He prays for himself (John 17:1–5); then he prays for his disciples, whom he has sent in mission to a hostile world (17:6–19); and finally he prays for future believers, notably their effectiveness and unity (17:20–26).

One of Jesus's shortest prayers occurs in the passion narrative as he dies on the cross: "My God, my God, why have you forsaken me?" (Matt. 27:46). This short prayer cites the opening verse of Psalm 22, a psalm of lament. In lament psalms, a person who is faithful to God laments or complains to God about the hostile reactions from some enemies (e.g., Ps. 22:6–8, 12–18). The psalmist also complains that God does not respond or provide deliverance from these enemies (e.g., Ps. 22:2, 11, 19–22). But at the end of the psalm, God abandons passivity and springs into action to deliver the psalmist. The psalm ends with the psalmist giving thanks to God (22:22–31).

By praying the opening verse of Psalm 22, Jesus is constructed as someone who is faithful to God, who experiences murderous opposition from enemies, along with God's absence in his crucifixion. It is the latter experience that verse 1 of the psalm highlights. Jesus cries out for divine intervention. The irony is that he addresses his lament that God has forsaken him to the God whom he experiences as having forsaken him. But as the psalm concludes,

God is present to vindicate the psalmist. Likewise, God vindicates the crucified Jesus in resurrection.

This recognition that vindication follows abandonment in Psalm 22, and that resurrection follows crucifixion in the Gospel passion narrative, highlights an important insight about Jesus's use of Psalm 22:1 as a short prayer. This one verse is not the only echo of Psalm 22 in Matthew 27; the passion narrative evokes the use of the whole psalm. Other details connect Psalm 22 and the passion narrative. Jesus is surrounded throughout by enemies who seek and accomplish his death (Matt. 27:1–3; Ps. 22:12–13, 16–18). They divide his clothing (Matt. 27:35; Ps. 22:18), shake their heads at him (Matt. 27:39; Ps. 22:7), and mock and deride him (Matt. 27:41–43; Ps. 22:6–8). He is surrounded by evildoers (Matt. 27:38, 44; Ps. 22:16). And Matthew 28 narrates his vindication in resurrection.

Jesus's brief prayer in the words of Psalm 22:1 therefore has multiple functions. It exhibits Jesus the Jew as a pray-er. He draws on one of Israel's psalms for his prayer. The prayer constructs him as one who experiences God-forsakenness. Yet by quoting the opening line of Psalm 22, Jesus's prayer evokes the narrative of the whole psalm, which comprises faithfulness to God, sociopolitical hostility, the experience of divine abandonment, and the experience of vindication. In turn, evoking the psalm functions as an important intertext for the passion and resurrection narratives.

Matters for Reflection

1. The prayers of Early Judaism are diverse and frequent. What sorts of prayers are prayed, in what contexts, and concerning what matters?
2. Name early attempts to set the time and wording of Jewish communal prayer.
3. What early Jewish practices related to prayer appear also in New Testament writings?
4. In what ways are the prayers in the New Testament similar or different from those early Jewish practices?

CHAPTER 13

People: Women and Non-Jews/Gentiles

In the previous chapters we have addressed some troubling misunderstandings and misrepresentations of Early Judaism by Christians, and we have troubled these misunderstandings by drawing attention to continuities—and some discontinuities—between texts from Early Judaism and the New Testament. In this final chapter we trouble some Christian misunderstandings of two groups: Jewish women and non-Jews/gentiles. We provide some better-informed correctives even as we also recognize considerable ambivalence in the presentations of these groups.

Women

Among some Christian groups and students in our classes, misunderstandings about the roles of women in the time of Jesus abound, such as the following:

- Jewish women were restricted to their homes, were not permitted to appear in public, and were certainly not permitted to speak with men.
- Jewish women were not permitted to own property, bear witness in court, or teach Torah.
- Women were subject to oppressive purity laws concerning menstruation and childbirth.
- Jesus's treatment of women was regarded as radically liberative, even scandalously so.

Some Christians have seen Jesus as the liberator of Jewish women, setting them free from their terrible lot. In fact, Jesus's treatment of women was fairly typical of the mixed attitudes and practices of the time.

Women in Early Judaism

Most of those who wrote and copied early Jewish literature were males. And most of these males belonged to the elites who had the time, skill, and means for such literary activities as well as an interest in preserving male privileges. This situation was not unique to Jews; it was common for Hellenistic and Roman cultures.

Male-authored sources offer us a range of views on women. Some are positive; others, from a modern reader's perspective, are misogynistic.

For instance, Ben Sira, a wisdom teacher from Jerusalem, claims,

> It is a disgrace to be the father of an undisciplined son,
>   and the birth of a daughter is a loss.
> A sensible daughter obtains a husband of her own,
>   but one who acts shamefully is a grief to her father.
> An impudent daughter disgraces father and husband
>   and is despised by both. (Sir. 22:3–5)

Ben Sira's perspective focuses on the father. As far as he is concerned, a daughter who does not conform to male expectations is "impudent" and disgraces him. Ben Sira is concerned for the father's honor, not the daughter's well-being. Sira blames the first woman, Eve, for human sin:

> From a woman sin had its beginning, and because of her we all die. (25:24)

Ben Sira also praises the "good wife," though his focus is on the wife bringing status and honor to the husband and not on her own accomplishments and satisfaction:

> Happy is the husband of a good wife;
>   the number of his days will be doubled.
> A courageous wife brings joy to her husband,
>   and he will complete his years in peace.
> A good wife is a good portion;
>   she will be granted as a portion to the man who fears the Lord.
> Whether rich or poor, his heart is content,
>   and at all times his face is cheerful. (Sir. 26:1–4)

Statements denigrating women are frequent also in the writings of Philo:

A wife is a selfish creature, excessively jealous and adept at beguiling the morals of her husband and seducing him by her continued impostures. (*Hypoth.* 11.14)

In Philo's view, an ideal wife is

- best suited for indoor life and careful not to show herself in public;
- not a busybody;
- reluctant to intervene in her husband's conflicts with others; and
- careful not to assume men's roles during war or an emergency. (*Spec. Laws* 3.169–74)

Philo came from a wealthy and powerful family. The lifestyle he envisions here expresses a male fantasy and does not reflect the lives of most women who were non-elite women. They were not restricted to houses but had public agency and roles.

Philo describes an ideal Jewish community, which he calls Therapeutae. This community includes men and women identified as Therapeutrides. Their gatherings conclude with a reenactment of the Israelites' singing after the crossing of the Red Sea (Exod. 15). Both male and female members of the community participate in this singing, and both groups experience spiritual ecstasy (*Contempl. Life* 83–89).

> Philo was a Jew who lived in first-century CE Alexandria. In his many writings, Philo explains the Torah using tools and ideas borrowed from Hellenistic philosophy.

Josephus's statements on women are also ambivalent. Some are offensive even if they have some resonance in some contemporary cultures. Writing about the Torah's view on marriage, he claims,

> The woman, says the Law, is in all things inferior to the man. Let her accordingly be submissive, not for her humiliation, but that she may be directed; for the authority has been given by God to the man. (*Ag. Ap.* 2.201)

He also posits that women can't serve as witnesses in a court (*Ant.* 4.219). This claim, however, is not accurate, as one of the Dead Sea Scrolls relies on women as witnesses against their husbands (1QSa 1:11).

Yet Josephus also writes about the powerful, elite women of the ruling Hasmonean and Herodian families. These women exercised agency and power in political life. One of the Hasmonean women was Queen Alexandra, who ruled Judea for nine years (76–67 BCE) after the death of her husband, Alexander Jannaeus (*Ant.* 13.398–432). Subsequently, Herodias married Herod Antipas, and when John the Baptist criticized the marriage as unlawful, Herodias and Antipas executed John (Josephus, *Ant.* 18.116–19; Matt. 14:1–12). Another Herodian woman, the sister of Agrippa II named Bernice, had an affair with

Titus, the Roman emperor (79–81 CE). Josephus also tells us about Queen Helene of Adiabene (*Ant.* 20.17), who was one of a number of elite female sympathizers and converts into Judaism.

Other early Jewish writings feature a series of memorable female figures who are typically described as beautiful and pious. For example, Esther became queen of Persia. In a context of hostile opposition to Jews, she used her position and risked her life to save her people.

There is also Ruth the Moabite, who was admirably loyal to her mother-in-law and who, through a levirate marriage to Boaz, became King David's ancestor.

In Genesis Apocryphon, Sarah, Abraham's wife, is a somewhat complex character, exhibiting fear, wisdom, intellectual insight, forethought, and skillfulness. A lengthy passage describes her great beauty (1QapGen 20:1–8), which serves to emphasize her attractiveness to various men and her main value as Abraham's sexual partner.

Susanna of the apocryphal story bearing her name also has to negotiate male lust. Two judges seek to seduce her. Unsuccessful, they condemn her to death, yet God hears her fervent prayer for vindication and answers instantly (Sus. 42–44). The corrupt judges are put to death.

In the book of Tobit, Tobit's daughter-in-law Sarah has had a tragic life. A demon Asmodeus has killed each of her seven husbands on their wedding night. Sarah is accused of murdering her husbands. She prays, God answers, Sarah marries Tobit's son Tobias, and the demon is exorcised from her (Tob. 3:11–17).

The book of Judith introduces a brave and pious widow whose name, Judith, means, quite simply, "a Jewess." She competently manages her own affairs. She regularly purifies herself by immersion in water (Jdt. 9). She prays (chap. 9) and eats only kosher foods (chap. 10). When the men fail to protect her and her city against the invading Assyrians, she takes agency, formulates a plan, courageously enters the enemy's camp, cunningly seduces the Assyrian general Holofernes, and kills him.

Also showing great courage and faithfulness is the mother of the seven sons tortured on the orders of the Hellenistic king Antiochus IV Epiphanes. The sons refuse to obey the king's orders to break the law and eat pig's meat. Their mother watches as her sons are tortured and slaughtered. She encourages them to stand firm, knowing that God will raise them from the dead. Having seen the death of her sons, she, too, dies as a martyr (2 Macc. 7).

Finally, some data point to women participating in civic affairs. Several early Jewish texts speak of women as the breadwinners of the family (Tob. 2:11). The archives of Babatha and Salome Komaise found in the Judean

Desert indicate that women could divorce their husbands and own real estate. Women took part in town affairs (Jdt. 6:16) and community meetings (1QSa 1:4–5). The Dead Sea Scrolls group endowed certain "mothers" with some authority (4Q270 [4QD^c] 7 i 13–15). And in the second temple, which was rebuilt by Herod, a special space was provided for Jewish women to worship. It was called the Court of Women (Josephus, *J.W.* 5.198–99).

Women in the Early Jesus-Movement

The New Testament texts reflect the same gender dynamics as are evident in the texts of Early Judaism. While society was patriarchal and organized by and for the benefit of men, women had a variety of roles and a substantial presence and agency in the public domain.

For example, Jesus feeds a large crowd comprising at least five thousand people. The Gospel text notes that the total did not include the women and children who were also present (Matt. 14:21). That verse expresses the pervasive patriarchy in counting the men, even as it acknowledges the presence of women.

In other scenes, women exercise agency for their lives and are present in the public domain. A woman approaches Jesus in public to procure healing for her demon-possessed daughter (Matt. 15:22). Jesus's mother attends a wedding with him and, presumably, with other women, including a bride! And when the wine runs out, she takes the initiative to ensure Jesus does something about it (John 2:1–11).

Another woman who "had been suffering from hemorrhages for twelve years" touches Jesus's cloak in the midst of a crowd (Mark 5:25–27). There is no mention of her being escorted or "protected" by a man, nor is there mention of concerns about purity, no requirement that she should have stayed at home or should have been shouting "Impure," no ban on her touching Jesus, no identification of the reason for her bleeding. Christian interpreters supply such elements to frame the scene negatively.

Rather, she is a woman with agency who has some resources. No husband or father is mentioned. She has engaged "many physicians." She has "spent all that she had" in seeking her own healing. Now she approaches Jesus in public, touches his garment, and seeks healing from him.

Where did her economic resources come from? Other evidence, such as business documents, attests to women running businesses, receiving inheritances, owning property. As did women across the ancient world, Jewish women worked in providing products (jewels, cloth, garments, perfume, food, pottery) and selling services (food, grooming, hairdressing, childcare, medical care, midwifery, sex work). They also provided labor and knowledge in agricultural work. And married women had marriage contracts called "ketuboth," which protected them economically if they divorced.

Mary and Martha seem to own their own home in a village (Luke 10:38). They welcome Jesus and provide hospitality. There's no reference to any domestic help. The absence of the latter might suggest that while they had some property, they were not very wealthy. The parable of the woman who loses a coin indicates she has a house, some money—though not an abundant amount since she searches for a lost coin—and friends who gather with her to celebrate (Luke 15:8–10).

Some other women seem to have considerable wealth. A group of women accompanied Jesus and the male disciples in public on travels through cities and villages (Luke 8:2–3). They provided for them "out of their own resources." Supplying food and other necessities for a group implies that they had and controlled some level of economic resources. Three women are named, two without any connection to a husband or father. A third, Joanna, is identified as the wife of Chuza, the steward of the ruler Herod. That link suggests she had some status and wealth.

As companions of Jesus and the disciples, these women accompanied Jesus into synagogues, where women customarily gathered with men. And women play an important role as witnesses to Jesus's resurrection and are entrusted with its proclamation to the male disciples (Matt. 28:7–10, 16).

What is significant about these scenes—and there are others—is that none of them is remarkable concerning the roles of women. The only surprise might be for contemporary (mis)interpreters who hold uninformed stereotypes about subjugated Jewish women. As a male, Jesus's interaction with women was typical and neither radical nor revolutionary.

Jesus's record, however, is not unblemished. He chooses an inner group comprising only male followers. A gentile woman approaches Jesus to request healing/exorcism for her demon-possessed daughter (Mark 7:25–26). Jesus has retreated from the public and is not at all receptive to her approach (7:24). He rejects her request by imaging the woman and her daughter as dogs (that's like calling a woman in our time a bitch). Some male interpreters have tried (and failed) to defend Jesus by downplaying the offensiveness of the comparison. It is not a joke or an endearment. It is offensive, indefensible, and unacceptable for a male to use this language for a woman. Nor is the scene rehabilitated when the woman turns the image back on Jesus and outwits him so that he carries out her wishes and heals the daughter (7:28–30).[1]

---

1. The discussion of the scene is rich and complex. See Warren Carter, *Mark*, Wisdom Commentary 42 (Collegeville, MN: Liturgical Press, 2019), 187–200.

Women in Paul

Paul attests leadership roles for women in the Jesus-communities. There are women who pray and prophesy in the worship of the Corinthian Jesus-assembly (1 Cor. 11:5). In Romans 16, Paul greets several women whom he describes as working hard in the gospel work: Prisca (16:3); Mary (16:6); Junia, one of the apostles (16:7); Tryphaena and Tryphosa (16:12); Persis (16:12); and Julia (16:15). Several of these women are Jews (Prisca, Mary, Junia), and several have names commonly used for slaves (Junia, Persis, Julia). Paul uses the verb "work" to describe his own ministry of preaching, church planting, and pastoral work (1 Cor. 15:10; Gal. 4:11). This use suggests these women also undertook these ministry and leadership roles.

Again, there is nothing remarkable about these roles. Jewish women exercised leadership in synagogues. And non-Jewish women exercised leadership in various groups and civic enterprises.

A further emphasis in some New Testament texts is consistent with another cultural attitude to women: that of a patriarchal society, which readily asserts the power and interests of men at the expense of women.

First Corinthians 14:34–35 teaches that "women should be silent in the churches. For they are not permitted to speak but should be subordinate. . . . For it is shameful for a woman to speak in church." The verses are much debated. There is considerable doubt that Paul wrote these words. More important, they do not fit the context of the verses on either side of them. If they were removed, the verses before and after them would form a good sequence. And they contradict what Paul previously said in recognizing that women pray and prophesy in the communities (1 Cor. 11:5; cf. Rom. 16). Probably, then, the verses were added later by someone who wanted to maintain cultural patriarchal structures and reinforce male power against Paul's affirmation that all, men and women, are gifted for the good of the Jesus-communities.

With their emphasis on the silenced, subordinate women, the verses are consistent with passages in some later New Testament texts attributed to Paul but not written by Paul. These later New Testament texts seek to restrict the roles and appearance of women; they advocate modest dress, minimal adornment, silence and submission to men, responsibility for the existence of sin, domestication, and the bearing of children (1 Tim. 2:8–15). Ephesians (5:22–33) and Colossians (3:18) employ household codes known since Aristotle and among Jewish writers like Josephus and Philo to authorize the submission of women to men. These New Testament texts co-opt cultural values of misogyny and patriarchy to claim divine sanction for male superiority and the subjugation of women.

Such ambivalence toward women and their roles cannot function to justify continued patriarchy and misogyny.

Gentiles/Non-Jews

Some Christians have understood Judaism to be exclusive and excluding. Jews were the chosen covenant people, so the claim is made, distinct from and uninterested in all other nations ("the gentiles") with their practices of idolatry. While Jewish attitudes to non-Jews or "the nations" in early Jewish literature and the Hebrew Bible were ambivalent and not uniform, a strong tradition affirmed gentile inclusion in the divine purposes.

For example, there were non-Jews who lived among Israel. Torah calls them "alien" residents and commands the Israelites to love them as themselves (Lev. 19:34). At the same time, it demands an annihilation of certain Canaanite nations and prohibits intermarrying with them (Deut. 7:1–3). These emphases attest a deep suspicion of the nations as a corrupting influence that would lead Israel to idolatry (Deut. 7:4) and into their immoral behavior (Lev. 18:1–30).

Or again, biblical prophets speak of the future divine judgment on the nations (Jer. 10:25) yet also envision a time when they will recognize the true God and learn God's ways (Isa. 2:1–4; Mic. 4:1–4). After the exile, prophetic voices call Israel to be "a light to the nations" (Isa. 42:6; 49:6) and to welcome foreigners who "hold fast" to God's covenant (Isa. 56:3–7). And at the same time, Ezra and Nehemiah condemn mingling and intermarrying with the "peoples of the land" (Ezra 9:1–2).

Gentiles/Non-Jews in Early Judaism

Early Jewish writings express similar diverse attitudes toward non-Jews. Their authors negotiated non-Jews while living in a world in which Jews were subjected to foreign imperial powers. These texts construct Jewish experiences ranging from peaceful coexistence to deadly persecution.

Instances of these negotiations are everywhere in the early Jewish literature. Here we can provide only a few examples.

In the book of Jubilees, God chooses Israel at the creation of the world (Jub. 2:21). Israel is God's "treasured people from all the nations," the "firstborn son" whom God has "sanctified" to be in covenant relationship with God. God expresses favor for Israel in appointing "spirits"—demons—to rule over all the nations "to lead them astray." However, this is not the case with Israel. Over them, God has "made no angel or a spirit to rule because he alone is their ruler" (15:31–32).

All this, argues Jubilees, requires Israel's separation from the nations. On his deathbed, Abraham commands Jacob,

> Separate from the nations, and do not eat with them. Do not act as they do and do not become their companion, for their actions are something that is impure

and all their ways are defiled and something abominable and detestable. . . .
Be careful, my son Jacob, not to marry a woman from all the descendants of
Canaan's daughters. (Jub. 22:16, 20)

The separation means avoiding eating with the non-Jews; not acting as they do, especially not worshiping idols; and not intermarrying.

These three behaviors that mark a Jewish way of life and identity separate from non-Jews recur in many early Jewish texts.

- Bel and the Dragon, Letter of Jeremiah, and Wisdom of Solomon attack the folly of worshiping idols.
- Jubilees, Tobit (4:12), Genesis Apocryphon (6:6–8), Testament of Kohath (4Q542 1 i 5, 9), and Visions of Amram (4Q543 1a–c 5–6) promote marrying only one's kin.
- Daniel 1, Tobit 1:11, and Letter of Aristeas 142 emphasize the avoidance of nonkosher foods.

As a contrast with Jubilees' demand for separation from the nations, some Jews exhorted a very different relationship to the nations:

> Let us go and make a covenant with the nations around us, for since we separated from them many disasters have come upon us. (1 Macc. 1:11)

This is not the only attitude to the nations in 1 Maccabees, but the text claims that "many" Jews subscribed to it.

Like 1 Maccabees, other texts offer different perspectives within the same text. The Letter of Aristeas, for example, explains that the divine laws given through Moses created a barrier, "iron walls," "a fence" between Israel and all other nations:

> Therefore the lawgiver [i.e., Moses] . . . fenced us around with unbroken palisades and with iron walls so that we might not intermingle at all with any other nations. (Let. Aris. 139)

These "iron walls" protect Israel

> so that [they] might not become perverted, being polluted by nothing or associating with worthless people. (Let. Aris. 142)

Yet at the same time, the Letter of Aristeas presents Jews responding positively to the invitation from the Hellenistic ruler of Egypt to go to Egypt and translate Hebrew Scriptures into Greek. The ruler is well-disposed toward the receptive Jews. He releases Jewish captives, offers generous hospitality to the translators, and puts the translations in his library.

Another pattern of Jewish interaction with gentiles is evident in 3 Maccabees. Unlike in the Letter of Aristeas, in 3 Maccabees the Hellenistic king seeks to destroy the Jews. The book reports "a hostile rumor" that Jews "hindered others from the observance of their customs" (3:2), stood out in their "worship and foods," and were disloyal to the king (3:6–7).

How do Jews respond? Third Maccabees says,

> The Jews, however, continued to maintain goodwill and unswerving loyalty toward the dynasty, but because they worshiped God and conducted themselves by his law, they kept their separateness with respect to foods. For this reason they appeared hateful to some, but since they adorned their style of life with the good deeds of upright people, they were established in good repute with everyone. (3 Macc. 3:3–5)

Note that 3 Maccabees carefully differentiates between "some" non-Jews who believed the harmful gossip about the Jews (3:6–7) and other non-Jewish citizens who held Jews "in good repute." Third Maccabees goes on to note significant interaction between Jews and gentiles and to praise those gentiles who offered help:

> And already some of their neighbors and friends and business associates had taken some of them aside privately and were pledging to protect them and to do everything in their power to help. (3 Macc. 3:10)

We have come a long way from the Jubilees' demand for a complete separation from the nations to Jewish-gentile cooperation, both in good times (being neighbors and business associates) and bad times (non-Jews offering protection).

While 3 Maccabees highlights the gentiles' appreciation for Jewish good citizenship, other early Jewish sources speak of non-Jews being attracted to Jewish beliefs and their way of life. Josephus argues that Judaism welcomed newcomers:

> The consideration given by our legislator (Moses) to the equitable treatment of aliens also merits attention. It will be seen that he took the best of all possible measures at once to secure our own customs from corruption, and to throw them open ungrudgingly to any who elect to share them. To all who desire to come and live under the same laws with us, he gives a gracious welcome, holding that it is not family ties alone which constitute relationship, but agreement in the principles of conduct. (*Ag. Ap.* 2.209–10)

He adds,

> We, on the contrary, while we have no desire to emulate the customs of others, yet gladly welcome any who wishes to share our own. That, I think, may be taken as a proof both of humanity and magnanimity. (*Ag. Ap.* 2.261)

Josephus reports many varied expressions of gentile interest in Judaism that Jews readily received. He tells of non-Jews visiting the Jerusalem temple and offering sacrifices there (*J.W.* 4.324; 5.15–18). He reports of non-Jews—often kings and dignitaries—providing financial support for the Jerusalem temple (*Ant.* 12.141). Some non-Jews, both wealthy (*Ant.* 20.195) and simple folks (*J.W.* 2.259–61), observed some aspects of Judaism, such as Sabbath (*Ag. Ap.* 2.282–84). And finally, there were those who embraced the Jewish way of life. The sources call them "proselytes" or converts.

Readers of the Bible will recall the story of Ruth the Moabite, who adopted the Israelite way of life and became the great-grandmother of King David (Ruth 4). Scholars think that this story reflects a wider phenomenon of gentile conversion to Judaism. In fact, Josephus boasts that there were "many" who agreed "to adopt our laws" (*Ag. Ap.* 2.123–24). The most famous converts he knew of were the members of the royal family of the ancient kingdom of Adiabene (*Ant.* 20.17–96).

Proselytes are mentioned in multiple early Jewish texts (e.g., Tob. 1:8; Jdt. 14:10).

Philo, in particular, celebrates the attractiveness of Judaism to gentiles. How reflective of actual circumstances Philo's claims might be is another matter. Nevertheless, he speaks at length about the interest that non-Jews showed in Jewish laws and about how some non-Jews even followed some Jewish laws, such as the Sabbath and the Day of Atonement:

> They attract and win the attention of all, of barbarians, of Greeks, of dwellers on the mainland and islands, of nations of the east and the west, of Europe and Asia, of the whole inhabited world from end to end. For, who has not shown his high respect for that sacred seventh day, by giving rest and relaxation from labor to himself and his neighbors, freemen and slaves alike, and beyond these to his beasts? . . . Again, who does not every year show awe and reverence for the fast? (*Moses* 2.20–24)

He argues that Jews should hold receptive and open gentiles as the "dearest friends and closest kinsmen":

> So therefore, all these who did not at the first acknowledge their duty to reverence the Founder and Father of all, yet afterwards embraced the creed of one instead of a multiplicity of sovereigns, must be held to be our dearest friends

and closest kinsmen. They have shown the godliness of heart which above all leads up to friendship and affinity, and we must rejoice with them, as if, though blind at the first they had recovered their sight and had come from the deepest darkness to behold the most radiant light. (*Virtues* 179)

Finally, Philo envisions a time when all the nations will embrace Judaism:

I believe that each nation would abandon its peculiar ways, and, throwing overboard their ancestral customs, turn to honouring our laws alone. For, when the brightness of their shining is accompanied by national prosperity, it will darken the light of the others as the risen sun darkens the stars. (*Moses* 2.44)

A tangible expression of a welcoming attitude toward non-Jews was the special area or outer court of the second temple, which was rebuilt by King Herod, where non-Jews were allowed (Josephus, *Ag. Ap.* 2.103). A stone tablet inscribed in Greek—now in the Istanbul Archaeological Museums—warned the non-Jewish visitors against trespassing the limits of that area (see fig. 13.1). Not everyone was happy with the gentile involvement with the temple. A text from the Dead Sea Scrolls community, 4QMMT (4Q394 3–7 i 11–12), seems to oppose gentile gifts to the temple.

The book of Tobit also argues that in the end of the days all the nations will turn to Israel's God:

Then all the nations in the whole world will all be converted and will truly fear God. They will all abandon all their idols who deceitfully have led them into their error, and in righteousness they will praise the eternal God. (Tob. 14:6–7)

The Animal Apocalypse seems to go one step further, claiming that at some point in the eschatological drama the very distinction between Jews and non-Jews will disappear (1 En. 90:38).

Still other sources, such as Psalms of Solomon, include gentiles in the eschatological future, on the one hand (17:31–34), yet also completely exclude them, on the other. A time will come when Israel will dwell in the land, "and no resident alien and foreigner shall sojourn with them any longer" (Pss. Sol. 17:28). The same two groups, foreigners and proselytes, are excluded from the eschatological temple in 4QFlorilegium, a text composed by the Dead Sea Scrolls community (4Q174 1–2 i 3–4).

Figure 13.1. A warning on the Jerusalem temple: "Let no foreigner enter within the parapet and the partition which surrounds the Temple precincts. Anyone caught [violating] will be held accountable for his ensuing death."

onceinawhile / CC BY-SA 3.0 / Wikimedia Commons

Gentiles/Non-Jews in the New Testament

While the beginnings of the Jesus-movement centered on Galilee and Judea with Jewish followers, soon non-Jews joined the movement. Controversy resulted among Jesus-followers over the interactions of Jewish Jesus-followers with gentile Jesus-followers and what practices were expected of the latter.

PETER VERSUS PAUL

A major clash took place in Antioch over Jewish followers and gentile followers eating together (Gal. 2:11–14). Jerusalem-based Jesus-followers under the leadership of James decided that shared meals were not acceptable. James's representatives persuaded Peter, Barnabas, and other Jewish Jesus-believers to stop the practice and separate themselves from gentile Jesus-followers. Paul was furious with this division and considered Peter's retreat from shared meals a violation of the gospel.

What was the fight about?[2]

Particular food practices had long marked Jewish identity. There were forbidden foods like pigs. Slaughtering animals required the draining of blood. Jews living among gentiles generally avoided food that might have been offered to gentile idols. Faithfulness to these practices was courageously demonstrated in the 160s BCE when the Seleucid/Syrian tyrant Antiochus IV Epiphanes tried to ban these practices prescribed by Torah. Stories reinforced separation from gentile food and eating with gentiles (Dan. 1:8–16; Tob. 1:10–15; Jdt. 10:5; 12:1–20; 2 Macc. 7; Jub. 22:16, "Eat not with them").

---

2. This section is informed by James D. G. Dunn, *The Epistle to the Galatians*, Black's New Testament Commentaries (London: A. & C. Black, 1993), 115–31.

It would be easy to conclude that all Jews rejected sharing meals with gentiles. But human interactions and social practices are not so neat. No doubt there was a variety of practice, with some being very strict and others more relaxed. Gentiles and Jews interacted with one another in cities across the Roman Empire. As we have seen, some gentiles were drawn to synagogue communities and practices (Josephus, *Ag. Ap.* 2.282; *J.W.* 7.45). Some gentiles adopted Jewish practices of food selection and preparation and shared in meals. Conversely, Jews living in the diaspora mixed with gentiles in various socioeconomic contexts. No doubt some did not hesitate to share meals with gentiles.

Peter's eating with gentile converts in Antioch, then, is not surprising. Why the backlash from James and other Jewish Jesus-followers in Jerusalem? Perhaps they were worried that the removal of all markers of Jewish identity would mean the loss of the tradition of Jewish separation from gentiles. Restoring separate meals ensured Jewish Jesus-believers would honor their traditions and identity. Their desire to maintain separate eating suggests they saw two distinct groups of Jesus-followers based on ethnicity.

Why was Paul appalled? Perhaps because he emphasized the unity of communities of Jesus-believers, whether Jewish or gentile, much more than James seems to have thought. Paul seems to have seen one movement, in which gentile believers belonged to the God of Israel but were not required to take on Jewish identity expressed in markers such as food purity practices.

Likewise, Paul indicated to the Corinthian and Roman believers that conscience should guide them regarding food offered to idols. They could eat this meat as long as other believers were not scandalized (1 Cor. 8–10; Rom. 14). And when he heard of nasty fights among Jesus-believers in Rome over observance of food laws, Sabbaths, and festivals, he urged them to respect diverse approaches to these practices. Faithfulness to Jesus, not adopting Jewish identity markers, ensures gentile participation in the people of God. He did not argue against Jewish Jesus-followers continuing these practices, but he did not think them necessary for gentile believers (Rom. 14:1–15:13).

The same logic seems to inform Paul's attitude to circumcision. He argues strongly in Galatians that male gentile Jesus-followers do not need to be circumcised. Faithfulness to Jesus, not adopting markers of Jewish identity such as circumcision or food purity observance, integrate gentiles into the people of God.

Paul, of course, describes himself as an apostle to the gentiles (Rom. 1:5; 16:26). His priority was not with Jews who were born into God's covenant and guided in faithful living by the Torah. Paul's focus was on how gentiles were included in the purposes of the God of Israel without converting to the practices of Judaism.

Paul was convinced that God is the God of all people, both Jews and gentiles:

> Or is God the God of Jews only? Is he not the God of gentiles also? Yes, of gentiles also, since God is one. (Rom. 3:29–30)

God relates with both Jews and gentiles through faithfulness:

> And he will justify (set in right relationship) the circumcised (Jews) on the ground of faithfulness and the uncircumcised (gentiles) through that same faithfulness. (Rom. 3:30, authors' trans.)

Accordingly, Paul is adamant that gentile inclusion does not mean Jews are excluded from the divine purposes. Both are included:

> I want you to understand this mystery . . . : a hardening has come upon part of Israel until the full number of the gentiles has come in. And in this way all Israel will be saved. . . . For the gifts and the calling of God are irrevocable. . . . For God has imprisoned all in disobedience so that he may be merciful to all. (Rom. 11:25–26, 29, 32)

Gospels

The Gospels were written several decades after Paul's letters. A couple of them were probably written for largely gentile audiences. They largely assume that both Jews and gentiles are welcome in the Jesus-movement. Mark's Jesus announces that before his return, "the good news must first be proclaimed to all nations" (Mark 13:10). Matthew's Jesus initially says his mission is only to Israel (15:24), but subsequently the risen Jesus commands his disciples, "Go therefore and make disciples of all nations" (Matt. 28:19). Luke's Gospel has a sequel in which the Spirit empowers followers to worldwide mission: "You will be my witnesses in Jerusalem, in all Judea and Samaria, and to the ends of the earth" (Acts 1:8–9). John's risen Jesus declares, "As the Father has sent me (in mission into the world), so I send you (in mission into the world)" (John 20:21, authors' trans.).

While these instructions are clear, we must remember that we do not know the stories behind the texts. Did readers of the Gospels, Jews and gentiles, readily agree and obey? Or did some dissent? Are the commands so clear precisely because there were disagreements about who should be included and on what basis? Or do they reinforce widespread understandings and practices?

Matters for Reflection

1. In light of the content in this chapter, how would you describe the roles of women in Early Judaism?
2. How do the views on women in early Jewish writings relate to those of the New Testament texts?
3. In light of the content in this chapter, how would you describe understandings of gentiles in Early Judaism?
4. Are these understandings reflected also in the New Testament?

Postscript

Thirteen chapters.
    Thirteen essays (of) troubling misunderstandings.
    We could readily continue with thirteen more.
    It would be facile to claim that Christian interpreters alone are responsible for constructing these troubling misunderstandings of Early Judaism. While there is some truth in this claim, it overlooks the contribution of the New Testament texts themselves. As we have seen,

- New Testament texts claim Jews crucified Jesus.
- New Testament texts call Jews children of the devil.
- New Testament texts declare salvation exists only through Jesus.
- New Testament texts insist on prayer only in Jesus's name.

We can understand the circumstances in which such claims were made, and we can appreciate how they functioned to shape the identity of the early Jesus-movement by defining other Jews negatively. But in order not to continue these hateful constructions, it is equally important for us as readers and interpreters of these texts to bring informed understandings, discerning spirits, charitable mindsets, and expansive hearts to our readings of the texts.
    We invite you to explore other beliefs and practices that early Jewish texts and New Testament writings share. The bibliography we provide in the following pages is a good start.
    We believe that such exploration is crucial for better understanding of both Judaism and Christianity. It is critical for identifying (and) troubling misunderstandings.

In a world in which antisemitism continues to threaten our humanity, it is something we must do.

We began this book by evoking images of Ecclesia and Synagoga. Several of those images showed hostile interactions. But one recent image, displayed on the cover of this book, is marked by a different interaction—one of mutuality, respect, and partnership. The friendly conversation between the two in this latter image is possible only through informed understandings of the troubling misunderstandings that made the vicious images possible for hundreds of years.

APPENDIX

The Dead Sea Scrolls and Hungry Caterpillars

When we cite Dead Sea Scrolls in this book, we use several scholarly conventions. These conventions can be confusing.

Convention 1. Some writings found among Dead Sea Scrolls have several names. One example is one of the compositions we cite often in this book—Community Rule. Scholars also refer to it as Serekh HaYahad, a Hebrew name meaning the "Rule of the Yahad." This Hebrew name is commonly abbreviated as "S."

Convention 2. Scholars use numbers and letters to refer to individual Dead Sea Scrolls:

- Numbers refer to the cave in which a scroll was found;
- Numbers are assigned to a scroll.

For example, 1Q33 stands for a scroll that was found in Cave 1 at Qumran; its number is 33. What is not so simple is that, in addition to 1Q33, this composition also has two names, one in Hebrew and one in English. The Hebrew name is Milhamah ("war"). In English it is often called the War Scroll. That is why scroll 1Q33 is frequently referenced as 1QMilhamah or simply 1QM.

Throughout this book we tried to provide both the number and the name of each scroll we cite.

What happens if scholars publish a given scroll but later identify another fragment that belongs to it? In some cases they give the newly identified fragment the same scroll number but add the French word "bis." To tell the reader that they belong to one and the same scroll, we refer to them as follows: 1Q34 + 1Q34bis.

Convention 3. When we quote from the Bible, we usually use chapter and verse. This method does not work for the Dead Sea Scrolls. Ancient scribes organized these writings into columns; columns comprise lines. So numbers in Dead Sea Scrolls citations also indicate columns and lines. For example, 1QM 1:2 refers to the copy of the War Scroll from Qumran Cave 1, column 1, line 2.

Often, all we have left of a given scroll are fragments. Each fragment is assigned a number. The designation 4Q161 (4QpIsa^a) 8–10 15–29, for example, stands for a scroll from Qumran Cave 4; the scroll's number is 161; its name is 4QpIsa^a (copy "a" of Pesher Isaiah from Qumran Cave 4); and we are referring to fragments 8–10 of this scroll, lines 15–29.

Sometimes a given fragment contains more than one column of text. We designate these columns using small Roman numerals. So in the designation 4Q169 (4QpNah) 3–4 i 6–8, the numbers 3–4 i 6–8 stand for fragments 3–4, in the first column, lines 6–8.

In some cases, scholars assemble several fragments together in an attempt to reconstruct a damaged text. They may signal it by using a plus sign (+). One example is 4Q444 (4QIncantation) 1–4 i + 5 2. Here fragments 1–4 have been placed alongside fragment 5.

Convention 4. Most of the Dead Sea Scrolls are badly damaged. The exposure to the elements, mice, and bugs destroyed much of these precious texts. To signal a hole in the leather or papyrus, scholars use square brackets: [ ]. These brackets tell us when text has been lost.

Now in some cases, scholars can reconstruct the missing text. There might be another copy of the same literary work. Or if a biblical passage is cited, we can restore the text using the biblical verse. As readers we should remember that such reconstructions are tentative.

Finally, in this book we refer only once to a scroll that was found outside of Qumran. This is the scroll from Masada, another location in the Judean Desert. This scroll is designated Mas 1k. "Mas" stands for Masada, while "1k" is the number assigned to this scroll.

Bibliography

In this book we use the following English translations of early Jewish texts:

Charlesworth, James H., ed. *The Old Testament Pseudepigrapha*. 2 vols. New York: Doubleday, 1983–85.
Josephus. *Josephus*. Translated by H. St. Thackeray et al. 9 vols. Loeb Classical Library. London: Heinemann, 1926–65.
Nickelsburg, George W. E. *1 Enoch 1: A Commentary on the Book of 1 Enoch, Chapters 1–36; 81–108*. Hermeneia. Minneapolis: Fortress, 2001.
Nickelsburg, George W. E., and James C. VanderKam. *1 Enoch 2: A Commentary on the Book of 1 Enoch, Chapters 37–82*. Hermeneia. Minneapolis: Fortress, 2012.
Philo. *Philo*. Translated by F. H. Colson and G. H. Whitaker. 10 vols. Loeb Classical Library. Cambridge, MA: Harvard University Press, 1929–62.
VanderKam, James C. *Jubilees: A Commentary on the Book of Jubilees*. 2 vols. Hermeneia. Minneapolis: Fortress, 2018.
Vermes, Geza, trans. *The Complete Dead Sea Scrolls in English*. London: Penguin, 2012.

Below we list additional sources, arranged in roughly chronological order, to facilitate further study.

Early Judaism

Hebrew Bible Introduction

Collins, John J. *Introduction to the Hebrew Bible*. 3rd ed. Minneapolis: Fortress, 2018.

Apocrypha

Harrelson, Walter J., ed. *The New Interpreter's Study Bible: New Revised Standard Version with the Apocrypha*. Nashville: Abingdon, 2003.

Klawans, Jonathan, and Lawrence Wills, eds. *The Jewish Annotated Apocrypha*. Oxford: Oxford University Press, 2020.

Pseudepigrapha

Feldman, Louis, James Kugel, and Lawrence Schiffman, eds. *Outside the Bible: Ancient Jewish Writing Related to Scripture*. 3 vols. Melrose Park, PA: Jewish Publication Society, 2013.

Panayotov, Alexander, James Davila, and Richard Bauckham, eds. *Old Testament Pseudepigrapha: More Noncanonical Scriptures*. Vol. 1. Grand Rapids: Eerdmans, 2013.

Dead Sea Scrolls

Wise, Michael O., Martin G. Abegg Jr., and Edward M. Cook, trans. *The Dead Sea Scrolls: A New Translation*. San Francisco: HarperSanFrancisco, 2005.

Josephus

Josephus. *Flavius Josephus: Translation and Commentary*. Edited by Steve Mason. 10 vols. Leiden: Brill, 1999–.

New Testament

Harrelson, Walter J., ed. *The New Interpreter's Study Bible: New Revised Standard Version with the Apocrypha*. Nashville: Abingdon, 2003.

Levine, Amy-Jill, and Marc Brettler, eds. *The Jewish Annotated New Testament*. 2nd ed. Oxford: Oxford University Press, 2017.

Early Judaism and Early Jewish Writings

Baumgarten, Albert I. *The Flourishing of Jewish Sects in the Maccabean Era: An Interpretation*. Leiden: Brill, 1997.

Chapman, Honora Howell, and Zuleika Rodgers, eds. *A Companion to Josephus*. Blackwell Companions to the Ancient World. Chichester, UK: Wiley & Sons, 2016.

Cohen, Shaye J. D. *From the Maccabees to the Mishnah*. 3rd ed. Louisville: Westminster John Knox, 2014.

Collins, John J. *The Apocalyptic Imagination: An Introduction to Jewish Apocalyptic Literature*. 3rd ed. Grand Rapids: Eerdmans, 2016.

———. *The Dead Sea Scrolls: A Biography*. Princeton: Princeton University Press, 2019.

———. *The Scepter and the Star: Messianism in Light of the Dead Sea Scrolls*. 2nd ed. Grand Rapids: Eerdmans, 2010.

Collins, John J., and Daniel C. Harlow, eds. *The Eerdmans Dictionary of Early Judaism*. Grand Rapids: Eerdmans, 2010.

deSilva, David. *Introducing the Apocrypha: Message, Context, and Significance*. 2nd ed. Grand Rapids: Baker Academic, 2018.

Elledge, Casey. *Resurrection of the Dead in Early Judaism 200 BCE–CE 200*. Oxford: Oxford University Press, 2017.

Gurtner, Daniel. *Introducing the Pseudepigrapha of Second Temple Judaism: Message, Context, and Significance*. Grand Rapids: Baker Academic, 2020.

Gurtner, Daniel, and Loren T. Stuckenbruck, eds. *T&T Clark Encyclopedia of Second Temple Judaism*. 2 vols. London: Bloomsbury T&T Clark, 2019.

Harrington, Daniel. *Invitation to the Apocrypha*. Grand Rapids: Eerdmans, 1999.

Hempel, Charlotte, and George J. Brooke, eds. *T&T Clark Companion to the Dead Sea Scrolls*. London: Bloomsbury T&T Clark, 2019.

Henze, Matthias, ed. *A Companion to Biblical Interpretation in Early Judaism*. Grand Rapids: Eerdmans, 2012.

———. *Mind the Gap: How the Jewish Writings Between the Old and New Testament Help Us Understand Jesus*. Minneapolis: Fortress, 2017.

Kamesar, Adam. *The Cambridge Companion to Philo*. Cambridge: Cambridge University Press, 2009.

Kugel, James L. *Traditions of the Bible*. Cambridge, MA: Harvard University Press, 1998.

Lim, Timothy, and John J. Collins, eds. *The Oxford Handbook of the Dead Sea Scrolls*. Oxford: Oxford University Press, 2010.

Nickelsburg, George W. E. *Ancient Judaism and Christian Origins: Diversity, Continuity, and Transformation*. Minneapolis: Fortress, 2003.

Perdue, Leo, and Warren Carter. *Israel and Empire: A Postcolonial History of Israel and Early Judaism*. London: Bloomsbury T&T Clark, 2015.

VanderKam, James C. *The Dead Sea Scrolls Today*. Grand Rapids: Eerdmans, 2010.

———. *An Introduction to Early Judaism*. Grand Rapids: Eerdmans, 2022.

New Testament

Beker, J. Christiaan. *Paul's Apocalyptic Gospel: The Coming Triumph of God*. Philadelphia: Fortress, 1982.

Carter, Warren. "Are There Imperial Texts in the Class? Intertextual Eagles and Matthean Eschatology as 'Lights Out' Time for Imperial Rome (Matt. 24:27–31)." *Journal of Biblical Literature* 122 (2003): 467–87.

———. *Mark*. Wisdom Commentary 42. Collegeville, MN: Liturgical Press, 2019.

———. *Matthew and the Margins: A Sociopolitical and Religious Reading*. Maryknoll, NY: Orbis Books, 2000.

———. *Seven Events That Shaped the New Testament World*. Grand Rapids: Baker Academic, 2013.

———. *What Does Revelation Reveal? Unlocking the Mystery*. Nashville: Abingdon, 2011.

Carter, Warren, and Amy-Jill Levine. *The New Testament: Methods and Meanings*. Nashville: Abingdon, 2013.

Cohen, Jeremy. *Christ Killers: The Jews and the Passion from the Bible to the Big Screen*. Oxford: Oxford University Press, 2007.

Dunn, James D. G. *The Epistle to the Galatians*. Black's New Testament Commentaries. London: A. & C. Black, 1993.

———. *The Theology of Paul the Apostle*. Grand Rapids: Eerdmans, 1998.

Eisenbaum, Pamela. *Paul Was Not a Christian: The Original Message of the Misunderstood Apostle*. New York: HarperOne, 2009.

Hanson, K. C., and Douglas Oakman. *Palestine in the Time of Jesus: Social Structures and Social Conflicts*. Minneapolis: Fortress, 1998.

Levine, Amy-Jill. "Holy Week and the Hatred of the Jews: How to Avoid Anti-Judaism this Easter." *ABC Religion and Ethics*, April 1, 2021, https://www.abc.net.au/religion/holy-week-and-the-hatred-of-the-jews/11029900.

———. *The Misunderstood Jew: The Church and the Scandal of the Jewish Jesus*. San Francisco: HarperSanFrancisco, 2006.

Nickelsburg, George W. E. *Ancient Judaism and Christian Origins: Diversity, Continuity, and Transformation*. Minneapolis: Fortress, 2003.

Reinhartz, Adele. "The Gospel of John: How 'the Jews' Became Part of the Plot." In *Jesus, Judaism, and Christian Anti-Judaism: Reading the New Testament After the Holocaust*, edited by Paula Fredriksen and Adele Reinhartz. Louisville: Westminster John Knox, 2002.

Ringe, Sharon. *Wisdom's Friends: Community and Christology in the Fourth Gospel*. Louisville: Westminster John Knox, 1999.

Rivkin, Ellis. *What Crucified Jesus? Messianism, Pharisaism, and the Development of Christianity*. New York: UAHC, 1997.

Saldarini, Anthony J. *Pharisees, Scribes and Sadducees in Palestinian Society: A Sociological Approach*. Wilmington, DE: Michael Glazier, 1988.

Sanders, Edward P. *Paul and Palestinian Judaism: A Comparison of Patterns of Religion*. Philadelphia: Fortress, 1977.

Scripture and Ancient Sources Index

Note: The order of the books of the Hebrew Bible follows the threefold division of the Torah (Genesis–Deuteronomy), the Prophets (Joshua–Malachi), and the Writings (Psalms–Chronicles).

Hebrew Bible

Genesis
1   151, 157
1:27   32
3   11
5:21–24   87, 131
6   11
6:1–4   99, 142, 174
6:2   99
12–15   27
12:1–3   77
12:3   23, 28
12:10–20   27
15:6   28
16:3   32
17:1–14   75
17:2–7   27
17:4–6   28
17:27   23
22   182
25:1   32
41:45   11
49:10   86–88

Exodus
6:2–9   75
15   173, 187
15:1–18   180
15:1–19   173–74
15:17–18   43
15:20–21   173, 180
15:26   69
16:22–26   72
16:29   72
17:7   182
19:5   68
19:5–6   72
19:6   62
19:16   150
20:1–21   75
20:8   71
20:10   72
24:8–11   23
34:21   72
35:3   72

Leviticus
4:3   84
4:5   84
15:18   72
16   69
18   32
18:1–30   192
19:18   29, 81
19:34   192
23:9–14   133
25   73
25:13   73, 144
26   69
26:12   48

Numbers
24:17   40, 85, 88
25:6–13   59
29:32–30:1   71
36:13   69

Deuteronomy
4–31   75
5:12–15   71
6:5   29, 81
7:1–3   192
7:4   192
7:7–8   68
7:9   68
15   73, 182
15:2   73, 144
16:13–14   71
20:17   31
21:7   122
21:22–23   115
24:1   32
24:4   27
27–29   44
27:26   78
27:29   44
28   69
28–29   124
28:9   147
28:29   124
28:47–53   151
33:2   110

Judges
5:1–31   180

209

1 Samuel

2:1 180
2:1–10 180
2:4 180
2:7–8 180

2 Samuel

7:1–10 41
7:1–16 37
7:3–16 41
7:5–16 88
7:12–13 85
7:13 43, 48
7:14 48
16:23 102

1 Kings

2:3 69
18 59
19:16 84

2 Kings

17:24–41 54
21:1–18 74
23:10 132

Isaiah

1:11–17 39
1:17 42
2:1–4 192
6:1 43
11:2 86
11:3–4 85, 86
11:4 85, 87
13:1 151
13:6–10 151
25:6–10 182
30:10 56
40–55 9
40:1 24
40:3–5 24–26
40:4 26
40:5 26
42:6 192
44:28–45:1 84
49:6 192
52:11 48
56 45

56:1 31
56:3–7 192
56:7 45
58:13 72
61:1–2 93

Jeremiah

7:1–15 39
7:11 45
10:25 192
17:21 72
23:5 85
25:11–12 143
31:31–34 22–23
31:34 23
33:3 171
33:15 85

Ezekiel

1:13 150
36:22–37 181
37:1–14 130
37:26–27 46
40–42 43

Amos

4:4–5 39
5:4 31
5:21–24 39

Micah

5:2 44
6:6–8 39
6:8 31

Habakkuk

1:5–11 20
2:3 21, 144–45

Malachi

1 40
1:7–9 40
1:10 40

Psalms

2:2 84
14:1 163

22 21–22
22:1 19, 21, 183–84
22:2 183
22:6–8 21, 183–84
22:7 21, 184
22:11 183
22:12–13 21, 184
22:12–18 183
22:16 184
22:16–18 184
22:18 21, 184
22:19–22 183
22:21b 21
22:22–31 183
69 21

Proverbs

8 156
8–9 155
8:2–3 156
8:5 156
8:18 156
8:20 156
8:22–31 156–57
8:32–36 157
9:13–18 163

Job

1–2 99–100
12:7–10 155–56

Ruth

4 195

Daniel

1 193
1:8 197
3:23 173
5:3 30
6:10 178–79
7 146
7:13–14 87–88, 92, 150
9:24–27 143
12 130
12:2 166
12:2–3 128
12:13 128

Ezra

1–10 9
3:2 69
9:1–2 192

Nehemiah

7:73–8:1 39
10 23

2 Chronicles

33:1–9 176
33:1–20 74
33:11–14 176
33:12–13 9
33:13 74
33:18–19 176
35–36 9

Jewish Apocrypha and Pseudepigrapha

Additions to Daniel

Bel and the Dragon
in toto 9, 193

Prayer of Azariah
1:20–22 173

Susanna
42–44 188

Additions to Esther

C 13:9–15 173
C 14:2 179
C 14:14 173
C 14:19 173

Apocryphal Psalms

151 9
154 176

Baruch

1:1 45
1:5 179
1:14 178
1:15–3:8 74
2:11–3:8 174
3 166
3–4 155
3:4 155
3:37–4:1 159
4:1 69–70
4:20 179

2 Baruch

1:1–5 45
4:1 45
25:2–29:2 89
29:3 89
29:4–8 89
29:6 89
30:1 89
40:1 89
40:2 89
40:3 89
50:2–51:6 132
51:10–12 132
54:15–19 11
71:2–74:2 89
72:2–3 89

1 Enoch

1–36 60
1:9 12
6–7 142
6–11 99–100, 142
6–15 104
6–16 11
6:1–2 99
6:7–8 98–99, 142
6:16 11
7:3 104
8:1–4 142
9 142
9–10 98, 100
9:1 98
9:6 104
10–11 142
10:1 99
10:1–3 98
10:1–14 100

10:4–22 98
10:16–11:2 142
14:8–23 43
14:22–23 98
15:8–11 104
15:9 100
15:9–11 100
15:10 100
15:16 60
16:1 100
20 98
22 130
22:1 130
26:1 38
26:4–27:4 132
32:3 132
37–71 87
39:6–7 87
39:12–13 98
40 98
42:1–2 162, 166
42:1–3 166
46:1 87
48:3–8 87
48:10 87
51:1 87
61:5 87
62:1 12, 87
62:2 87
62:7 87
62:12 87
69:20–24 98
69:28 87
71:14 87
72:1 98
82:9–20 98
85–90 44
85:1–90:41 143
89–91 56
89:6–7 56
89:28 87
89:59 143
89:73 39
90:17–37 143
90:26 132
90:28 144
90:29 44
90:38 196
91:11–17 145
93 56
93:3 145
93:3–10 145

93:10 160
93:10–11 56, 160
102:4 130
102:11 130
103:2 130
103:4 130
103:7 130
103:8 130
104:2 130
104:4 130
104:11 130

4 Ezra

3:20 11
4:40–5:13 88
7:28 88
7:29 88
7:29–32 131
7:36 132
7:79 88, 131
7:80 131
7:85 131
7:87 131
7:88 131
7:88–98 131
7:95 131
7:100 131
7:101 131
11:1–12:35 146
12–13 88
12:32 88, 146
12:32–33 88
12:34 146
13:1 88
13:3 88
13:9 88
13:10 88
13:13 88
13:26 88
13:35 88
13:37–38 88
13:40–47 88
13:48 88

Jubilees

1:1 71
1:7 69
1:17 43
1:29 43, 71
2:2 98

2:18 98
2:19 71
2:21 71, 98, 178, 192
2:30 98
6:17 71
8:12 38
8:19 38
10:1–14 100
10:8 100
10:10 100
10:11 100
10:12–14 100
12:20 101
12:22–24 28
15:27 98
15:31–32 100, 192
20:2 30
22:16 193, 197
22:20 193, 197
23:16 56
23:22–26 56
30:18 98
31:14 43, 98
50:6–13 71
50:10 72
50:11 72

Judith

4:8–13 179
4:9 179
4:11 179
4:13 179
4:15 179
6:16 189
6:19 181
9 174, 188
9–10 188
9:1 178–79
10–13 76
10:5 197
10:13 76
12:1–20 197
12:8 179
14:10 195
16:1–17 180

Letter of Jeremiah

in toto 193

Life of Adam and Eve (Greek)

18:1 11

1 Maccabees

1:11 193
1:23 37
2 75
2:23–27 59

2 Maccabees

3:6 37
3:10–12 37
3:15 179
7 129, 188, 197
7:7–11 129
7:16 129
7:19 129
7:20–23 129
7:29 130
10:4 179
12:39–45 130
13:12 179

3 Maccabees

2:1 179
2:1–20 74, 174
2:4–7 174
3:3–5 194
3:6–7 194
3:10 194

Prayer of Manasseh

7 177
9 177
11 177
12 177

Psalms of Solomon

9:9 27
17:4–5 86
17:7 86
17:9 86
17:11–18 86
17:11–20 12
17:21 86
17:22–23 86
17:25 86
17:26–27 86
17:30–31 86
17:33 86
17:34 86
17:36–37 86
17:40 86

Sirach

22:3–5 186
23:4 181
23:27 70
24:2 157
24:3 157
24:6 157
24:7–9 157
24:10 155, 157
24:12–17 157
24:23 69, 155
24:23–27 158
24:32–34 158
25:24 156
26:1 186
26:1–4 186
28:2 182
37:15 171
38:24–34 158
38:24–39:11 62
38:25–26 158
38:27 158
38:28 158
38:29–30 158
38:34 159
39:1–11 158
39:5–8 158
43:6–7 57
44:19 27–28
44:21 28
50:5–11 38
50:17 179
50:17–19 178
50:19 36
51:10 181
51:19 179

Testament of Solomon

18 60

Testaments of the Twelve Patriarchs

Testament of Benjamin

3:3–4 30

Testament of Dan

5:3 30

Testament of Issachar

5:1–2 30

Testament of Joseph

11:1 30

Tobit

1:8 195
1:10–15 197
1:11 193
1:18 181
2:11 188
3:1–5 174
3:1–6 74
3:7–8 101
3:11–12 179
3:11–16 174
3:11–17 188
3:16 171
4:12 193
7:12 181
8:1–3 102
8:1–9 178
8:5–7 174
8:15–17 174
9 174
12:14 182
13 174
13:4 181
14:6–7 196

Wisdom of Solomon

7:21–30 160
7:27 167
9 174
9:8 43
9:17 168
16:28 178

New Testament

Matthew

1:1 28
1:1–17 28
1:18 109
1:21 46
1:23 46
2 116
2:2–6 63
2:4 44
2:5–6 44
2:13 109
2:19 109
3:3 25
3:8 28
4:8–9 104
4:11 109
4:24 108
5:17–20 59
5:34 182
5:43 31
5:43–44 30
5:43–45 152
5:45 31
6:1 181
6:9–13 181–83
6:11 182
6:12 144
7:22 107
8:16 108
9:2–8 46
9:10–13 63
9:32 107
9:34 104, 108
10:8 107
10:28 132
11:18 103, 108
11:25 183
12:6 46
12:14 63
12:24 103–4, 108
12:28 105
12:38 63
13:16 136
13:36–43 152
13:39 109
13:41 109
13:47–50 152
13:49 109
14:1–12 187
14:21 189

15:1 63
15:17 62
15:22 189
16:21 44, 63
18:10 109
19:3 32
19:5–6 32
19:9 32
20:18 44, 63
21 44
21:1 35
21:12 44
21:15 63
21:23 44
22:1–11 45
22:7 124
22:30 109
22:34–40 29, 81
23:23 63
23:25 63
23:31 63
23:37–39 152
24–25 116, 149–52
24:1–3 35
24:2 44, 149
24:3 149
24:25 116, 149
24:28 151
24:29 151
24:30 152
24:31 81, 109, 152
24:32 152
24:36 109
25:30 152
25:31–46 81, 152
25:32–34 152
25:34 152
25:40 152
25:41 109, 152
25:46 152
26–27 21, 45
26:27 21, 45
26:28 23, 46
26:53 109
27 184
27:1–2 63
27:1–3 184
27:2 119
27:3 119
27:16–17 117
27:23 122
27:24 123

27:25 6, 114, 122–24
27:35 184
27:37 116
27:38 116, 184
27:39 184
27:41–43 184
27:44 116, 184
27:46 19, 21, 183–84
27:52–53 136
28 184
28:1 136
28:1–8 136
28:2 109
28:5 109
28:7–10 190
28:9 136, 139
28:11–15 136
28:16 190
28:16–20 136, 140
28:19 199
28:20 46

Mark

1:2–3 25
1:17 94
1:20 94
1:24 108
1:25 94
1:26 107
1:34 108
1:41 94
3:15 107
3:22 104, 108
3:28 94
4:25 94
4:29 94
4:34 94
5:1–20 106–7
5:25–27 189
6:13 107
7:25–26 190
7:25–31 94
8:27–30 92
9:14 107
9:38 107
9:41 92
10:2–12 32
10:5–9 32
10:6 32
10:8 107
11–15 116

11:22–25 179
12:28–34 81
12:35 92
13 149
13:10 199
13:21 92
14–15 21
14:15 21
14:24 23
14:53 92
14:58–61 92
14:62 92–93
15:1–38 21
15:7 117
15:8–9 120
15:11 120
15:12 120
15:13 120
15:14–15 120–21
15:16–32 21
15:24 21
15:26 116
15:27 116–17
15:29 21
15:32 93
15:34 19, 21
16:1–8 21

Luke

1–2 35
1:11–38 109
1:19 109
1:26–38 180
1:46–56 180–81
1:47–55 26
2:11 93
2:13–14 109
2:14 26
2:15 109
2:32 26
2:46 36
3:1–2 180
3:4–6 25
3:5 26
3:6 26
3:21 183
4:5–7 104
4:18 93
4:31–37 107
4:33–35 108
4:40–41 108

4:41 108
5:17–26 64
5:17–6:11 65
5:29–32 64
6:1–2 65
6:7 65
6:12 183
7:24 109
7:27 109
7:36 64
8:2 108
8:2–3 190
9:20 93
9:26 109
9:28–29 183
9:37–43 107
9:49–50 107
9:52 109
10:17–19 107
10:25–28 81
10:38 190
11:1–4 181
11:14–20 108
11:15 104
11:37 64
11:37–54 65
12:1 65
12:8–9 109
13:31 64
14:1 64–65
15:8–10 190
15:10 109
16:14 64
17:20 65
18:1–14 179
18:9–14 65
20:10 64
20:20 64–65
20:27 65
20:27–40 127
21:9–38 149
21:37 36
22:20 23
22:41–46 183
22:67–69 93
23:2–3 93
23:35 93
23:38 116
23:39 93
24:1–35 137
24:19–24 137
24:23 109

24:25–27   140
24:25–35   137
24:26   93
24:30   139
24:36–37   139
24:36–49   137
24:39–40   139
24:46   93
24:49   138, 140
24:50–53   137
24:51   139

John

1:1   165
1:1–2   165
1:3–4   165
1:10   167
1:11–12   166
1:12   167
1:14   166
1:18   165–66
1:19   167
1:35–51   167
1:39   166
1:48–49   166
2:1–11   166, 189
2:1–12   167
2:13   167
2:13–14   166
3:1   58
3:14   168
3:16   167
3:22–23   166
4:1–42   64
4:5–15   166
4:9   167
4:20   42
4:46–54   166–67
5–12   167
5:1–9   166
5:2–3   166
5:14   179
5:16–18   167
5:21   166
5:24   167
5:28–29   139
5:36   166
5:37   168
5:46–47   168
6:1–3   166
6:1–14   166

6:1–15   167
6:25   166
6:38   165
6:39   165
6:41   165, 167
6:41–42   168
6:44   165
6:46   165
6:47–48   167
6:51   165
6:57   165
7:2   167
7:13   167
7:20   108
7:28   168
7:28–30   167
7:30–32   167
7:35   167
8:23   168
8:28   168
8:31   167
8:38   166
8:39–47   29
8:40   29, 167
8:41–43   29
8:42–44   167
8:44   6, 97, 108
8:44–47   29
8:48   108
8:49   108
8:52   108
9:22   165, 167
10:10   166
10:20–21   108
10:30   165
10:31   167
10:32   166
11:19   167
11:25–26   167
11:31–33   167
11:41–43   183
11:45   167
12:1–8   166
12:34   168
12:42   165, 167
12:49–50   166
13–17   164
13:3   168
13:12–17   167
13:34–35   167
13:38   138
14:2–7   168

14:7   166
14:9   166
14:10   166
14:16–17   168
14:18   168
14:18–19   167
14:24   166
15:13–15   167
16:2   165
16:7   168
16:13   168
17:1–26   183
17:3   94, 166
18:12   167
18:17   138
18:25–27   138
19:12   116, 168
19:19   116
19:34   3
19:38   167
20:11–29   138
20:15–16   139
20:17   139
20:19   139
20:21   140, 199
20:22   140
20:24–29   138, 140
20:26   139
20:30–31   140
20:31   94
21:1–14   138
21:4–6   139
21:9   139
21:9–14   139
21:15–19   138
21:24   138

Acts

1:8–9   199
1:13–14   179
1:24–26   179
2   137–38
2:42   179
3:1   179
3:14–15   113
4:1–4   65
4:24–31   179
5:17   65
5:30   6
5:34–39   58, 65
7:38   110

7:53   110
7:59–60   179
9:3   60
9:3–6   60
9:17   179
9:40   179
10:2   179
11:26   84
12:12   179
13:2–3   179
14:23   179
15:5   65
16:13   179
16:16   179
16:25   179
18:3   60
20:36   179
21:5–6   179
22:6–9   60
22:17   179
23:6–8   58
23:6–10   65
23:8   60
26:5   58, 65
26:8   58
26:13–16   60
28:8   179

Romans

1:1   90
1:5   77, 198
1:8   179
1:18   78
1:28–32   78
3:1–4   75
3:2   75
3:24   90
3:29   23
3:29–30   77, 199
3:30   199
3:30–31   79
3:31   59
4:1   28
4:12   28
4:16   79
5:8   81
6:3   90
6:3–11   90
6:4   90, 147
6:5   90, 147
6:8   147

Scripture and Ancient Sources Index

7   59, 78
7:7   78
7:12   75
7:18–19   78
8:1   90
8:9–11   46
8:10   90
8:34   90
8:35–39   90
8:38–39   106
9:4   23, 75
9:5   75, 89
10:4   67, 79
10:17   90
11:25–26   149
11:28–32   149
12:4–8   91
12:5   91
13:8–10   80
14   198
14:1–15:13   198
14:2   81
14:5–6   81
14:8   81
14:14   81
14:15   81, 90
14:17   81
14:19   81
14:20–21   81
14:21   81
15:2–3   91
15:6   90
15:7   90–91
15:16   90
15:30   179
15:32   179
16   191
16:26   198

1 Corinthians

1:1   90
1:4   179
1:10–17   47
1:12   91
1:23   90
1:26–29   47
3   48
3:1–8   47
3:9   46
3:16   46
3:23   91
4:8   134
6:3   110
6:9   46
6:9–11   47
6:13–20   47
7:5   179
8–10   46, 198
8:11   90
8:12   91
9:6   60
10:18–22   106
11:1   91
11:5   191
11:25   23
12:12–13   90
12:12–31   91
12:14   91
13:1   110
15:1–34   133
15:3–5   90
15:10   191
15:12–22   90
15:20–28   146
15:22   90, 148
15:23   91
15:23–24   148
15:23–28   90, 147

2 Corinthians

1:3   179
1:11   179
3:14–16   23
5:10   90
5:14–15   91
6:16   48
6:16–18   47
11:3   90
11:14   109
12:7   109
13:3   90

Galatians

1:1   90
1:3   90
1:6   90
1:14   59, 78
1:15–16   60
2:9   77
2:11–14   197
2:16   77, 90
2:16–21   79
2:19   90
2:20   90
3:10–13   78
3:13   67, 115
3:19   110
3:24   78
3:26–29   91
3:29   91
4:11   191
4:14   109
4:19   90
5:1–6   77
5:24   91
6:2   91

Ephesians

2:4–6   134
2:15   67
5:22–33   191
6:18   179

Philippians

1:3   179
1:6   90
1:10   90
2:4–5   91
2:8   79
2:16   90
3   59
3:2–7   60
3:5–6   58
3:6   59, 78
3:8   90
3:9   90
4:6   179

Colossians

3:18   191
4:2–4   179

1 Thessalonians

1:2   179
2:9   60
2:14–15   113
4:13   147
4:13–5:11   147
4:16   148
4:16–17   147

5   148
5:2–3   148
5:3   148
5:4–5   148
5:8–11   148
5:9–10   90

1 Timothy

2:1–2   179
2:8–15   191

Hebrews

8:13   24

James

2:1–13   81
2:14–26   81
2:21–24   81
2:25–26   82
5:16   179

1 John

5:14–17   179

Jude

14–15   12

Revelation

2–3   109
5:2   110
5:11–12   110
6:1–8:3   153
7:1–3   110
7:11–12   110
8:2   110
8:6–9:21   110
10:1–2   110
12:1–9   105
12:7–9   111
13:2   105
13:8   105
13:11–18   105
14:6–12   110
16:12–16   105
18:2   105
18:8   153
18:9–24   153

18:11 108
19:22 153
20:1–3 110
21:1–4 49
21:10 110
21:22 49, 144
22:3 49

Dead Sea Scrolls

Aramaic Levi Document (ALD)

2:4–5 179
3:1 179
3:2 179
13:4–7 160
13:15 160

Community Rule (1QS)

1:2 178
1:8 68
1:10–11 31
1:22 73
1:25–3:1 73
3:13–4:26 73, 161
6:4 178
8:1–10 42
8:12–16 24–25
8:14 25
9:3–5 42
9:10–11 84
9:18 161
10:1 178
11:5 177
11:7 98

Damascus Document (CD)

1:1–11 22, 56
1:8–9 73
1:10–11 73
1:18–19 56
3:12–16 41
3:13–16 22
3:18 41, 73
3:19–20 41
4:13–5:6 31
4:21 32
5:1 32

5:6–8 40
6:14–21 22
7:6–7 55
7:18–20 85
10:14–11:18 72
11:16–21 40
12:22–33 55
16:4–6 101
19:10–11 85
19:33–20:1 23
19:34 23
20:12 23
20:12–13 23

Genesis Apocryphon (1Q20; 1QapGen)

0:1–18 175
19:7–8 175
19:14–17 27
19:14–21 27
19:23–24 27
20:1–8 188
20:2–8 27
20:9 27
20:12–16 27, 175
20:17 27
20:21–23 27
20:23 27
20:28–29 27
20:30 27
21:8–14 27
22:27–34 27

Pesher Habakkuk (1QpHab)

2:4 22–23
2:8–9 20
7:1–2 20, 161
7:1–5 161
7:3–5 20
7:5–8 144
7:9–14 145
7:10–13 21
7:13–14 161
8:8–13 39
9:5–6 39
12:2–3 39
12:6–10 39

Rule of Blessings (1QSb)

5:20–29 85

Rule of the Congregation (1QSa)

1:4–5 189
1:11 187
2:8–9 98, 177
2:11–22 85
2:17–21 178

Thanksgiving Hymns (Hodayot; 1QH^a)

10–17 175
11:19–23 175
11:21–23 98

War Scroll (1QM; 1Q33)

1:2 204
1:9–12 177
7:6 98, 177
12:7–9 177
14:12–14 178

1Q27 (1QMysteries)

1 i 3–4, 5–7 162–63

1Q34 + 1Q34bis (Festival Prayers)

1 + 2 6 177

2Q22 (4QNarrative and Poetic Composition)

in toto 175

4Q160 (4QVisSam)

4 i + 5 175

4Q161 (4QpIsa^a)

8–10 15–29 85, 204

4QPesher Nahum (4Q169)

3–4 i 115
3–4 i 6–8 56

4QFlorilegium (4Q174)

1–2 i 3–4 196
1–2 i 21 1–13 41, 43
1–2 i 21 7 69
1–2 i 21 10–13 85

4Q252 (4QCommGen A)

5:1–4 86

4Q259 (4QS^e)

3:4 25

4Q266 (4QD^a)

6 i 6–8 101
8 i 9 98
11 8–14 178

4Q270 (4QD^e)

7 i 13–15 189

4Q365 (4QReworked Pentateuch^c)

6a ii + 6c 1–7 174

4Q366 (4QReworked Pentateuch^d)

4 i 71

4Q370 (4QAdmonition on the Flood)

1 1–2 178

Scripture and Ancient Sources Index   217

4Q371–373a (4QNarrative and Poetic Composition^{a–d})

in toto   175

4Q378 (4QApocryphon of Joshua^a)

6 ii 4–8   175
13 i   175
19 ii   175
22 i   175

4Q379 (4QApocryphon of Joshua^a)

1   175
5   175
18   175

4Q380 (4QNon-Canonical Psalms A)

in toto   176

4Q381 (4QNon-Canonical Psalms B)

33a, b + 35 8–11   176

4Q382 (4Qpap paraKings)

15 5–8   175
23   175
30   175
38   175
49   175
105   175
110   175
111   175
115   175

4Q385 (4QPseudo-Ezekiel^a)

2 5–8   130

Some Precepts of the Law (4QMMT)

4Q394 (4QMMT^a)
  3–7 i 11–12   196
4Q394 (4QMMT^a)
  4:6–7   57
4Q398 (4QMMT^e)
  14–17 ii 3   69

4Q400 (Songs of Sabbath Sacrifice^a)

2 6–8   177

4Q408 (4QApocryphon of Moses^c)

3 + 3a   178

4Q417 (4QInstruction^c)

1 i 6–7   162

4Q510 (Songs of the Sage^a)

1 4–5   102

4Q525 (4QBeatitudes)

2 ii 3–4   159

4Q542 (Testament of Kohath)

1 i 5, 9   193

4Q543 (Visions of Amram)

1a–c 5–6   193

The Temple Scroll (11QT^a)

29:8–10   43
64:2–6   115

11Q11 (11QApocryphal Psalms)

5 4–13   102

11Q13 (11QMelchizedek)

in toto   73

11Q5 (11QPsalms^a)

19:15–16   101
27   175
28:11–12   68

Hellenistic Jewish Sources

Josephus

Against Apion

1.33–35   70
2.103   196
2.123–24   195
2.145   70
2.173–74   70
2.201   187
2.209–10   194
2.261   195
2.277   70
2.282   198
2.282–84   195

Jewish Antiquities

1.161–68   28
1.168   28
1.235   28
3.320   69
4.219   187
8.42–49   102
9.291   54
11.306–12   54
12.7–10   54
12.141   195
12.256   114
13.74–79   54
13.173   53
13.254–56   54
13.288–98   53
13.373–79   53
13.376–80   115
13.398–432   187
17.41–45   53
17.295–96   117
18.11   52
18.12–17   52–53
18.14   127
18.15   128
18.16   127–28
18.23–24   53
18.25   53
18.116–19   54, 187
18.120–21   151
20.17   188
20.17–96   195
20.195   195
20.251   36, 63

Jewish War

1.62–63   54
1.92–98   115
1.401   38
2.117   118
2.120–61   52–53
2.129   31
2.152–58   127
2.163   127–28
2.165   128
2.259–61   195
2.293–308   37
2.400   37
3.123   151
4.324   195
4.510   116
5.15–18   195
5.198–99   189
5.219   38
5.411–12   45
5.451   115, 117
6.126   118
6.282   37
6.300–309   39
6.316   150
6.409–11   45
7.29   116
7.45   198
7.154   116
7.202–3   114
7.358–60   45

Life

1–11   52
11–12   54
191   53

Letter of Aristeas
88 36
92 38
127 70
128–71 76
139 193
142 193
143–47 70
150 70
161 70
163 70
168–69 70

Philo

Hypothetica
11.14 187

On the Contemplative Life
28 55
83–89 187

On the Decalogue
110 30

On the Embassy to Gaius
317 37

On the Life of Abraham
68–88 28

On the Life of Moses
2.13 70
2.44 69
2.52 69

On the Special Laws
2.13 69
2.63 30

On the Virtues
179 196

Questions and Answers on Exodus
2.42 69

Roman Sources

Quintilian

Lesser Declamations
27.4.13 115

Virgil

Aeneid
1.236 106
1.278–83 106
2.717–19 123

Early Christian Literature

Apostolic Constitutions and Canons
2.61.1 125

John Chrysostom

Adversus Judaeos
5.1.6–7 125–26

Justin

Dialogue with Trypho
104 125
108 125

Melito of Sardis

On Pascha
72 125

Origen

Against Celsus
4.22 125